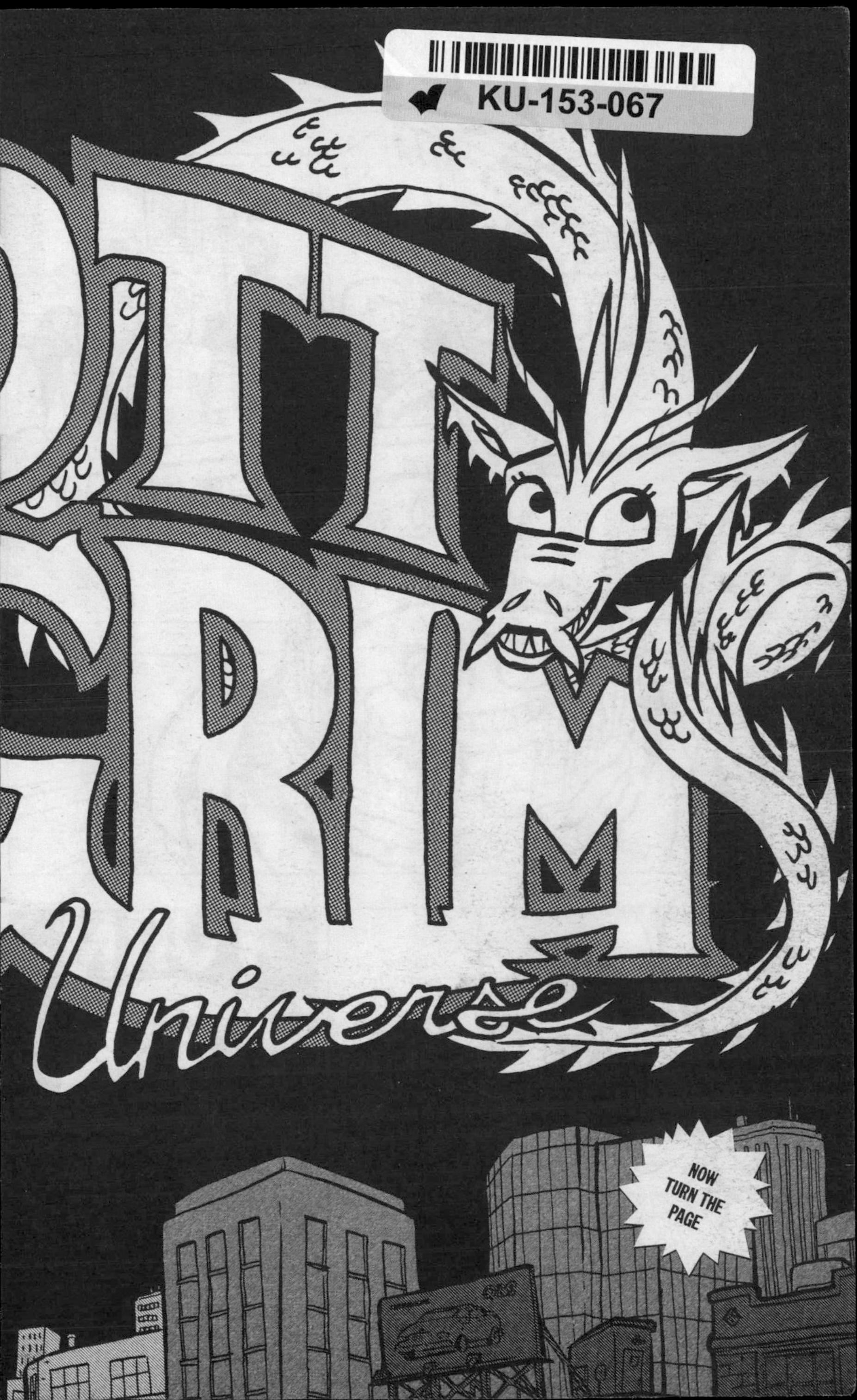
Universe
NOW TURN THE PAGE

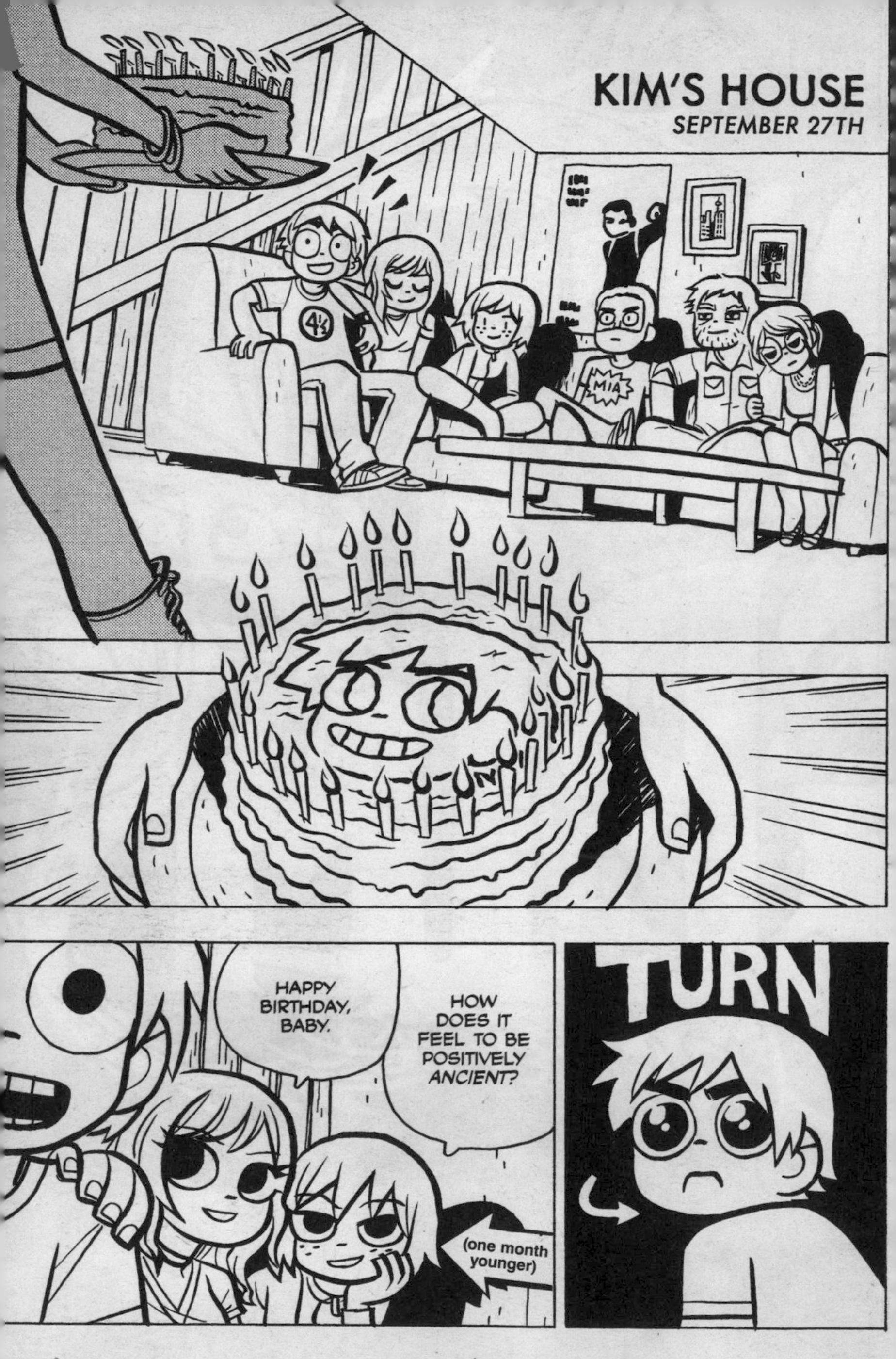
KIM'S HOUSE
SEPTEMBER 27TH
HAPPY BIRTHDAY, BABY.
HOW DOES IT FEEL TO BE POSITIVELY *ANCIENT*?
(one month younger)
TURN

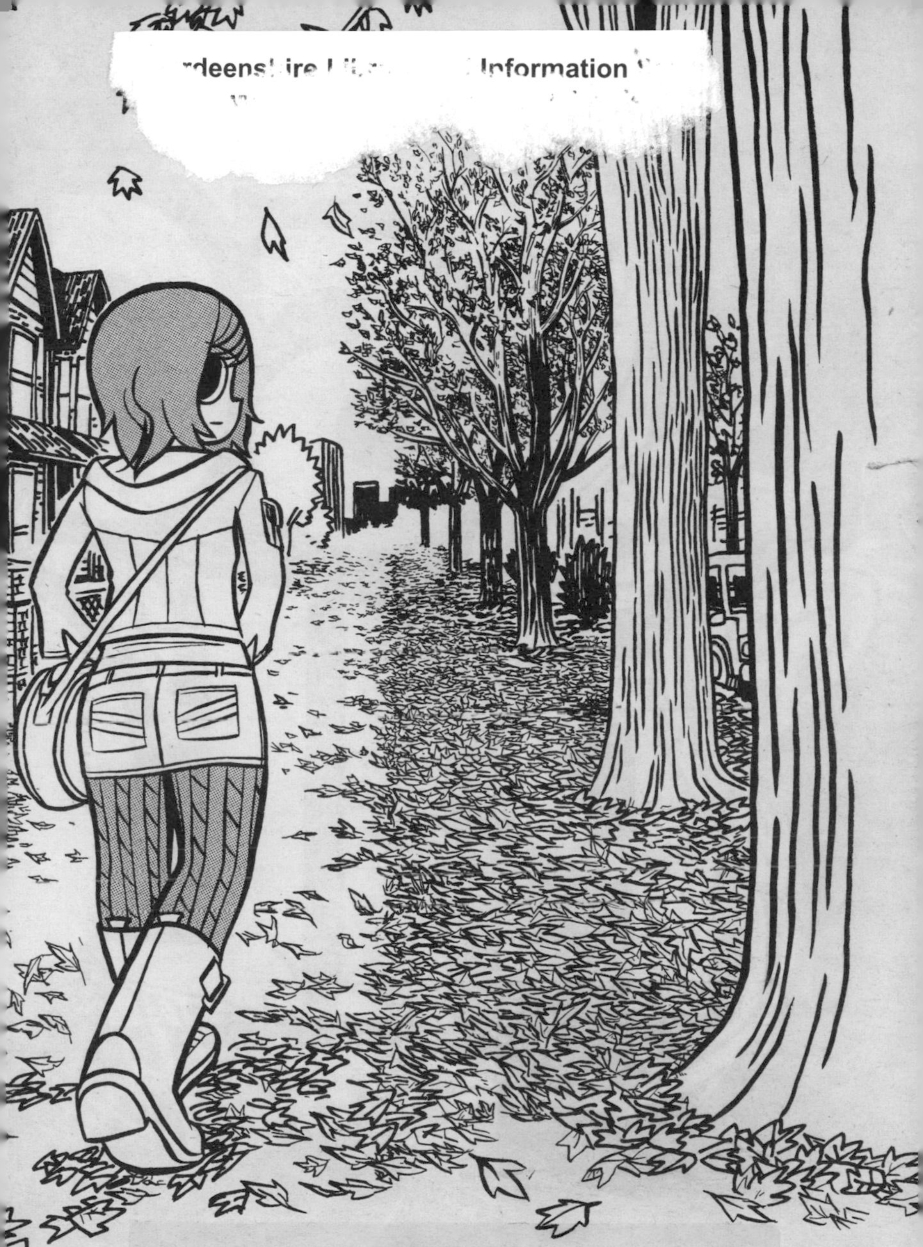

FOURTH ESTATE presents
BRYAN LEE O'

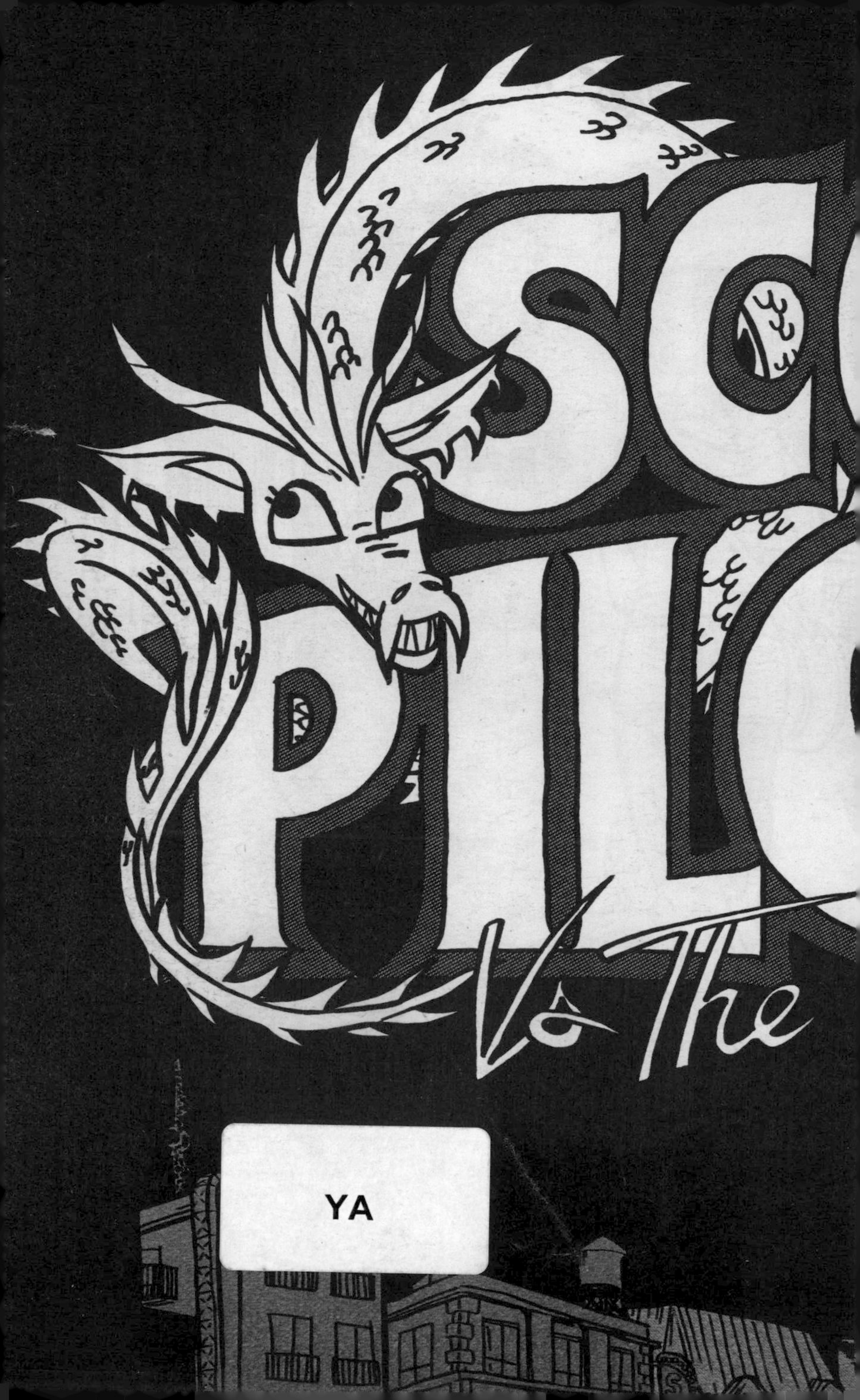
Vs The

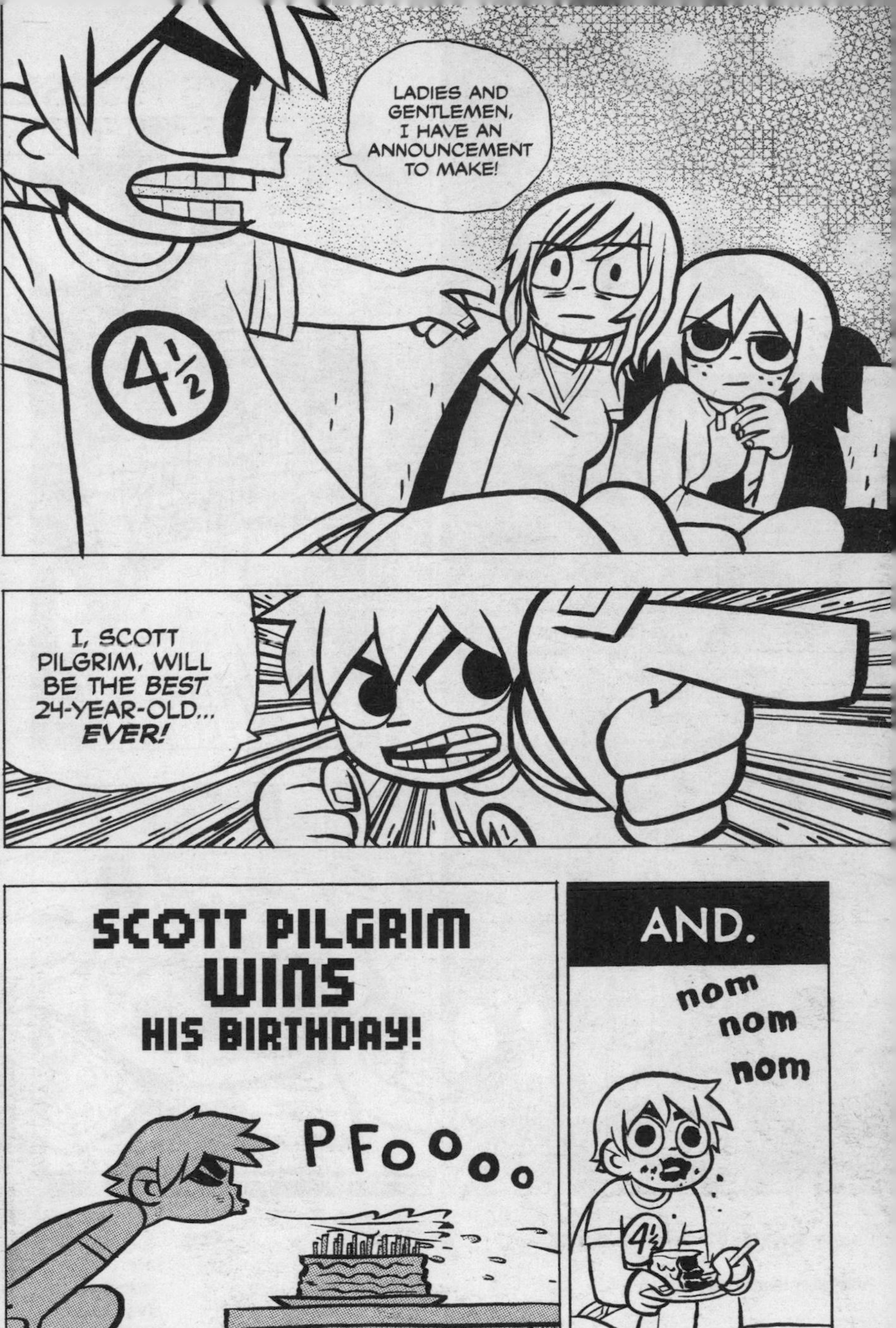
LADIES AND GENTLEMEN, I HAVE AN ANNOUNCEMENT TO MAKE!
I, SCOTT PILGRIM, WILL BE THE BEST 24-YEAR-OLD... EVER!
SCOTT PILGRIM WINS HIS BIRTHDAY!
PFOoooo
AND.
nom nom nom

26

PRECIOUS LITTLE LIFE

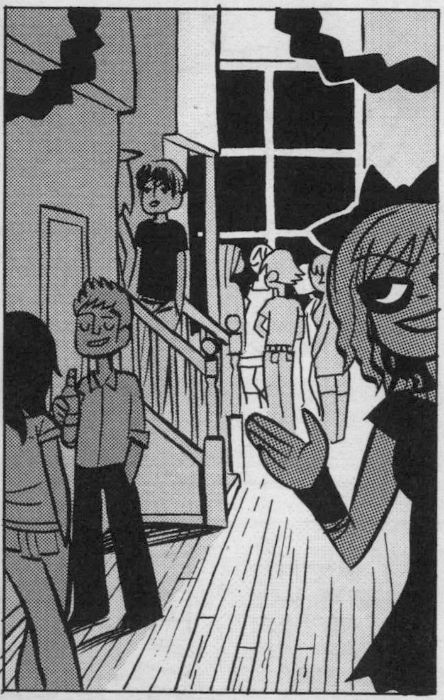

JULIE'S NEW APARTMENT
A studio loft in what was once a warehouse or something. Julie shares the small apartment with three other girls because, although it is out of their price range, they knew it'd be the BEST place to throw the COOLEST parties.

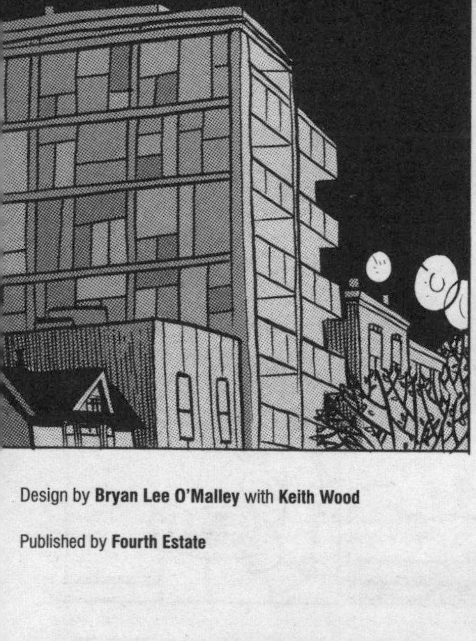

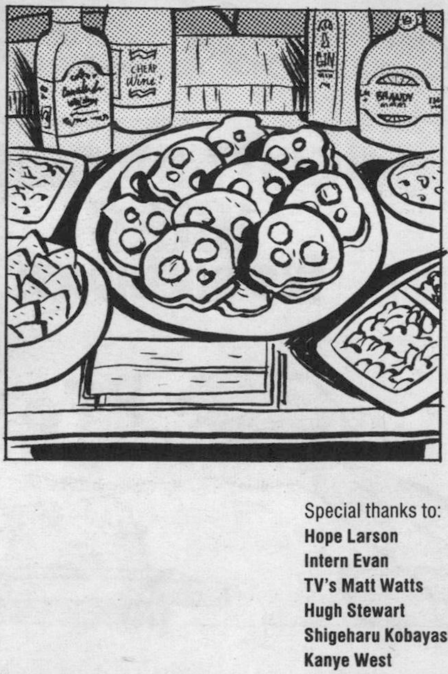
CHEAP Wine!

Design by **Bryan Lee O'Malley** with **Keith Wood**

Published by **Fourth Estate**

www.4thestate.co.uk | www.scottpilgrim.com | www.radiomaru.com

Special thanks to:
Hope Larson
Intern Evan
TV's Matt Watts
Hugh Stewart
Shigeharu Kobayashi
Kanye West
...AND YOU

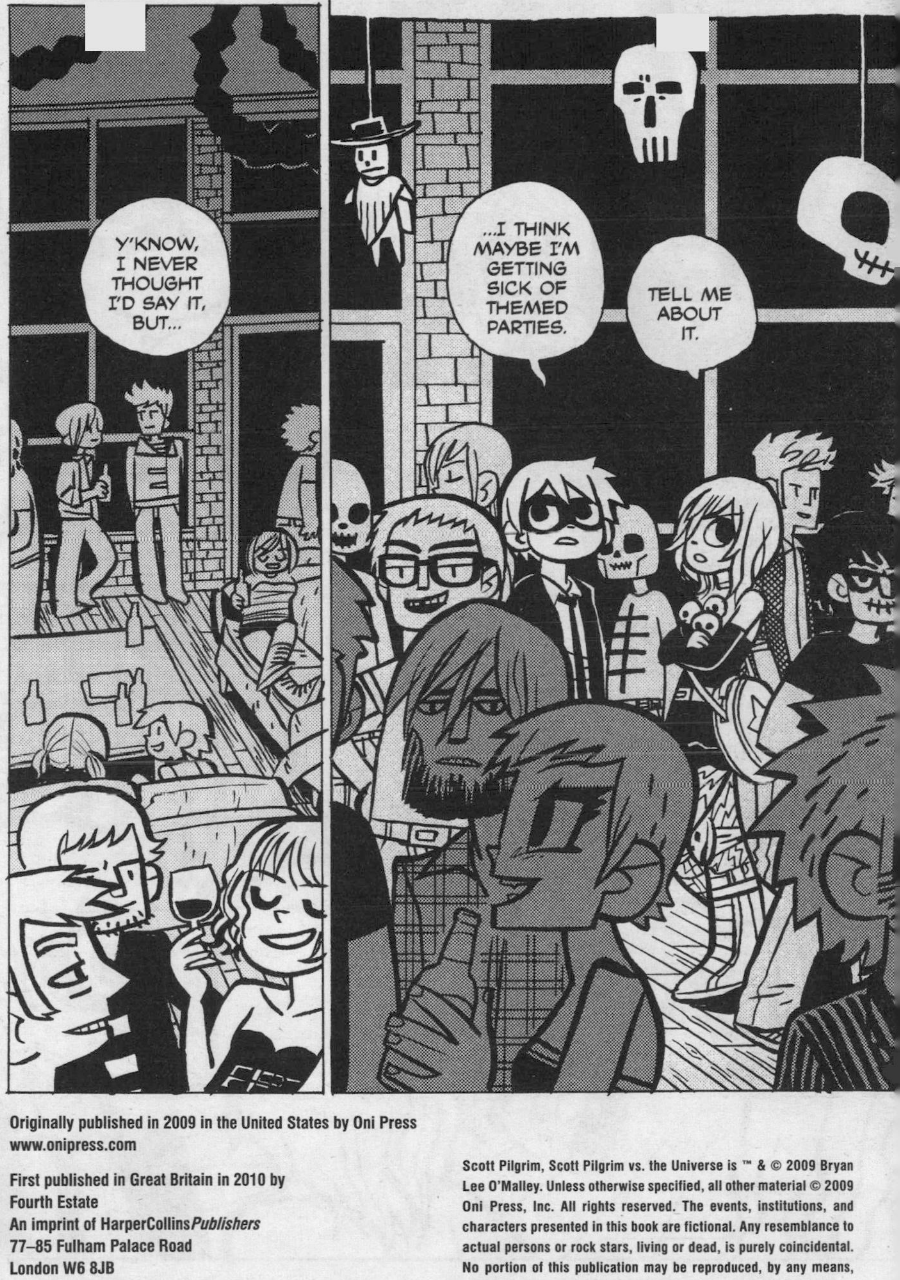
Y'KNOW, I NEVER THOUGHT I'D SAY IT, BUT...
...I THINK MAYBE I'M GETTING SICK OF THEMED PARTIES.
TELL ME ABOUT IT.

Originally published in 2009 in the United States by Oni Press
www.onipress.com

First published in Great Britain in 2010 by
Fourth Estate
An imprint of HarperCollins*Publishers*
77–85 Fulham Palace Road
London W6 8JB

14

ISBN 978-0-00-735147-3

Printed in Great Britain by
CPI Group (UK) Ltd, Croydon, CR0 4YY

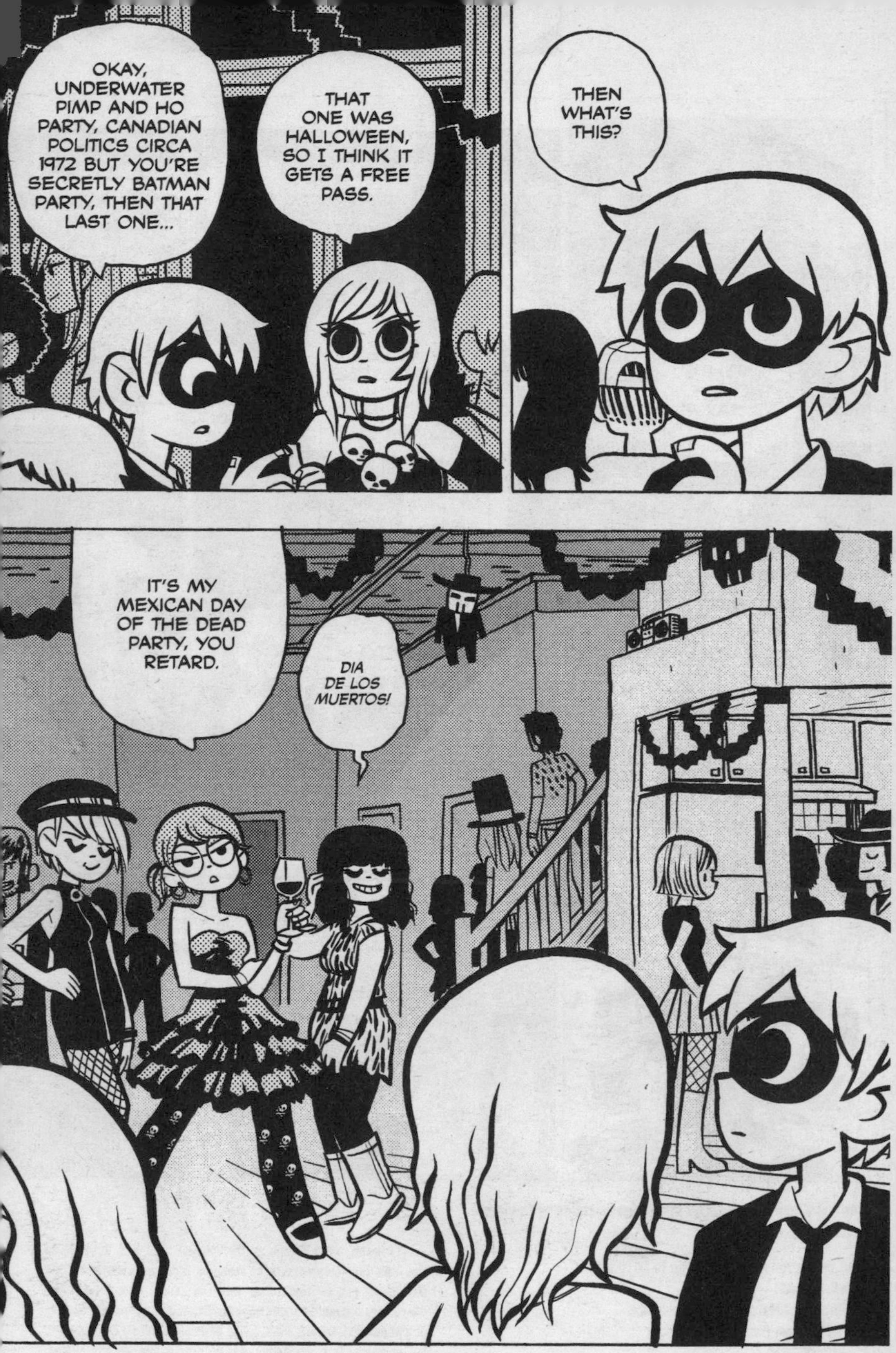
OKAY, UNDERWATER PIMP AND HO PARTY, CANADIAN POLITICS CIRCA 1972 BUT YOU'RE SECRETLY BATMAN PARTY, THEN THAT LAST ONE...
THAT ONE WAS HALLOWEEN, SO I THINK IT GETS A FREE PASS.
THEN WHAT'S THIS?
IT'S MY MEXICAN DAY OF THE DEAD PARTY, YOU RETARD.
DIA DE LOS MUERTOS!

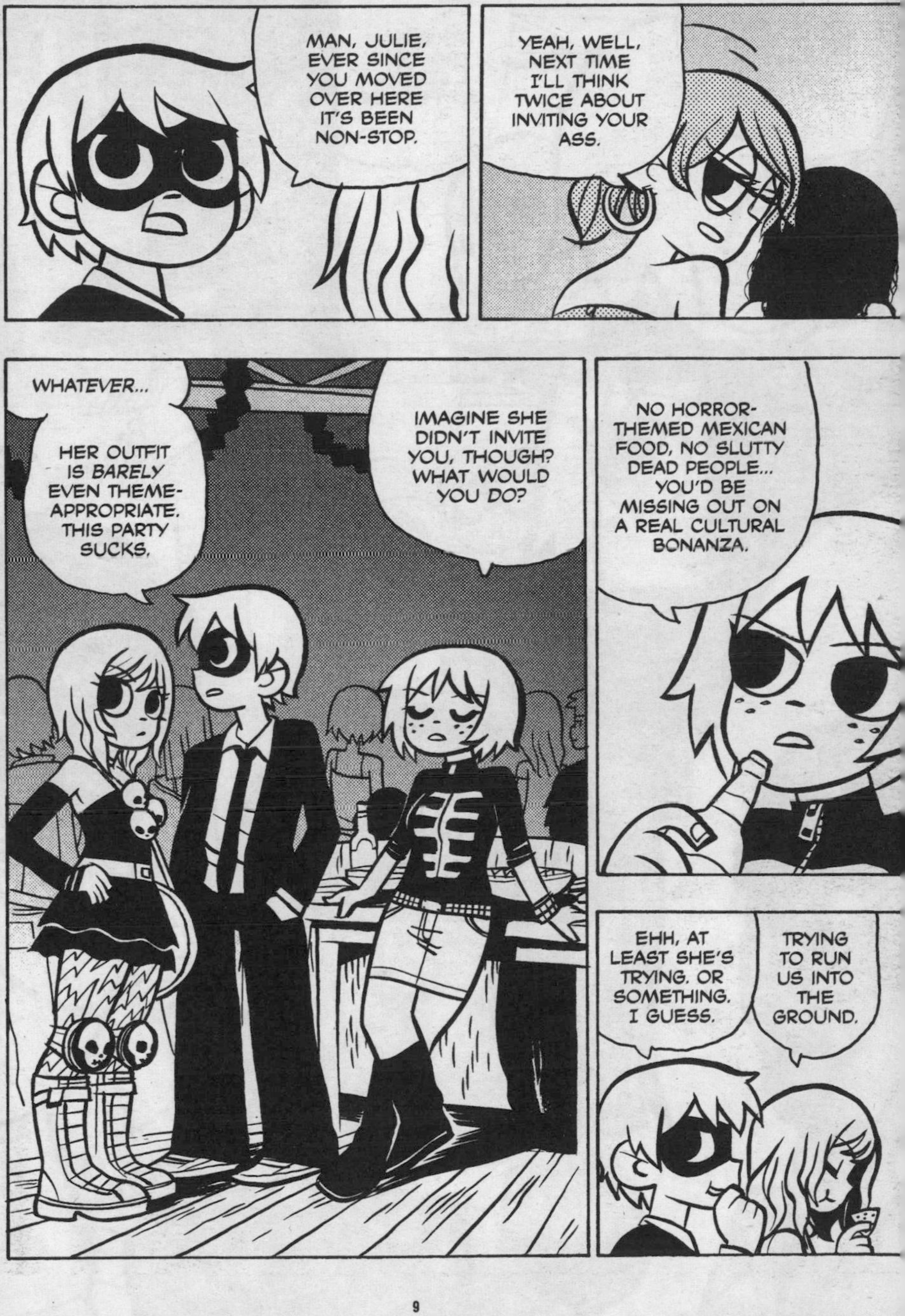
MAN, JULIE, EVER SINCE YOU MOVED OVER HERE IT'S BEEN NON-STOP.
YEAH, WELL, NEXT TIME I'LL THINK TWICE ABOUT INVITING YOUR ASS.
WHATEVER...
HER OUTFIT IS BARELY EVEN THEME-APPROPRIATE. THIS PARTY SUCKS.
IMAGINE SHE DIDN'T INVITE YOU, THOUGH? WHAT WOULD YOU DO?
NO HORROR-THEMED MEXICAN FOOD, NO SLUTTY DEAD PEOPLE... YOU'D BE MISSING OUT ON A REAL CULTURAL BONANZA.
EHH, AT LEAST SHE'S TRYING. OR SOMETHING. I GUESS.
TRYING TO RUN US INTO THE GROUND.

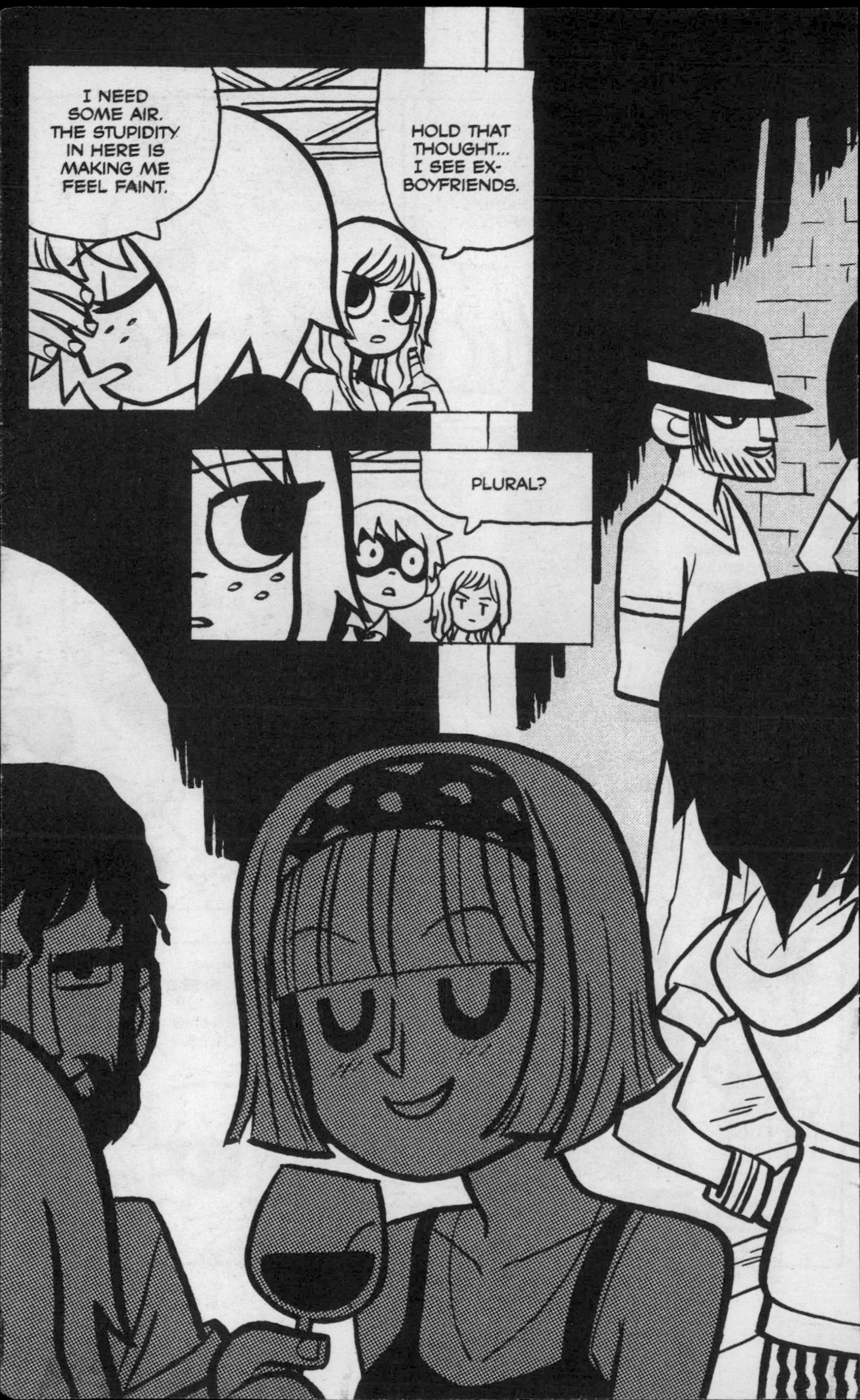
I NEED SOME AIR. THE STUPIDITY IN HERE IS MAKING ME FEEL FAINT.
HOLD THAT THOUGHT... I SEE EX-BOYFRIENDS.
PLURAL?

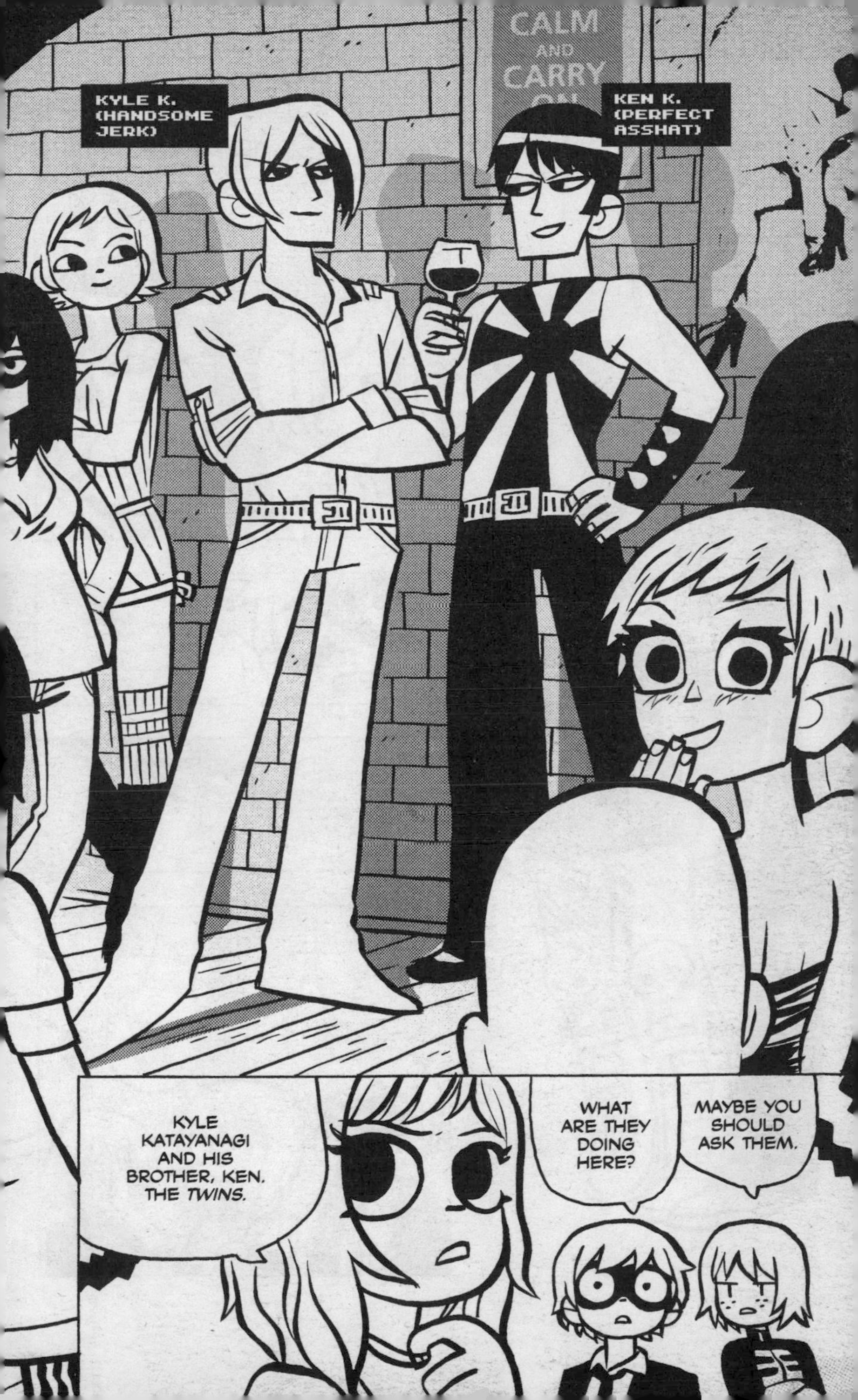
CALM
AND
CARRY
KYLE K. (HANDSOME JERK)
KEN K. (PERFECT ASSHAT)
KYLE KATAYANAGI AND HIS BROTHER, KEN. THE *TWINS.*
WHAT ARE THEY DOING HERE?
MAYBE YOU SHOULD ASK THEM.

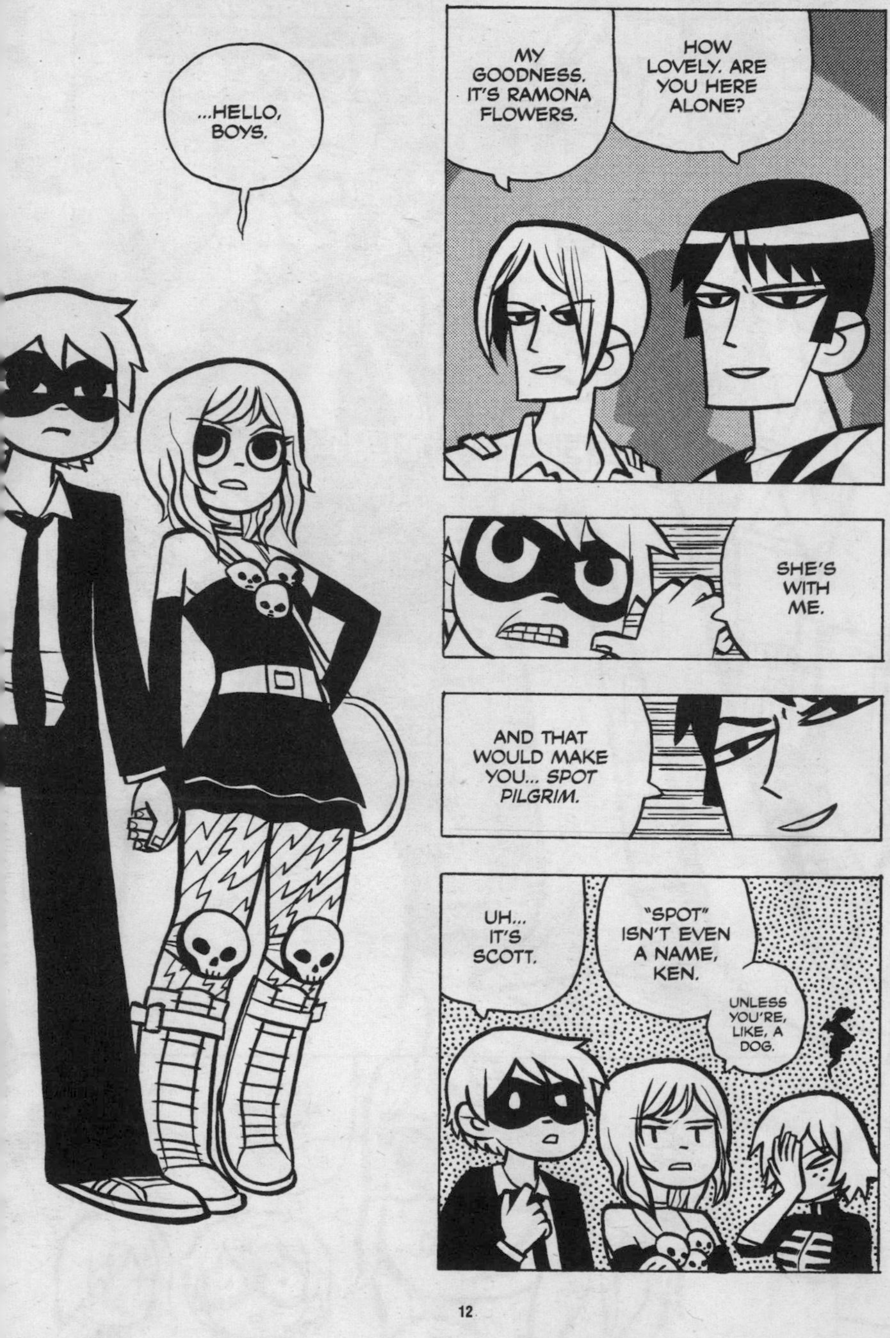
...HELLO, BOYS.
MY GOODNESS. IT'S RAMONA FLOWERS.
HOW LOVELY. ARE YOU HERE ALONE?
SHE'S WITH ME.
AND THAT WOULD MAKE YOU... *SPOT PILGRIM.*
UH... IT'S SCOTT.
"SPOT" ISN'T EVEN A NAME, KEN.
UNLESS YOU'RE, LIKE, A DOG.

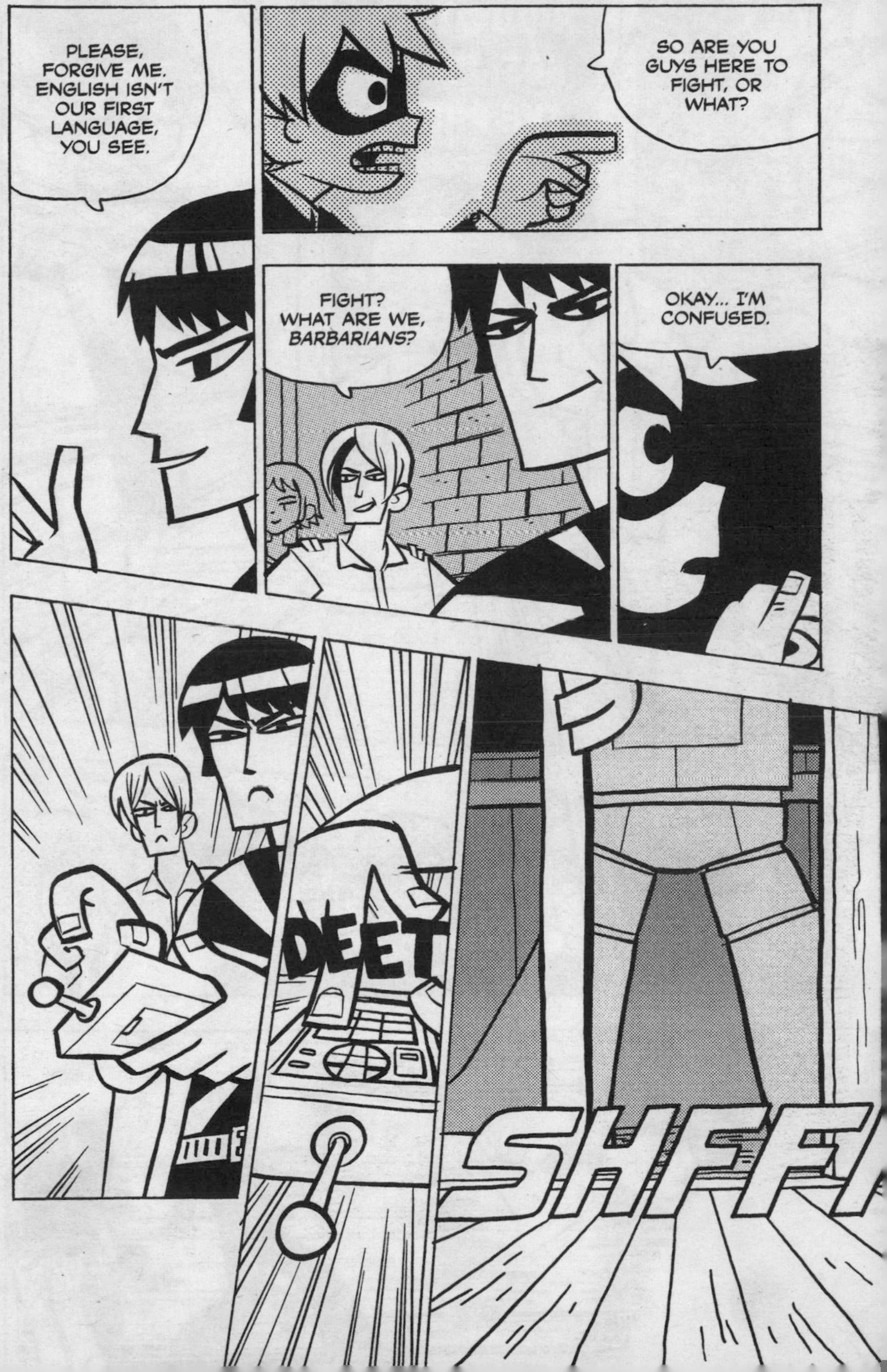
PLEASE, FORGIVE ME. ENGLISH ISN'T OUR FIRST LANGUAGE, YOU SEE.
SO ARE YOU GUYS HERE TO FIGHT, OR WHAT?
FIGHT? WHAT ARE WE, BARBARIANS?
OKAY... I'M CONFUSED.
DEET
SHFF!

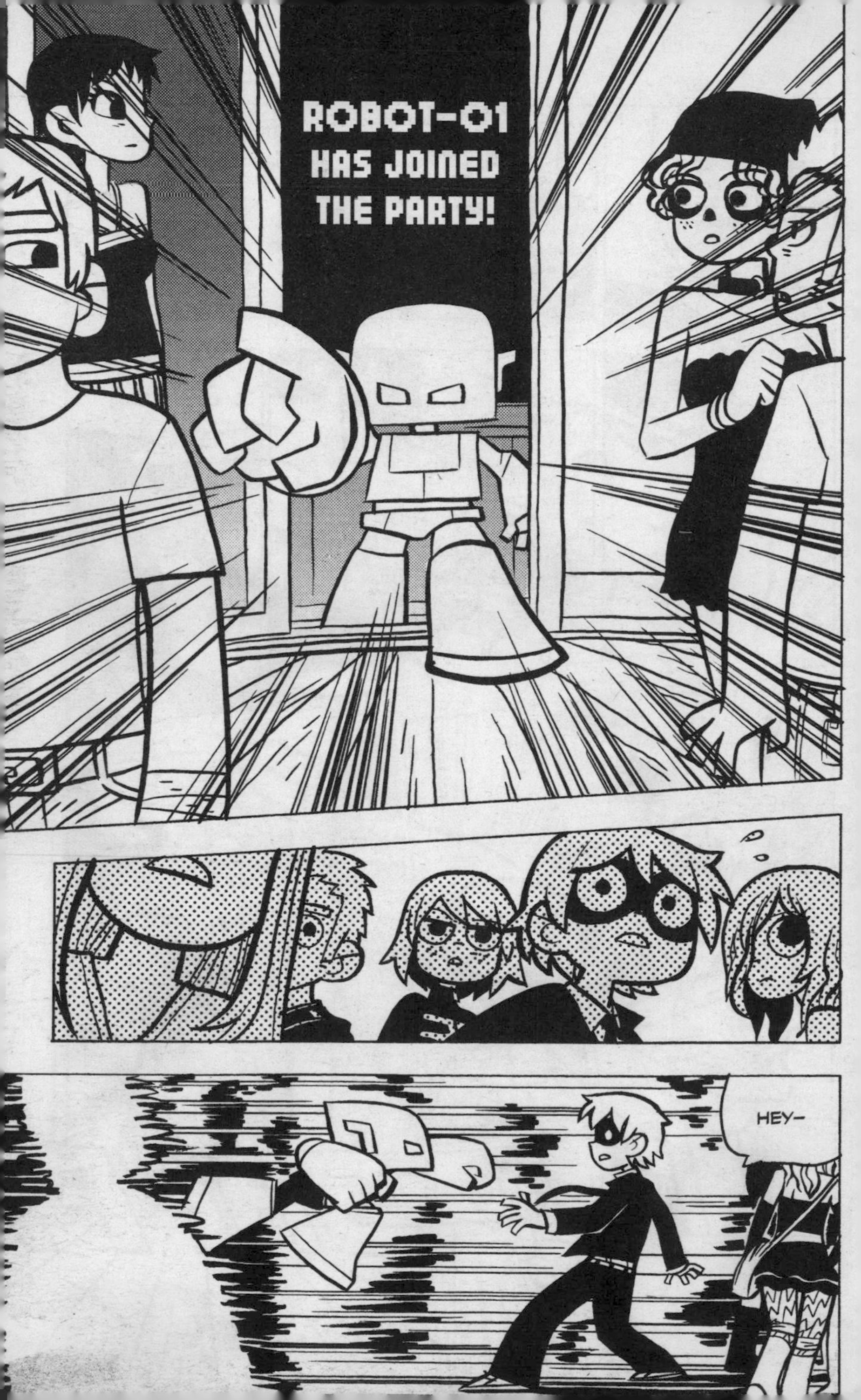
ROBOT-01 HAS JOINED THE PARTY!
HEY-

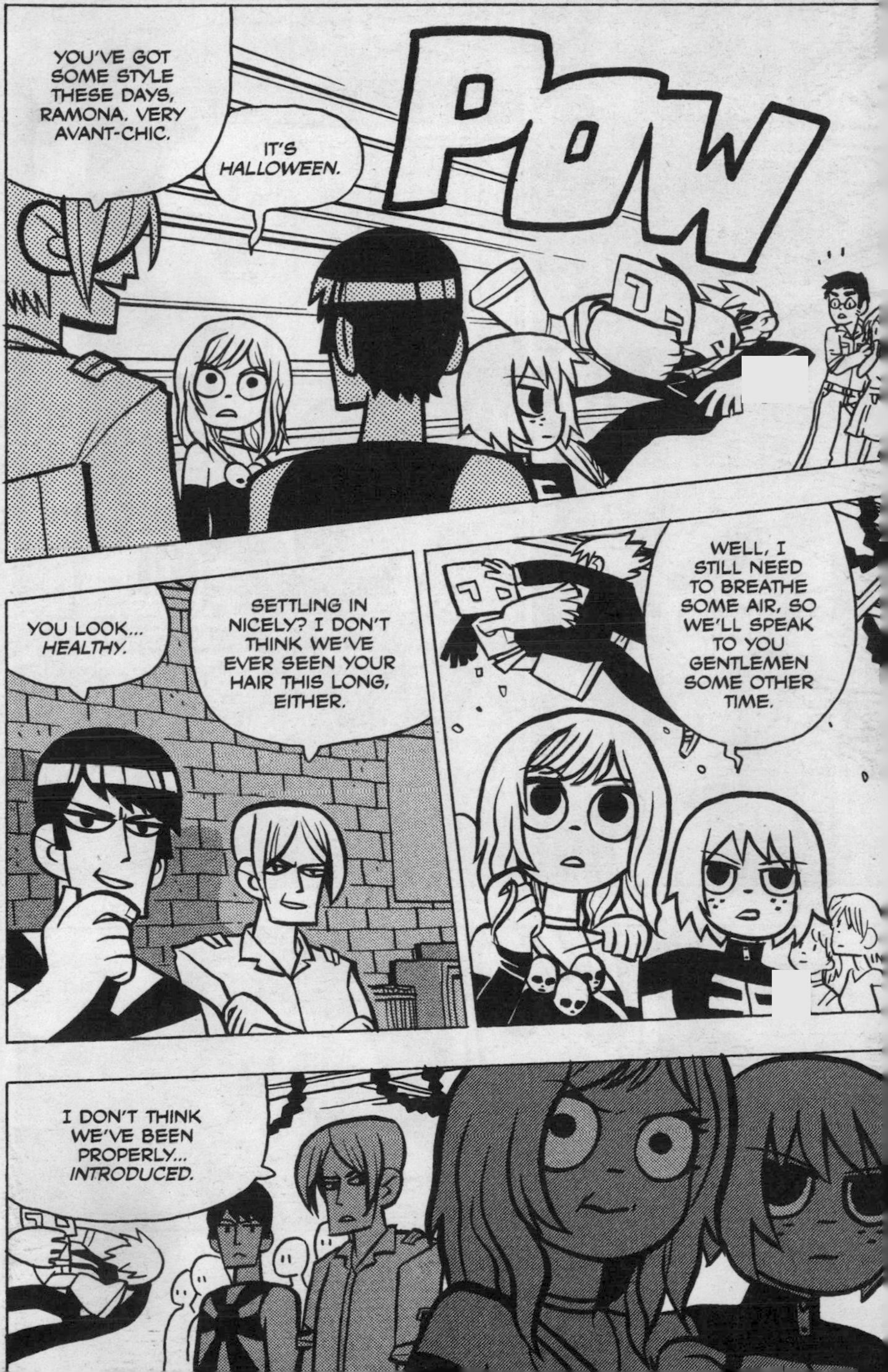
YOU'VE GOT SOME STYLE THESE DAYS, RAMONA. VERY AVANT-CHIC.
IT'S HALLOWEEN.
POW
YOU LOOK... HEALTHY.
SETTLING IN NICELY? I DON'T THINK WE'VE EVER SEEN YOUR HAIR THIS LONG, EITHER.
WELL, I STILL NEED TO BREATHE SOME AIR, SO WE'LL SPEAK TO YOU GENTLEMEN SOME OTHER TIME.
I DON'T THINK WE'VE BEEN PROPERLY... INTRODUCED.

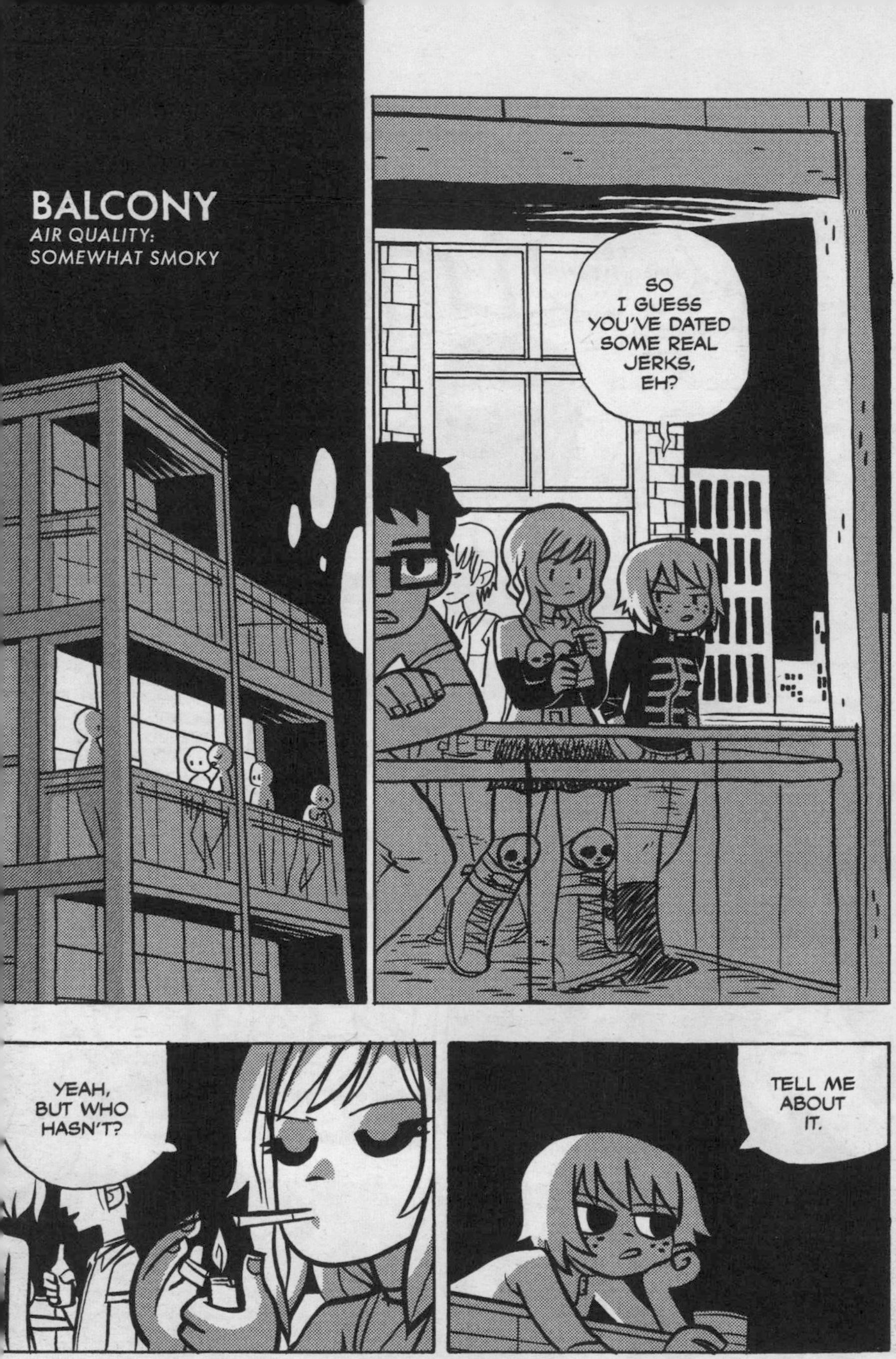
BALCONY
AIR QUALITY:
SOMEWHAT SMOKY
SO I GUESS YOU'VE DATED SOME REAL JERKS, EH?
YEAH, BUT WHO HASN'T?
TELL ME ABOUT IT.

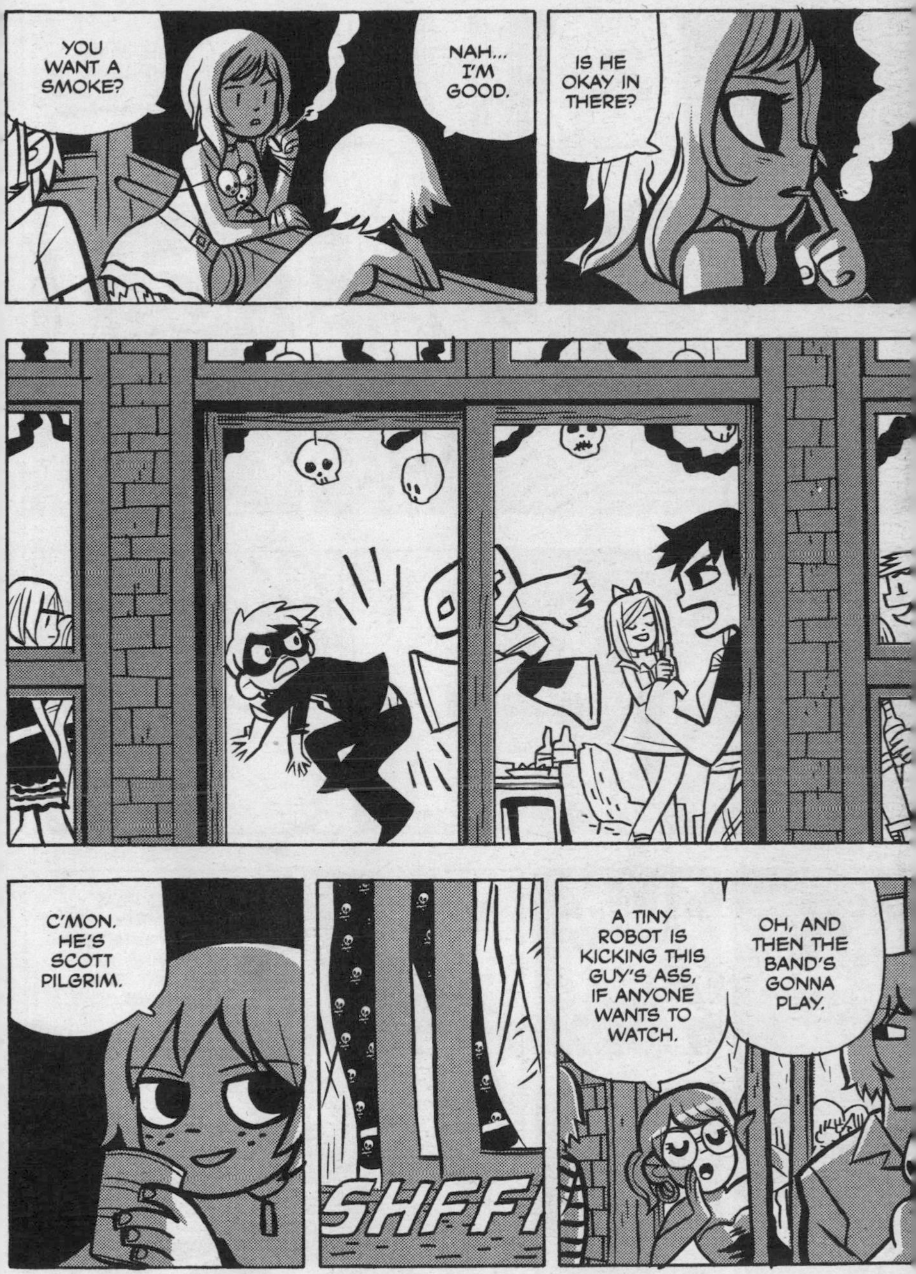
YOU WANT A SMOKE?
NAH... I'M GOOD.
IS HE OKAY IN THERE?
C'MON. HE'S SCOTT PILGRIM.
SHFFT
A TINY ROBOT IS KICKING THIS GUY'S ASS, IF ANYONE WANTS TO WATCH.
OH, AND THEN THE BAND'S GONNA PLAY.

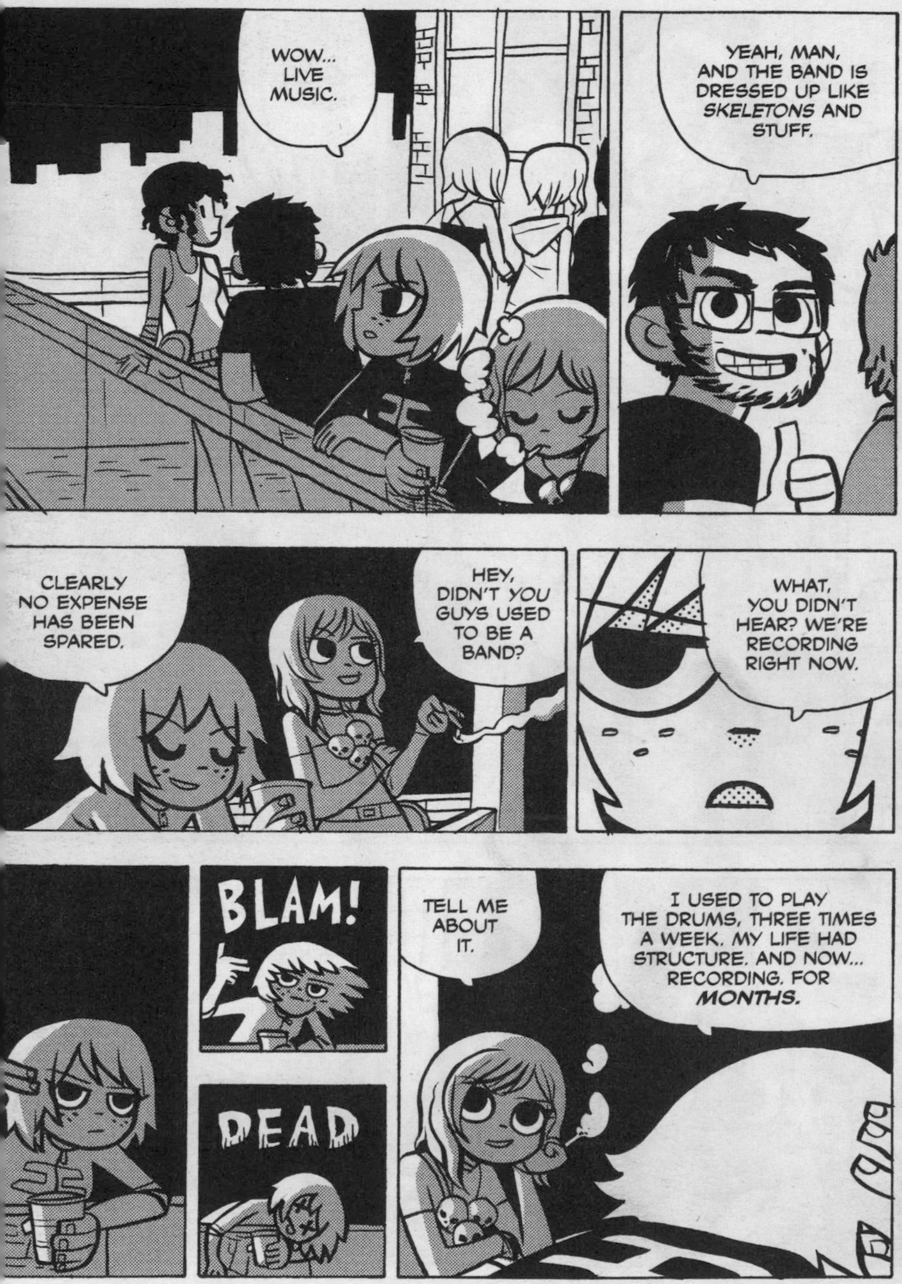
WOW... LIVE MUSIC.
YEAH, MAN, AND THE BAND IS DRESSED UP LIKE *SKELETONS* AND STUFF.
CLEARLY NO EXPENSE HAS BEEN SPARED.
HEY, DIDN'T *YOU* GUYS USED TO BE A BAND?
WHAT, YOU DIDN'T HEAR? WE'RE RECORDING RIGHT NOW.
BLAM!
DEAD
TELL ME ABOUT IT.
I USED TO PLAY THE DRUMS, THREE TIMES A WEEK. MY LIFE HAD STRUCTURE. AND NOW... RECORDING. FOR ***MONTHS.***

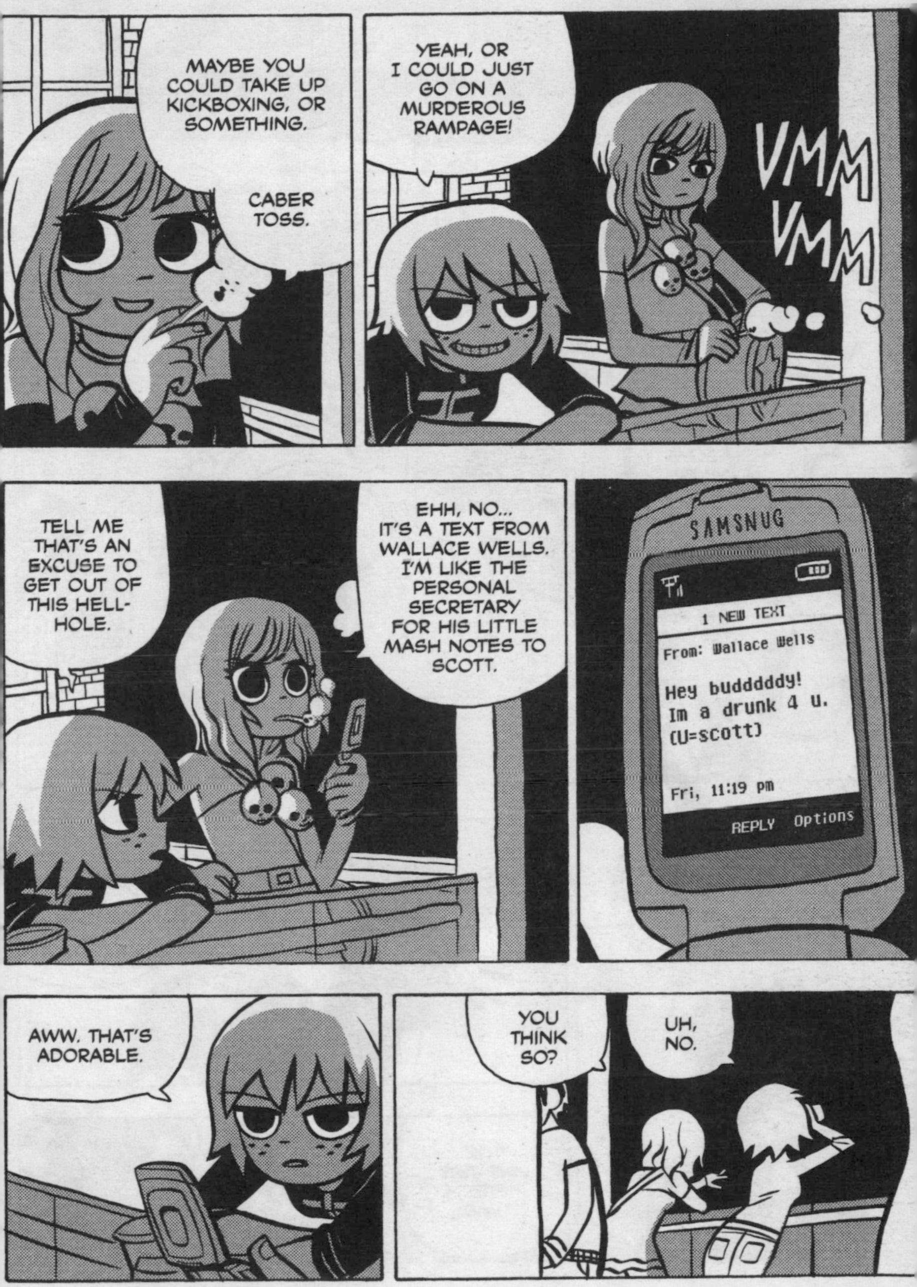
MAYBE YOU COULD TAKE UP KICKBOXING, OR SOMETHING.
CABER TOSS.
YEAH, OR I COULD JUST GO ON A MURDEROUS RAMPAGE!
VMM VMM
TELL ME THAT'S AN EXCUSE TO GET OUT OF THIS HELL-HOLE.
EHH, NO... IT'S A TEXT FROM WALLACE WELLS. I'M LIKE THE PERSONAL SECRETARY FOR HIS LITTLE MASH NOTES TO SCOTT.
SAMSNUG
1 NEW TEXT
From: Wallace Wells
Hey budddddy!
Im a drunk 4 u.
(U=scott)
Fri, 11:19 pm
REPLY
Options
AWW. THAT'S ADORABLE.
YOU THINK SO?
UH, NO.

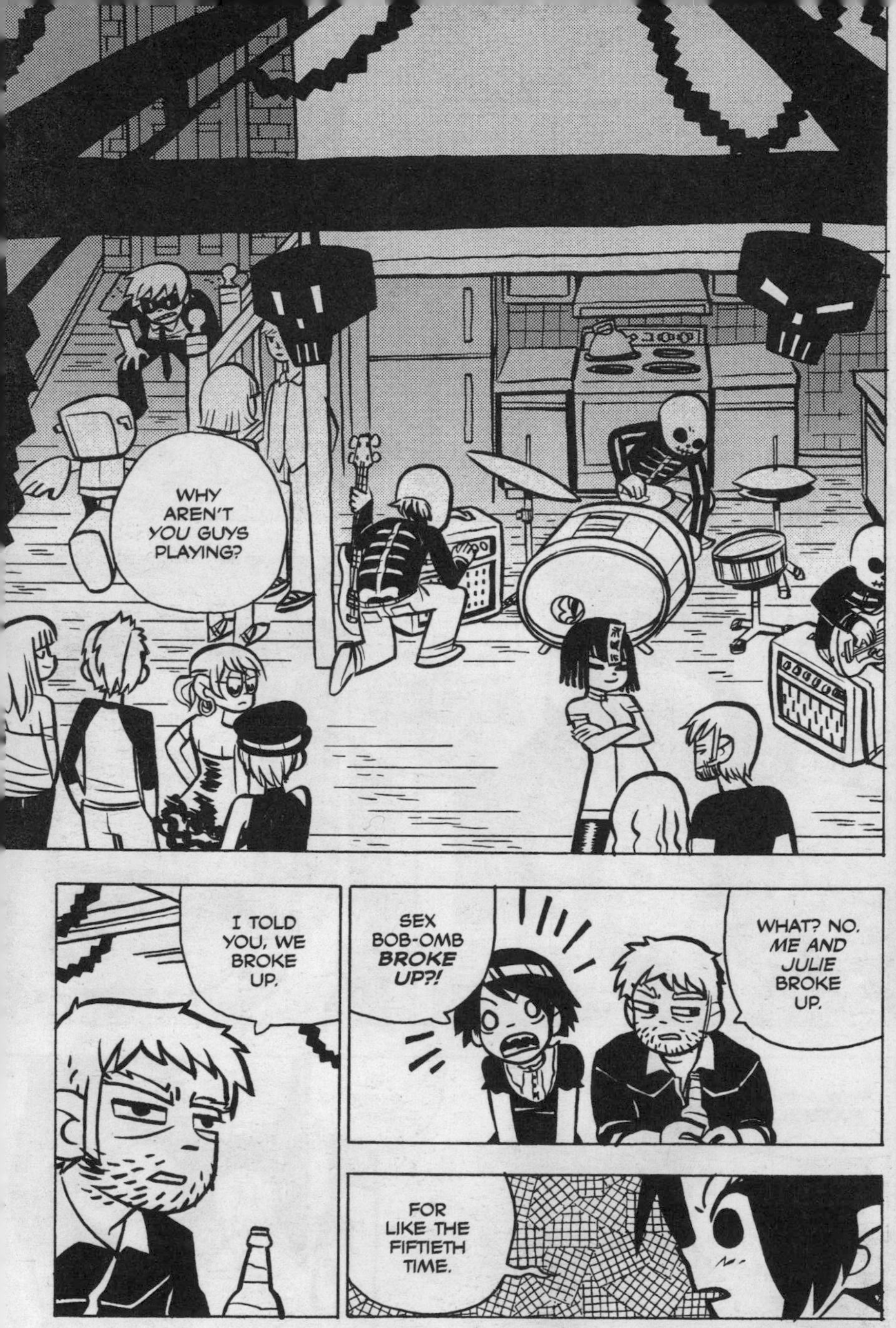
WHY AREN'T *YOU* GUYS PLAYING?
I TOLD YOU, WE BROKE UP.
SEX BOB-OMB **BROKE UP?!**
WHAT? NO. *ME AND JULIE* BROKE UP.
FOR LIKE THE FIFTIETH TIME.

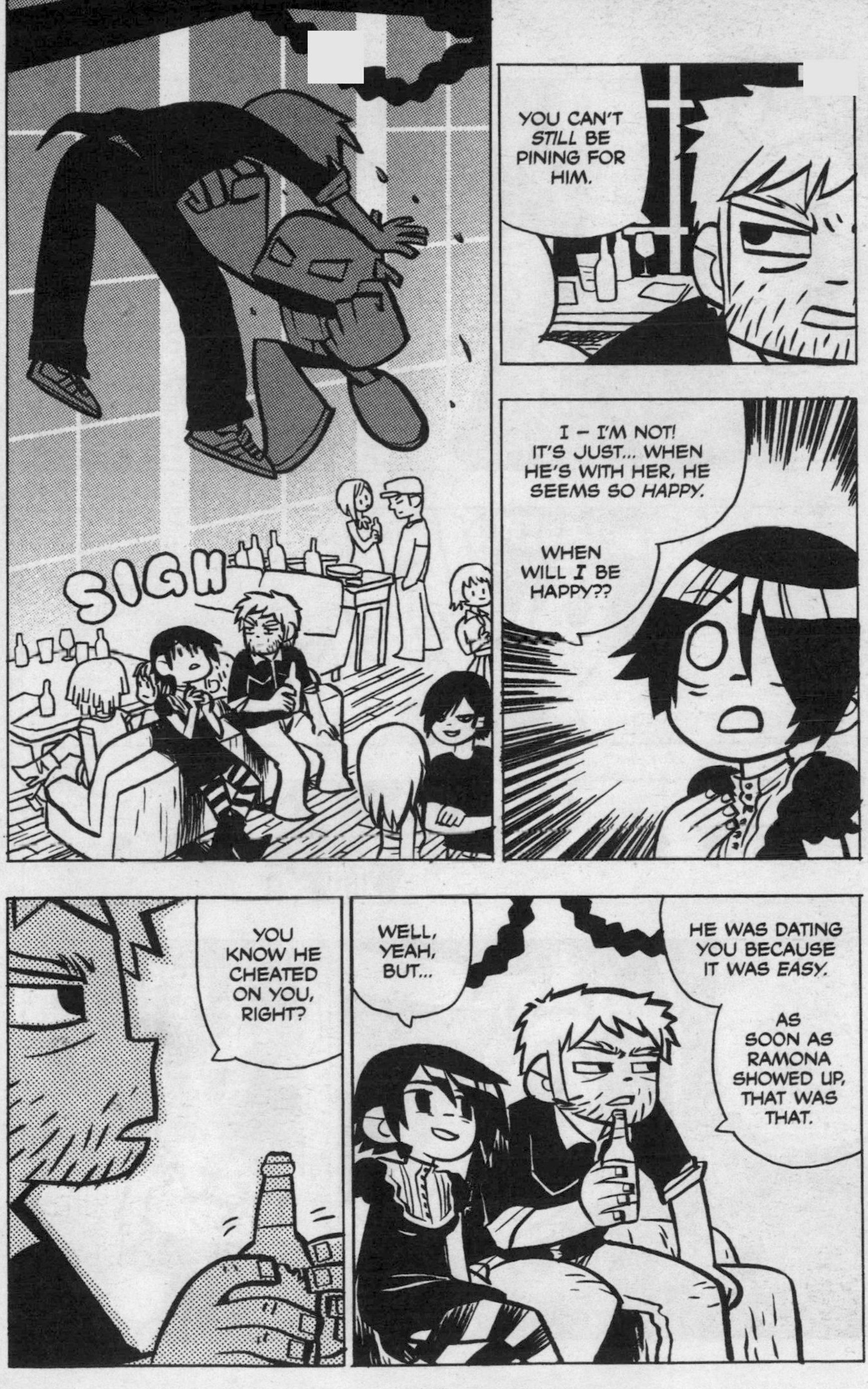
YOU CAN'T STILL BE PINING FOR HIM.
SIGH
I – I'M NOT! IT'S JUST... WHEN HE'S WITH HER, HE SEEMS SO HAPPY.
WHEN WILL I BE HAPPY??
YOU KNOW HE CHEATED ON YOU, RIGHT?
WELL, YEAH, BUT...
HE WAS DATING YOU BECAUSE IT WAS EASY.
AS SOON AS RAMONA SHOWED UP, THAT WAS THAT.

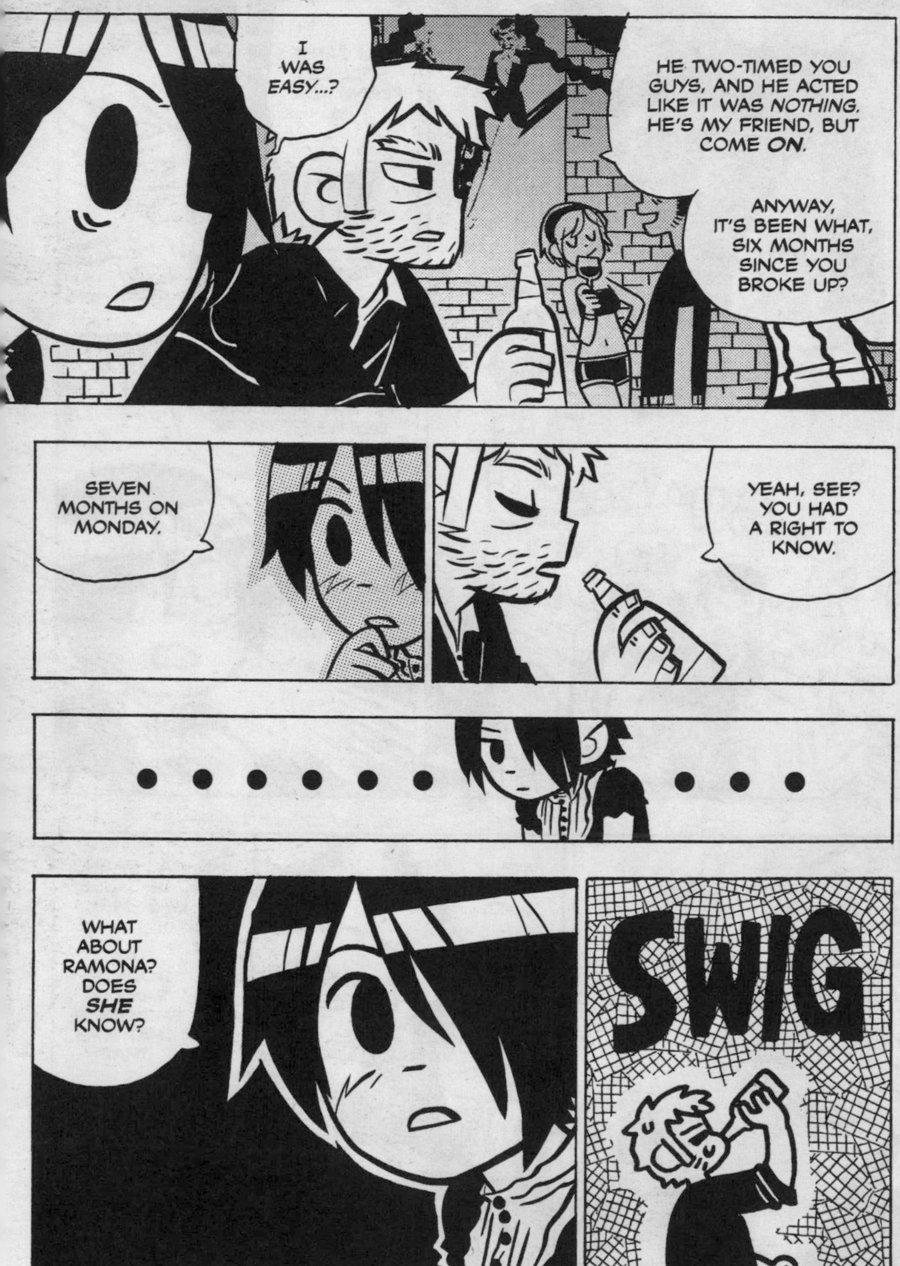
I WAS EASY...?
HE TWO-TIMED YOU GUYS, AND HE ACTED LIKE IT WAS *NOTHING*. HE'S MY FRIEND, BUT COME *ON*.
ANYWAY, IT'S BEEN WHAT, SIX MONTHS SINCE YOU BROKE UP?
SEVEN MONTHS ON MONDAY.
YEAH, SEE? YOU HAD A RIGHT TO KNOW.
WHAT ABOUT RAMONA? DOES *SHE* KNOW?
SWIG

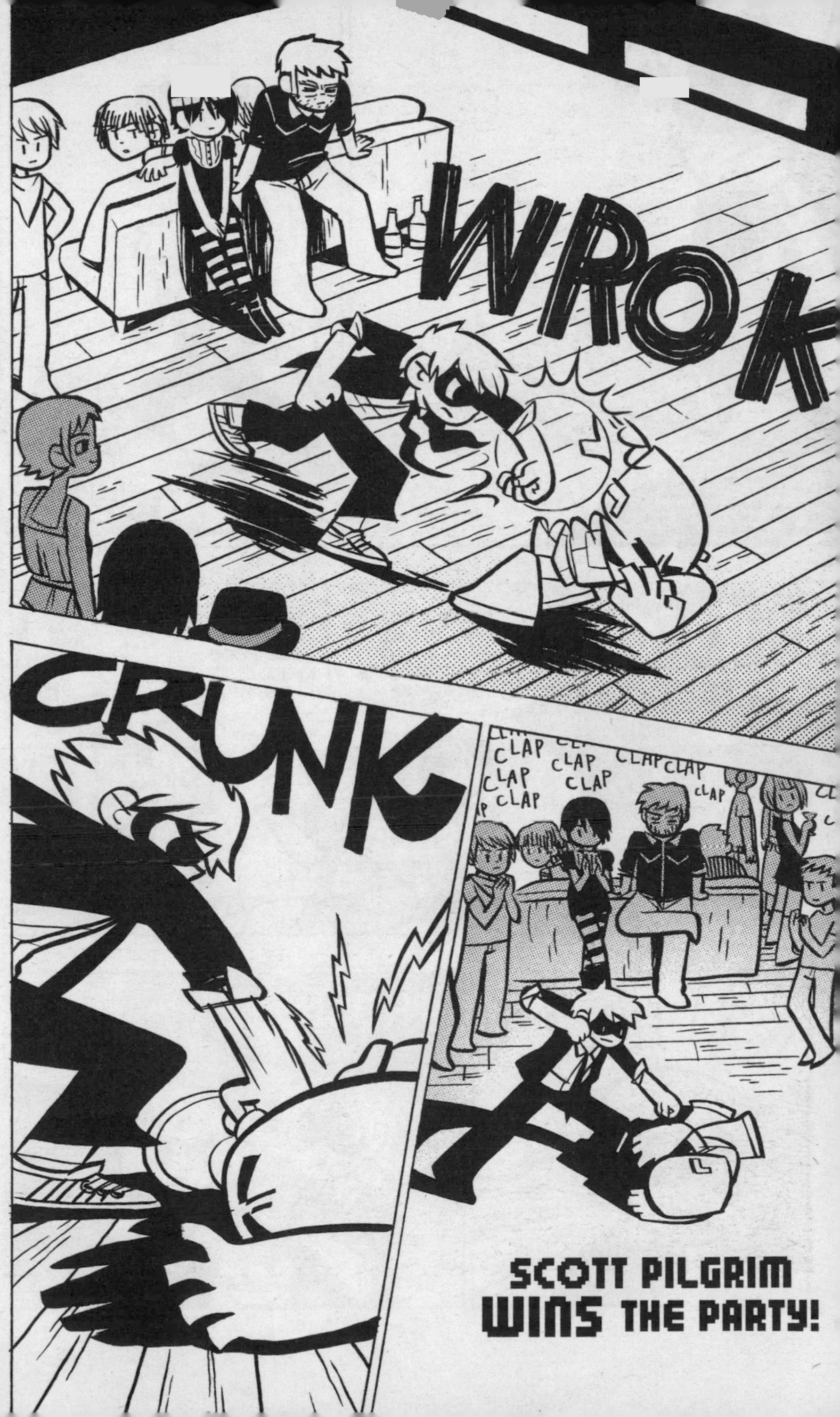
WROK
CRUNK
CLAP CLAP CLAP CLAP CLAP CLAP CLAP CLAP
SCOTT PILGRIM
WINS THE PARTY!

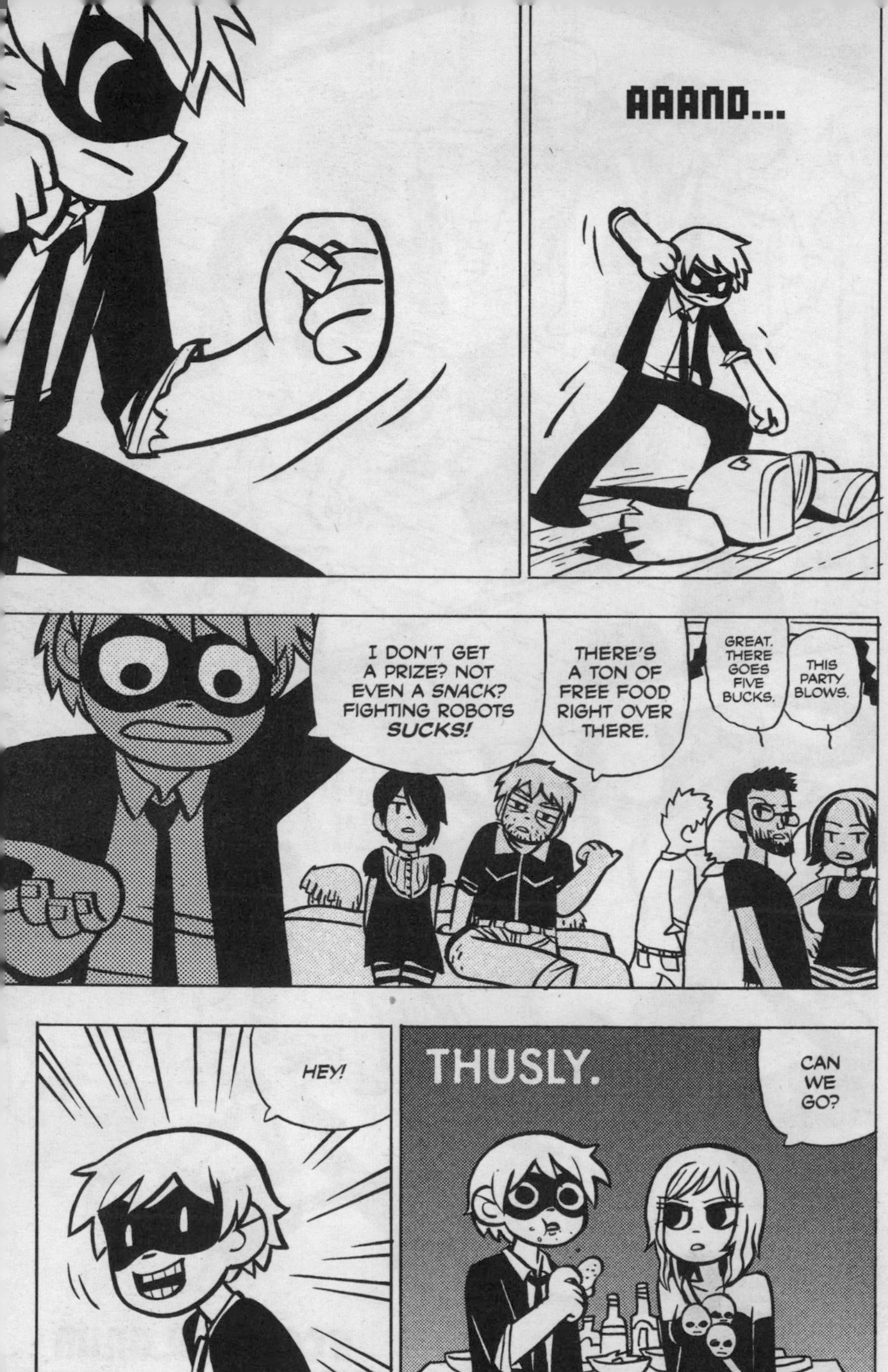
AAAND...
I DON'T GET A PRIZE? NOT EVEN A *SNACK*? FIGHTING ROBOTS *SUCKS!*
THERE'S A TON OF FREE FOOD RIGHT OVER THERE.
GREAT. THERE GOES FIVE BUCKS.
THIS PARTY BLOWS.
HEY!
THUSLY.
CAN WE GO?

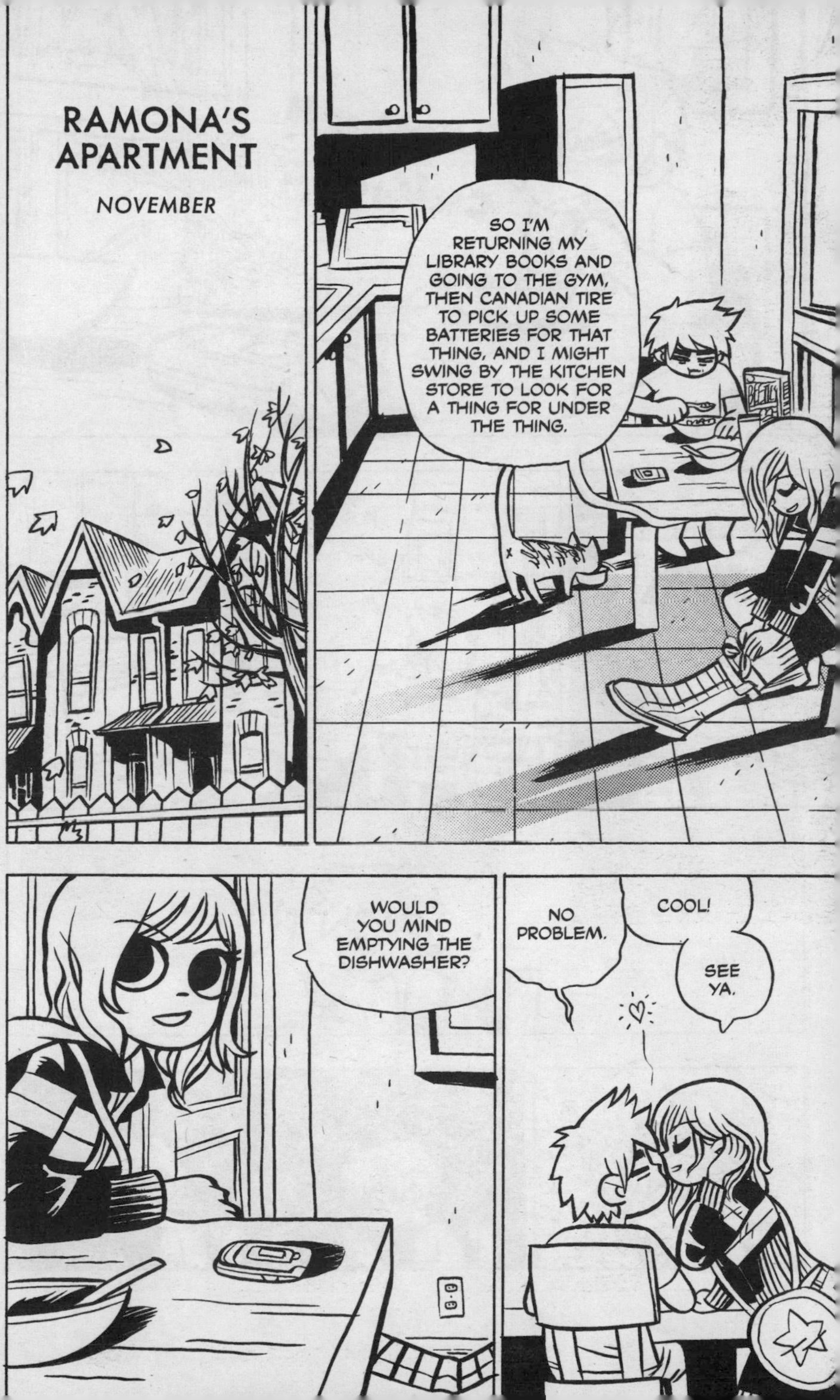
RAMONA'S APARTMENT
NOVEMBER
SO I'M RETURNING MY LIBRARY BOOKS AND GOING TO THE GYM, THEN CANADIAN TIRE TO PICK UP SOME BATTERIES FOR THAT THING, AND I MIGHT SWING BY THE KITCHEN STORE TO LOOK FOR A THING FOR UNDER THE THING.
WOULD YOU MIND EMPTYING THE DISHWASHER?
NO PROBLEM.
COOL!
SEE YA.

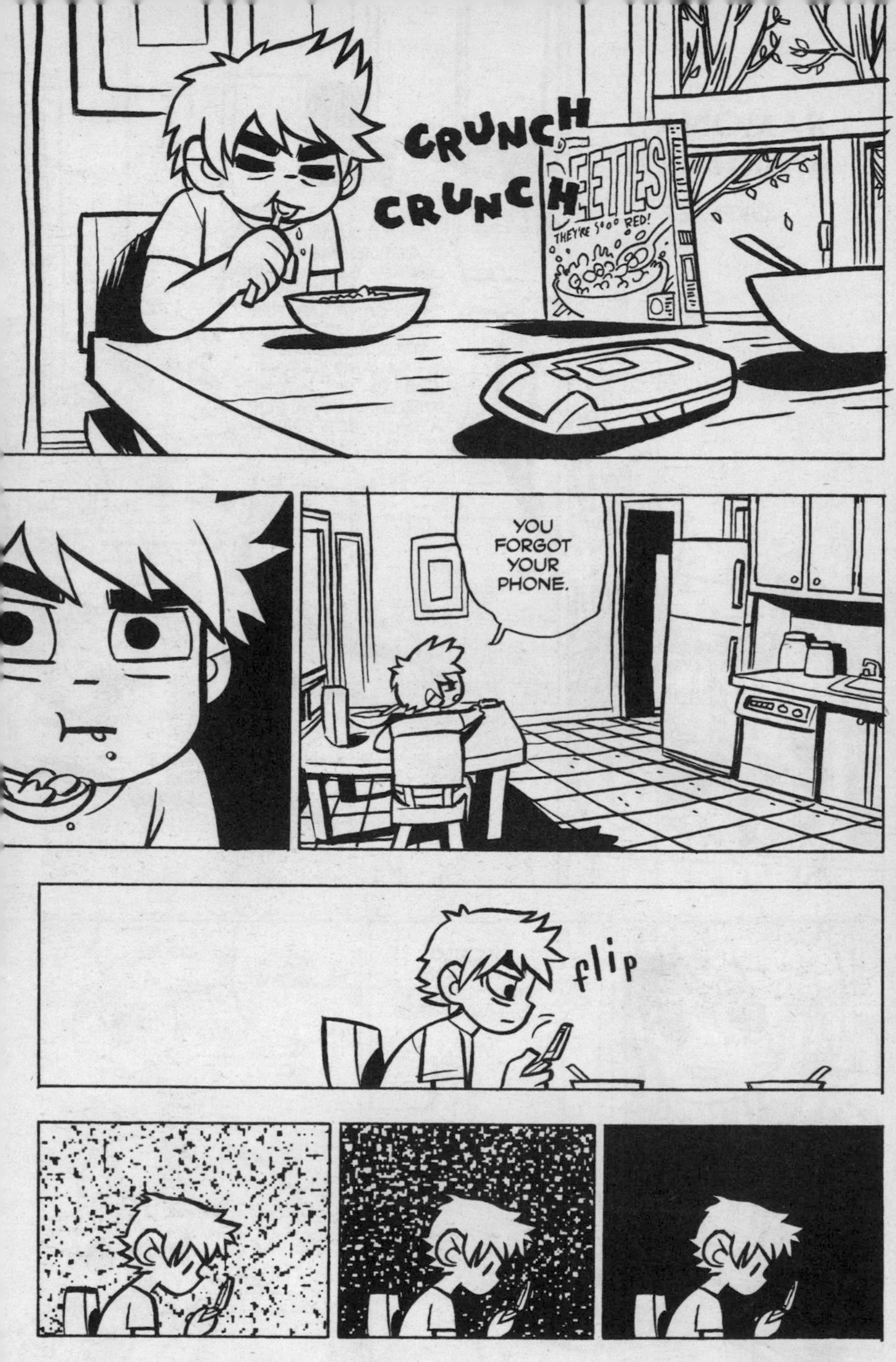
CRUNCH
CRUNCH
THEY'RE SOOO RED!
YOU FORGOT YOUR PHONE.
flip

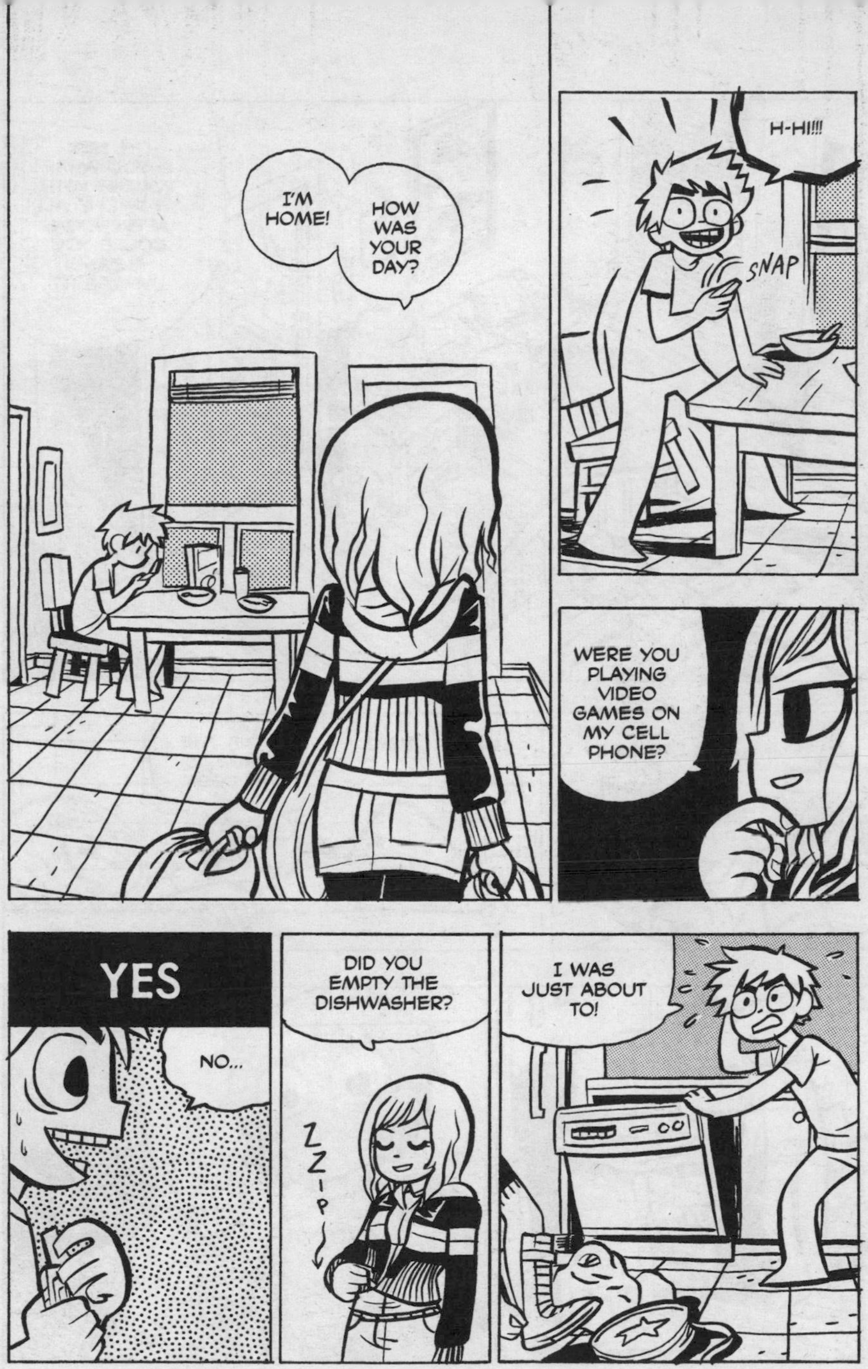
I'M HOME!
HOW WAS YOUR DAY?
H-HI!!!
SNAP
WERE YOU PLAYING VIDEO GAMES ON MY CELL PHONE?
YES
NO...
DID YOU EMPTY THE DISHWASHER?
ZZIP
I WAS JUST ABOUT TO!

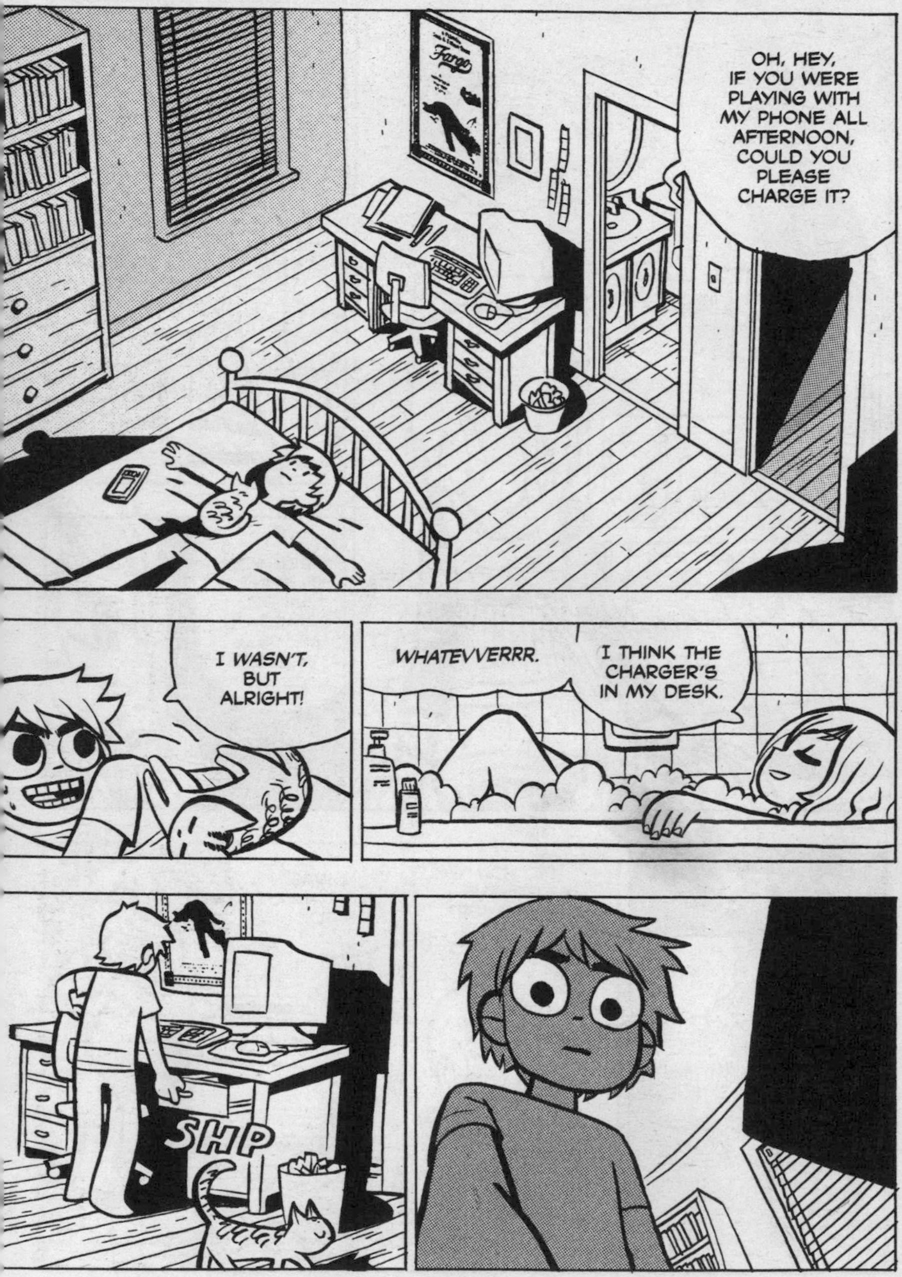
OH, HEY, IF YOU WERE PLAYING WITH MY PHONE ALL AFTERNOON, COULD YOU PLEASE CHARGE IT?
I *WASN'T*, BUT ALRIGHT!
WHATEVVERRR.
I THINK THE CHARGER'S IN MY DESK.
SHP

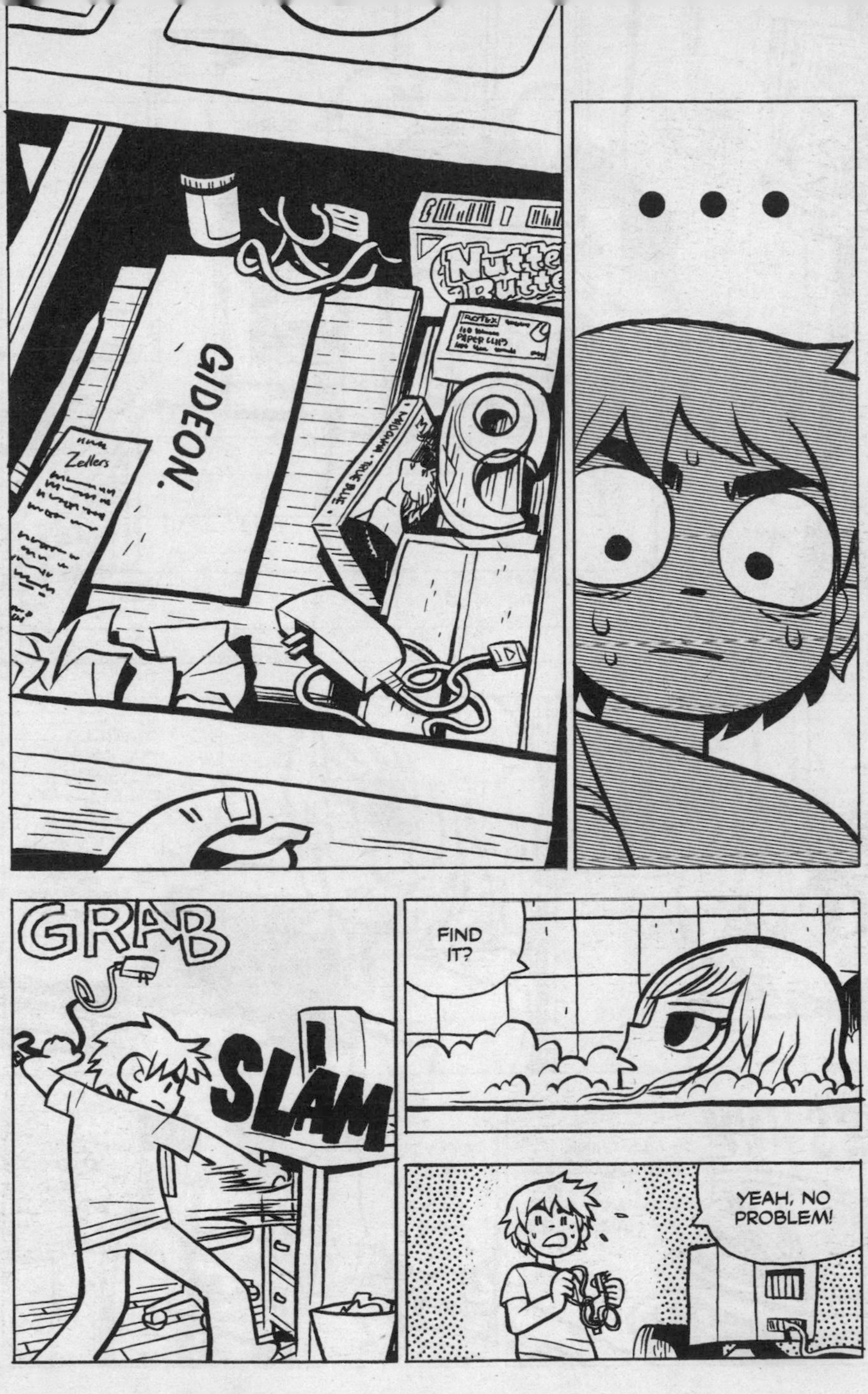
GIDEON.
Zellers
ROTEX
PAPER CLIPS
• • •
GRAB
SLAM
FIND IT?
YEAH, NO PROBLEM!

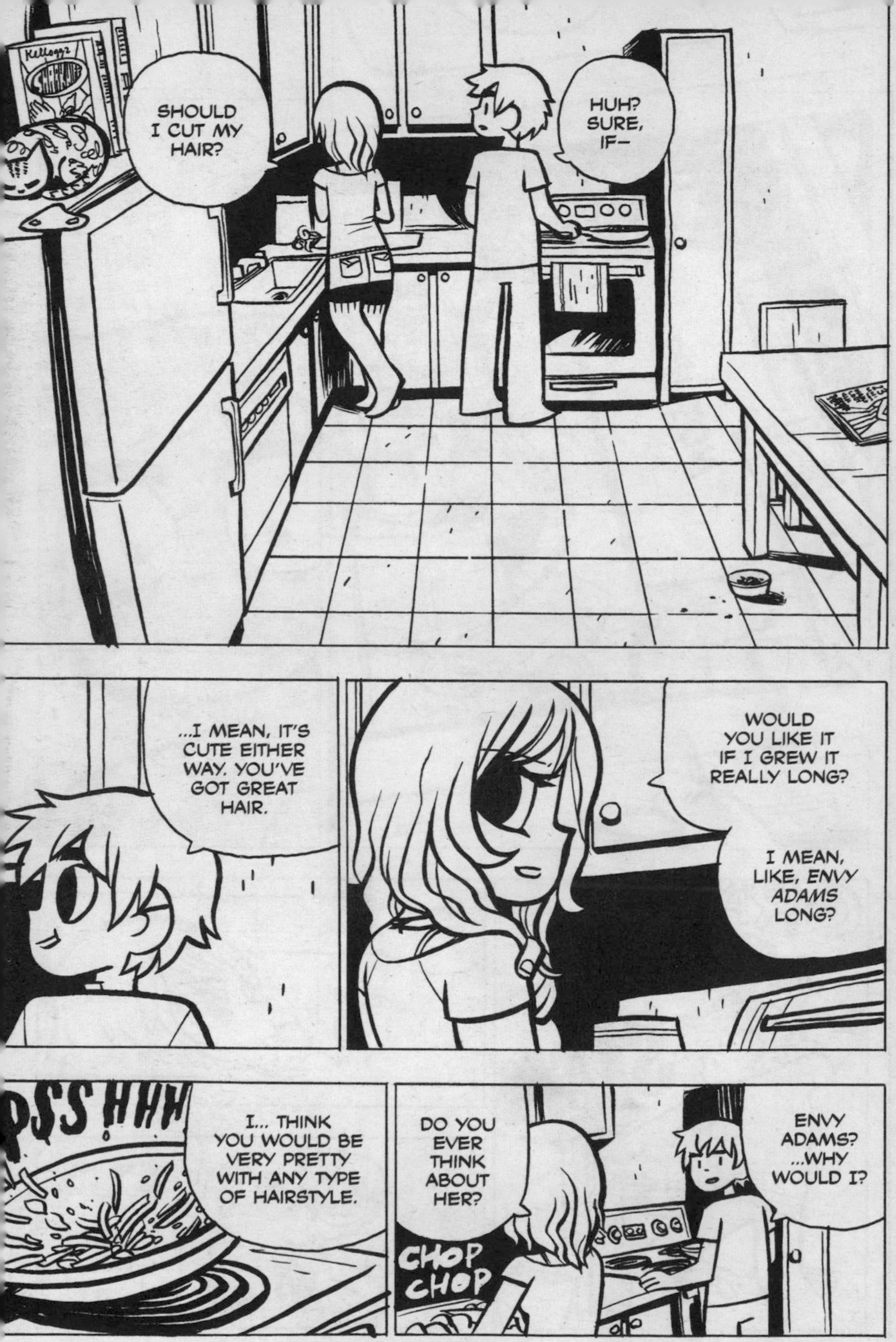
SHOULD I CUT MY HAIR?
HUH? SURE, IF—
...I MEAN, IT'S CUTE EITHER WAY. YOU'VE GOT GREAT HAIR.
WOULD YOU LIKE IT IF I GREW IT REALLY LONG?
I MEAN, LIKE, *ENVY ADAMS* LONG?
SSHHH
I... THINK YOU WOULD BE VERY PRETTY WITH ANY TYPE OF HAIRSTYLE.
DO YOU EVER THINK ABOUT HER?
CHOP CHOP
ENVY ADAMS? ...WHY WOULD I?

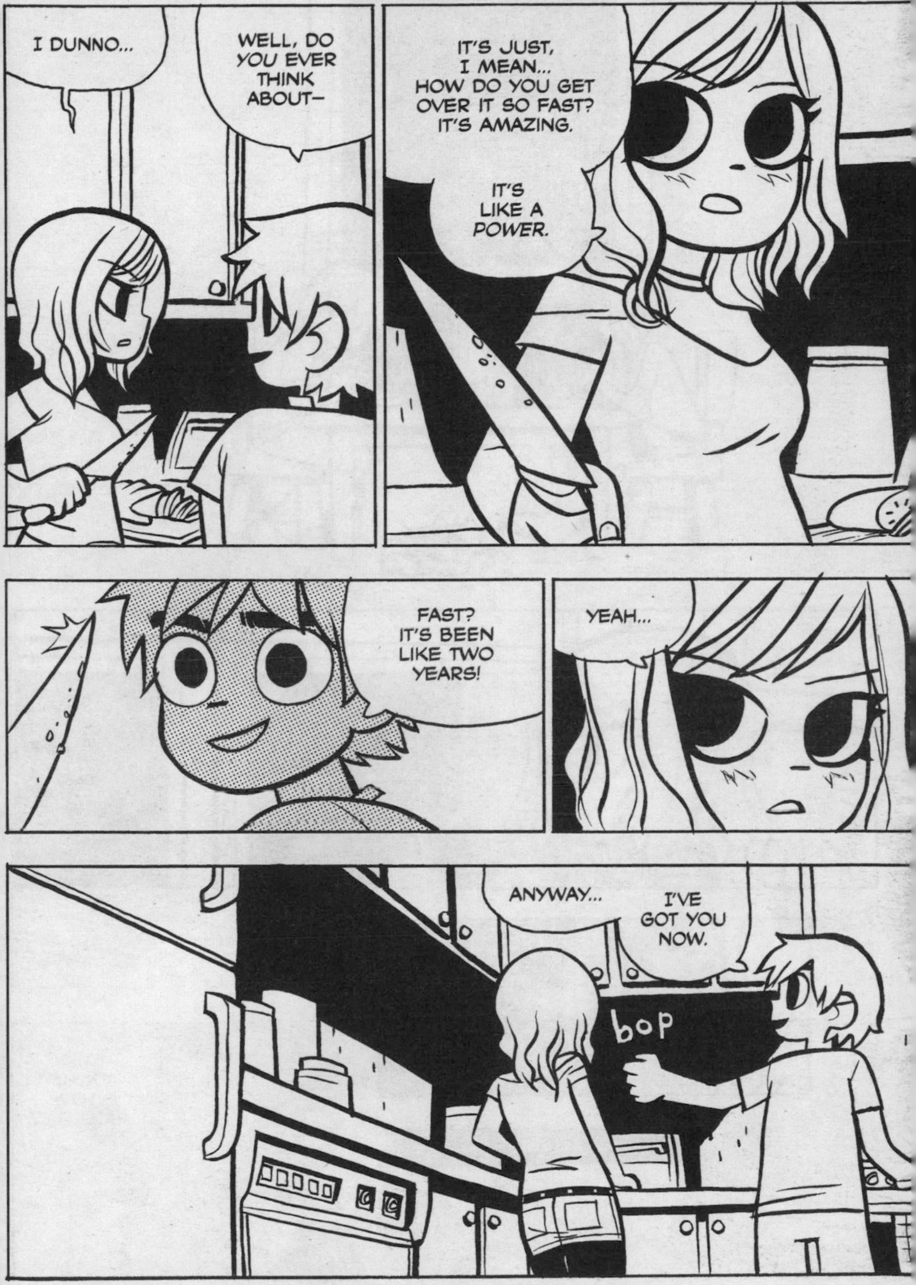
I DUNNO...
WELL, DO YOU EVER THINK ABOUT—
IT'S JUST, I MEAN... HOW DO YOU GET OVER IT SO FAST? IT'S AMAZING.
IT'S LIKE A POWER.
FAST? IT'S BEEN LIKE TWO YEARS!
YEAH...
ANYWAY...
I'VE GOT YOU NOW.
bop

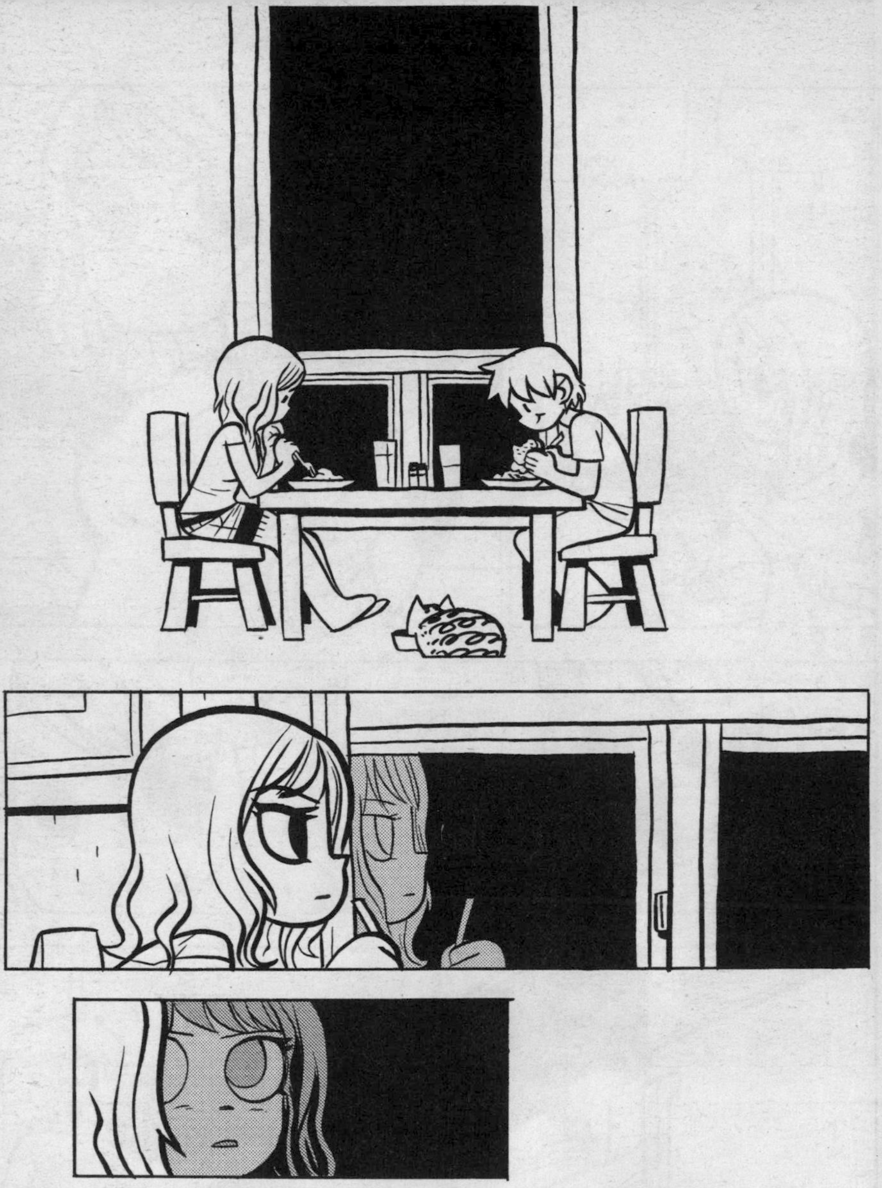

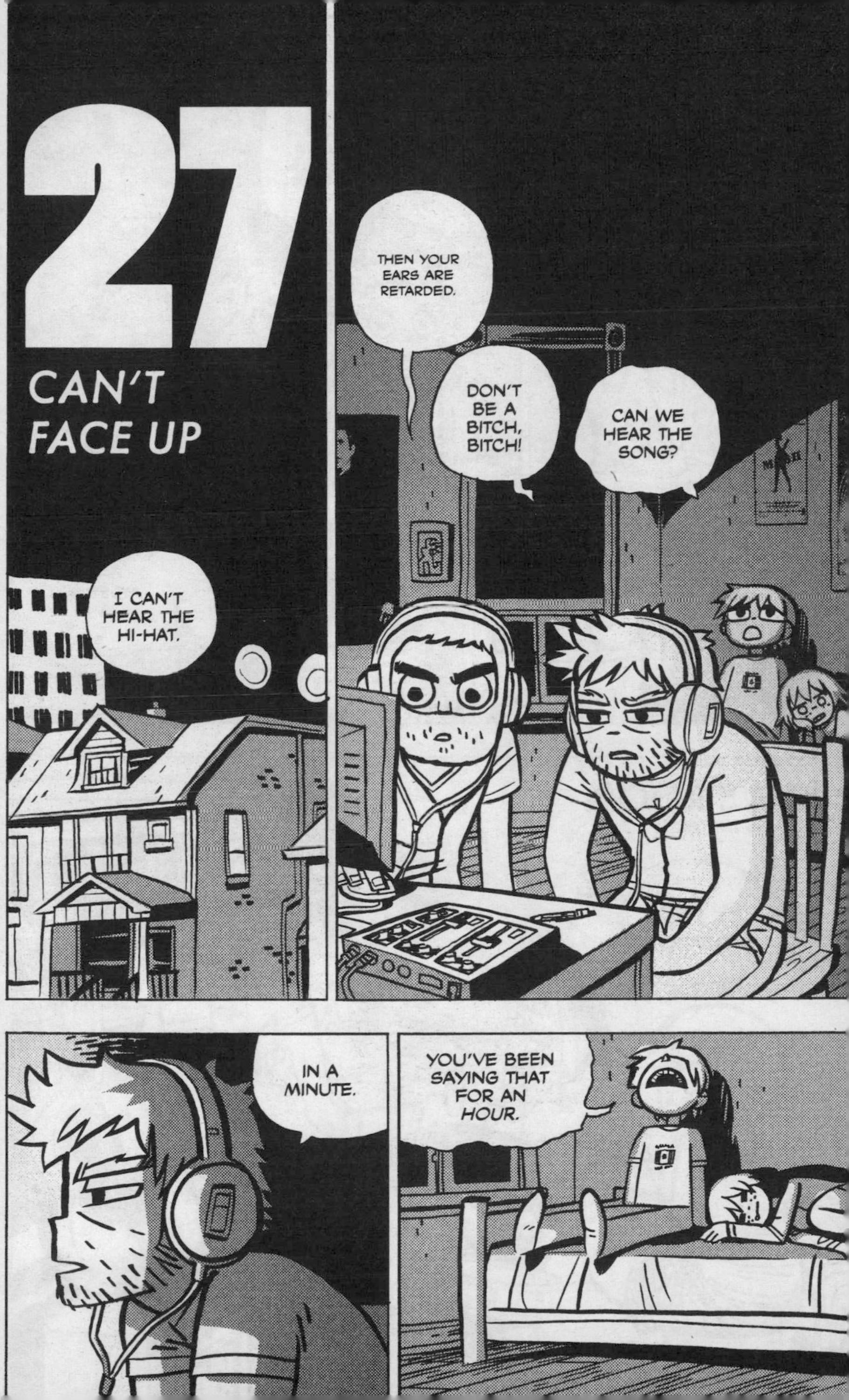
27
CAN'T FACE UP
I CAN'T HEAR THE HI-HAT.
THEN YOUR EARS ARE RETARDED.
DON'T BE A BITCH, BITCH!
CAN WE HEAR THE SONG?
IN A MINUTE.
YOU'VE BEEN SAYING THAT FOR AN *HOUR*.

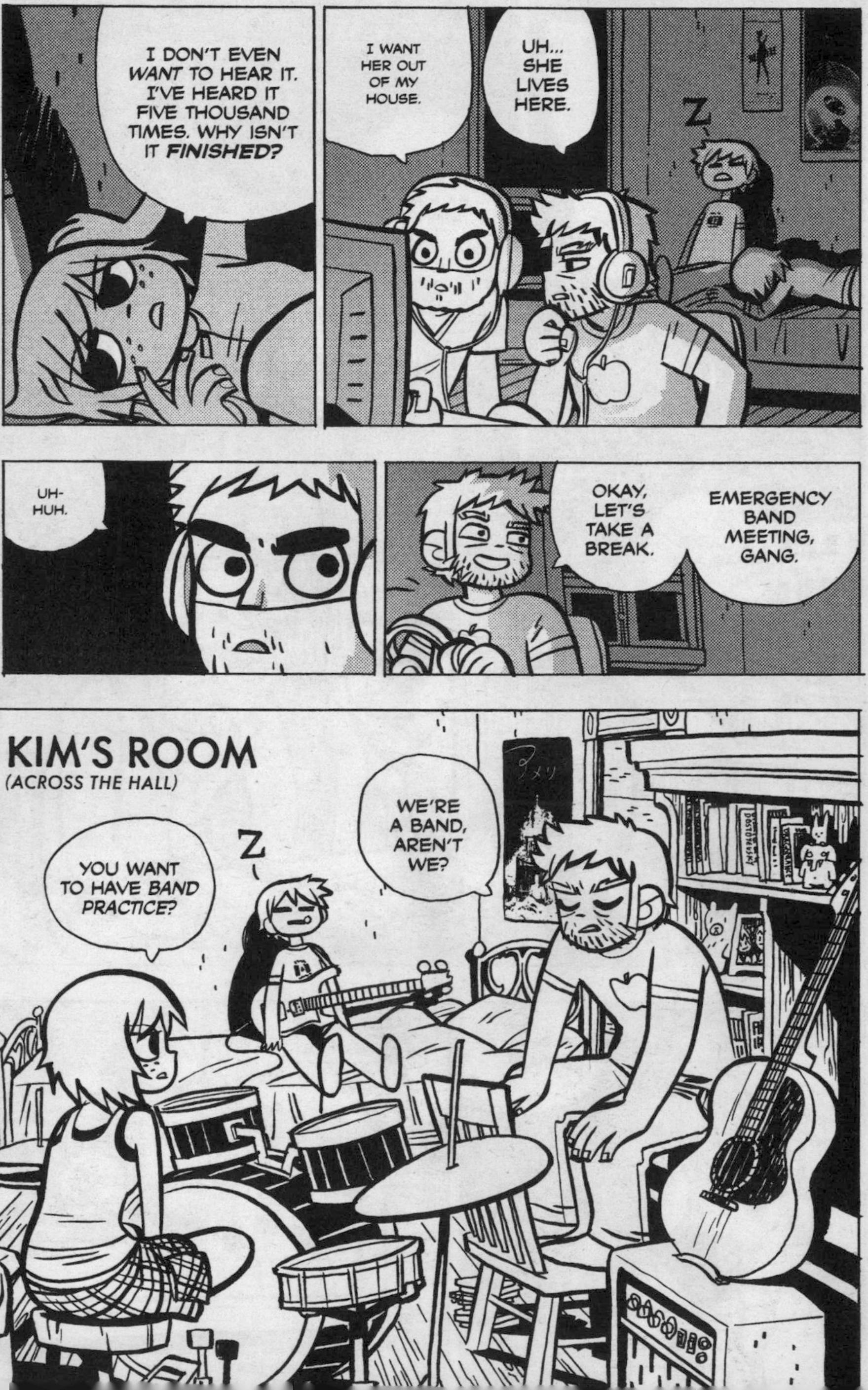

I DON'T EVEN WANT TO HEAR IT. I'VE HEARD IT FIVE THOUSAND TIMES. WHY ISN'T IT FINISHED?
I WANT HER OUT OF MY HOUSE.
UH... SHE LIVES HERE.
Z
UH-HUH.
OKAY, LET'S TAKE A BREAK.
EMERGENCY BAND MEETING, GANG.
KIM'S ROOM
(ACROSS THE HALL)
YOU WANT TO HAVE BAND PRACTICE?
Z
WE'RE A BAND, AREN'T WE?

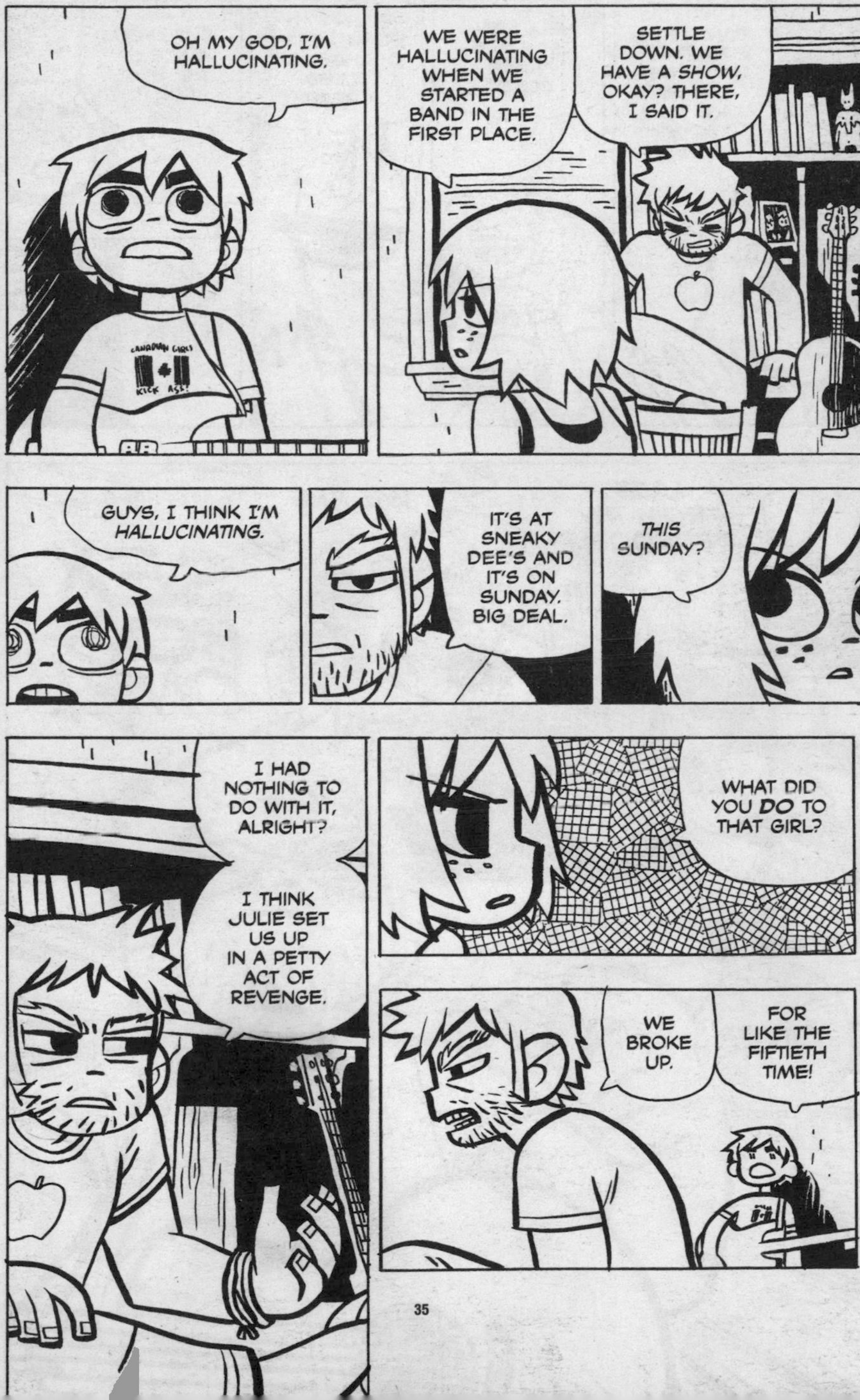
OH MY GOD, I'M HALLUCINATING.
CANADIAN GIRLS KICK ASS!
WE WERE HALLUCINATING WHEN WE STARTED A BAND IN THE FIRST PLACE.
SETTLE DOWN. WE HAVE A *SHOW*, OKAY? THERE, I SAID IT.
GUYS, I THINK I'M *HALLUCINATING.*
IT'S AT SNEAKY DEE'S AND IT'S ON SUNDAY. BIG DEAL.
THIS SUNDAY?
I HAD NOTHING TO DO WITH IT, ALRIGHT?
I THINK JULIE SET US UP IN A PETTY ACT OF REVENGE.
WHAT DID YOU *DO* TO THAT GIRL?
WE BROKE UP.
FOR LIKE THE FIFTIETH TIME!

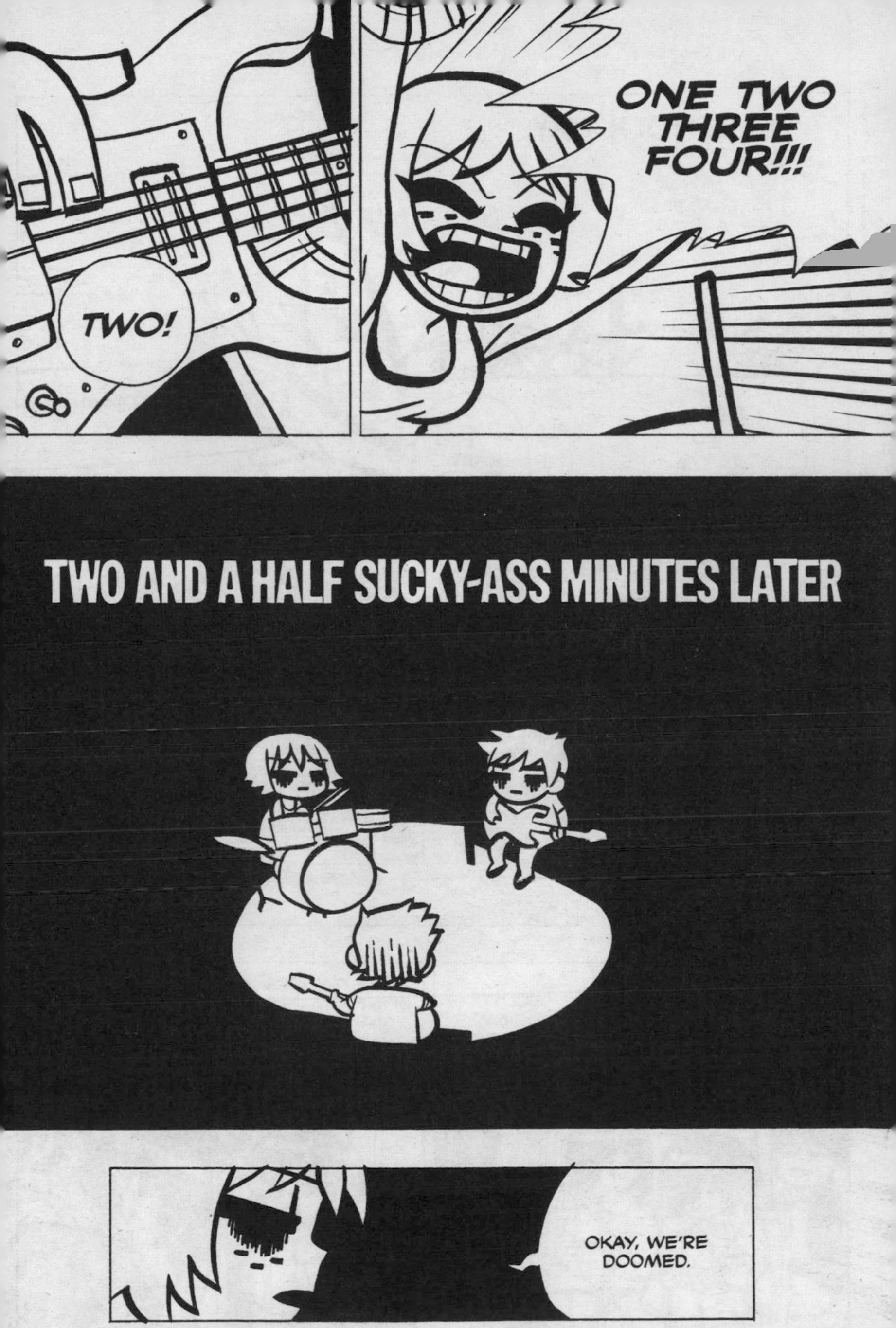
TWO!
ONE TWO THREE FOUR!!!
TWO AND A HALF SUCKY-ASS MINUTES LATER
OKAY, WE'RE DOOMED.

A SCHOOL DAY

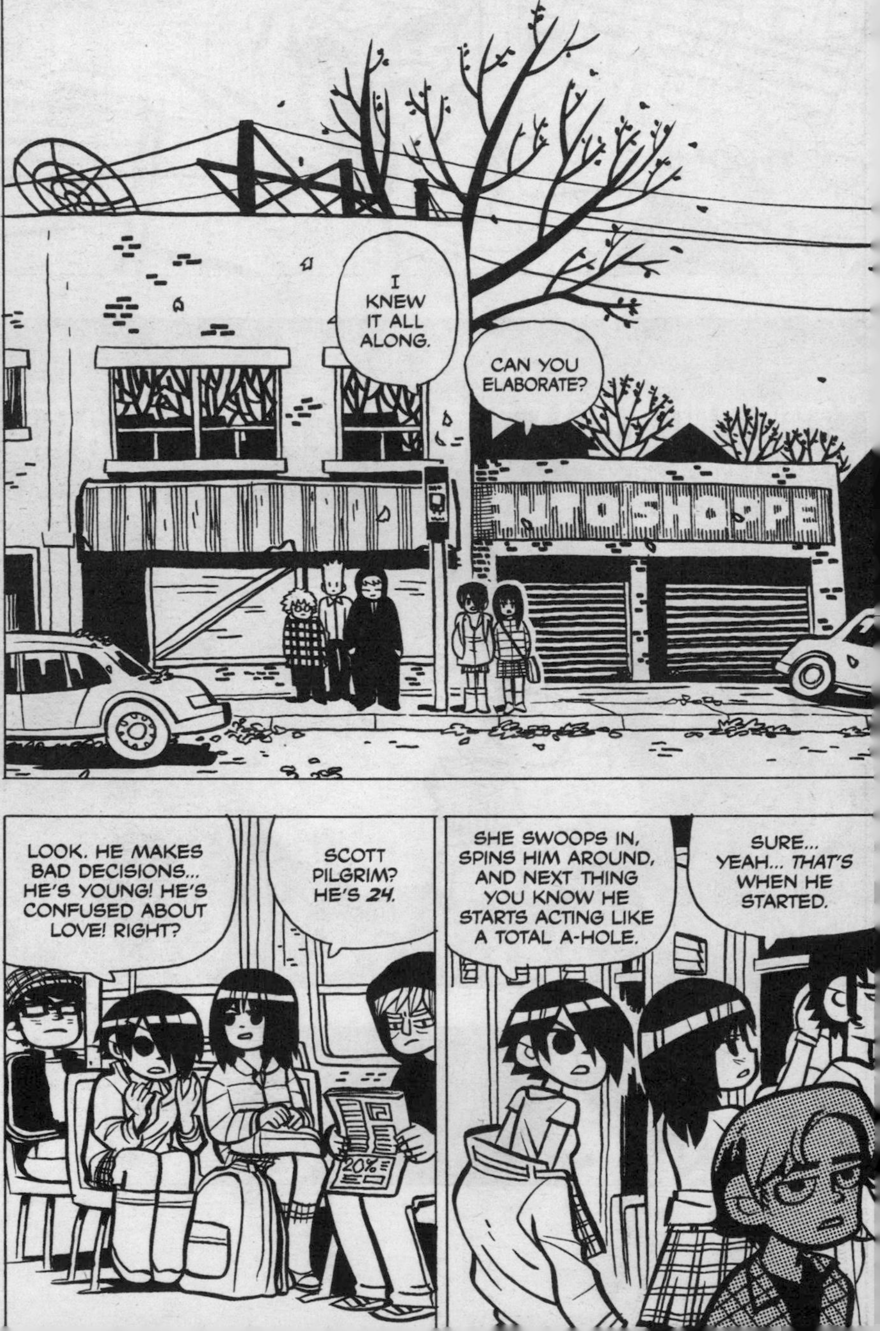

I KNEW IT ALL ALONG.
CAN YOU ELABORATE?
LOOK. HE MAKES BAD DECISIONS... HE'S YOUNG! HE'S CONFUSED ABOUT LOVE! RIGHT?
SCOTT PILGRIM? HE'S *24*.
20%
SHE SWOOPS IN, SPINS HIM AROUND, AND NEXT THING YOU KNOW HE STARTS ACTING LIKE A TOTAL A-HOLE.
SURE... YEAH... *THAT'S* WHEN HE STARTED.

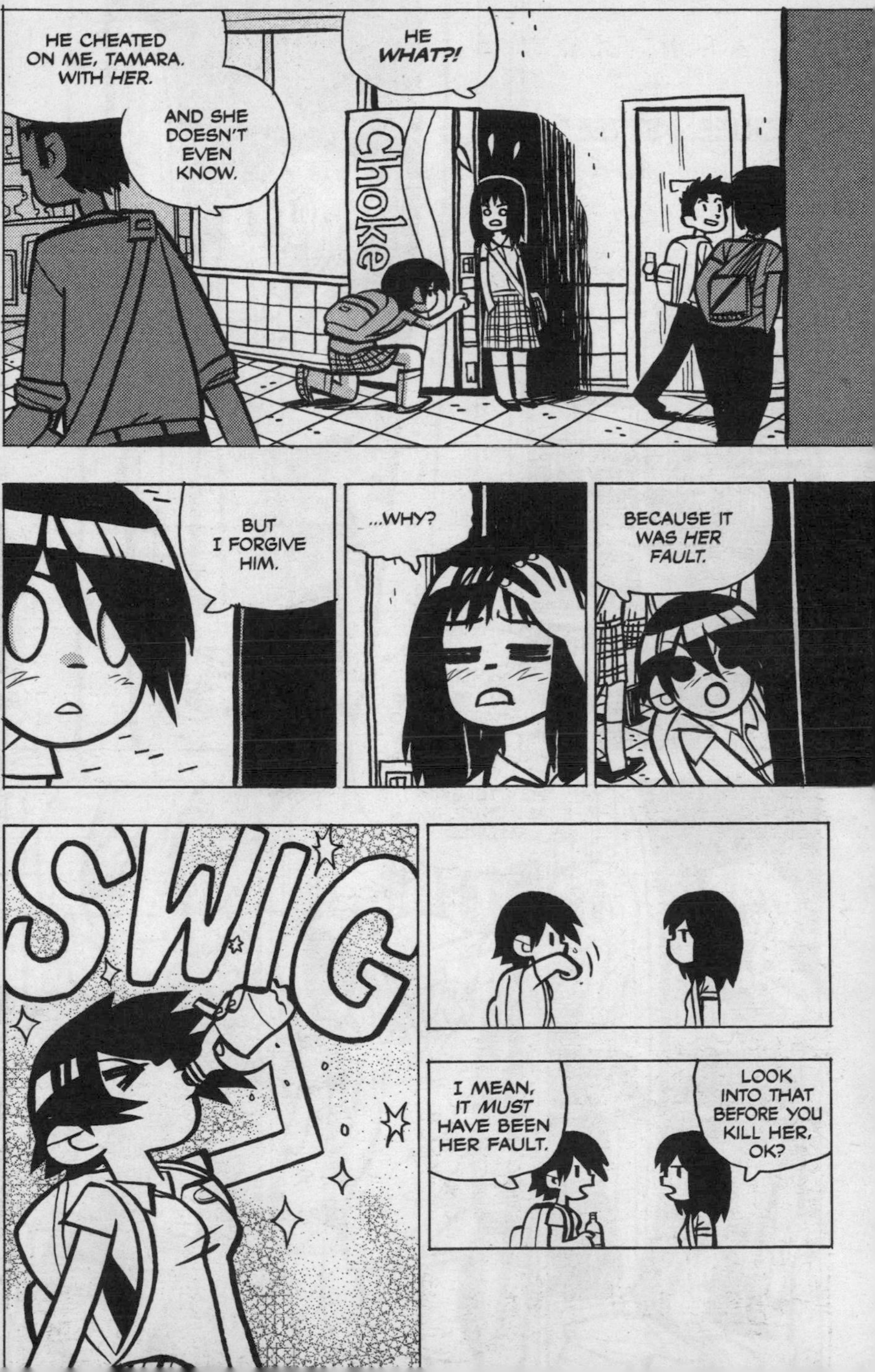
HE CHEATED ON ME, TAMARA. WITH *HER*.
HE *WHAT?!*
AND SHE DOESN'T EVEN KNOW.
Choke
BUT I FORGIVE HIM.
...WHY?
BECAUSE IT WAS *HER* FAULT.
SWIG
I MEAN, IT *MUST* HAVE BEEN HER FAULT.
LOOK INTO THAT BEFORE YOU KILL HER, OK?

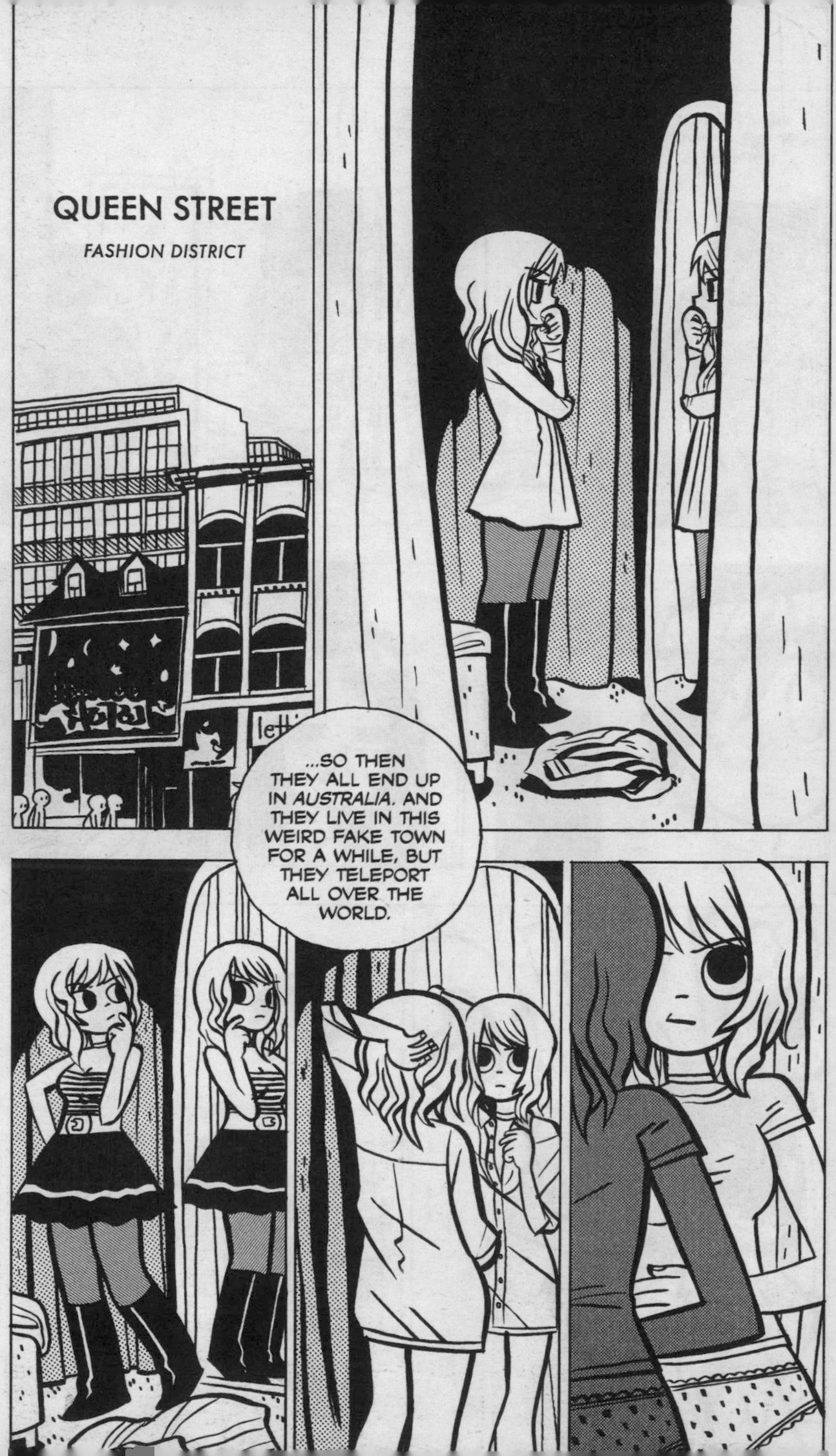
QUEEN STREET
FASHION DISTRICT
...SO THEN THEY ALL END UP IN AUSTRALIA. AND THEY LIVE IN THIS WEIRD FAKE TOWN FOR A WHILE, BUT THEY TELEPORT ALL OVER THE WORLD.

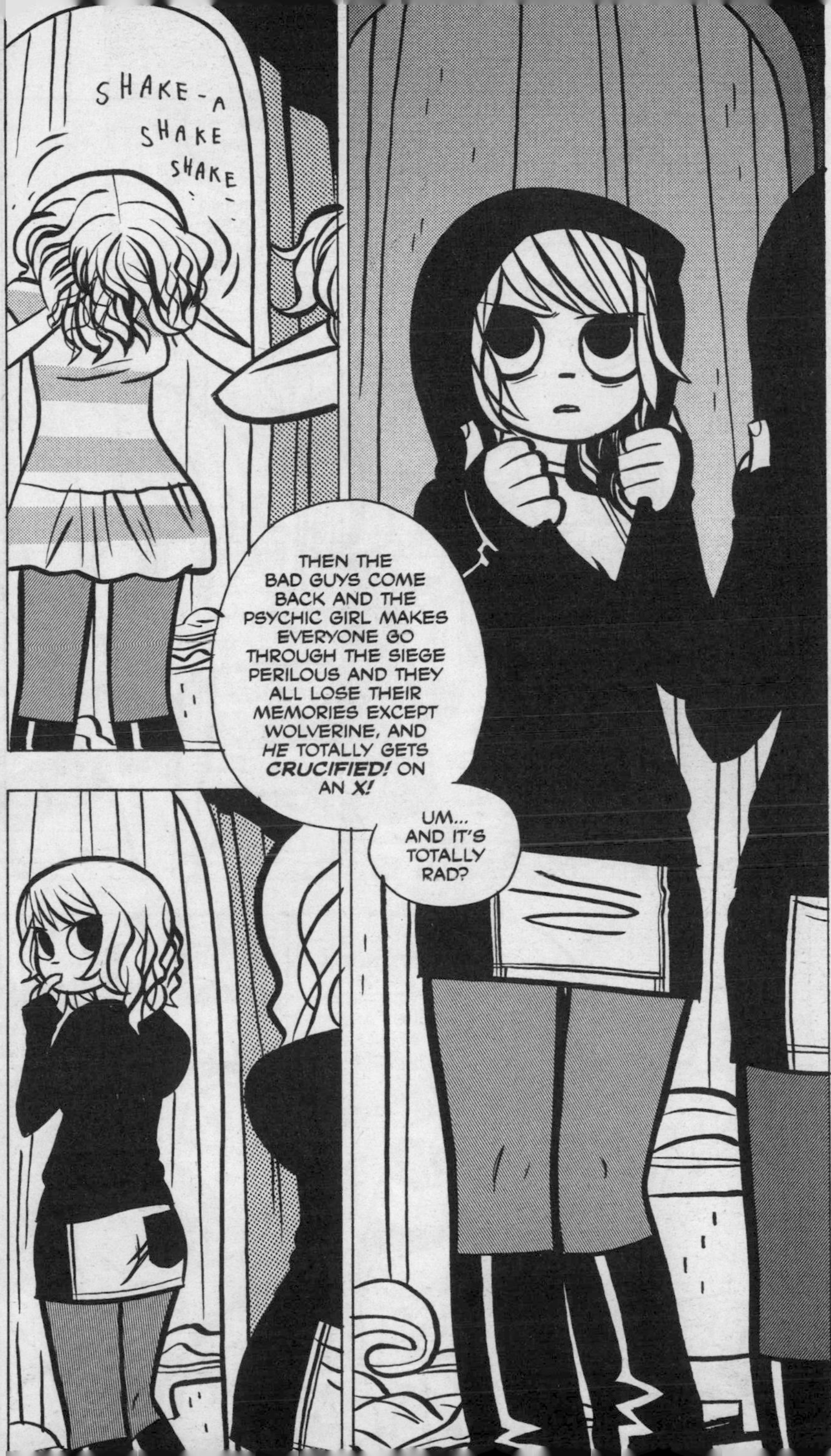
SHAKE-A SHAKE SHAKE
THEN THE BAD GUYS COME BACK AND THE PSYCHIC GIRL MAKES EVERYONE GO THROUGH THE SIEGE PERILOUS AND THEY ALL LOSE THEIR MEMORIES EXCEPT WOLVERINE, AND *HE* TOTALLY GETS ***CRUCIFIED!*** ON AN ***X!***
UM... AND IT'S TOTALLY RAD?

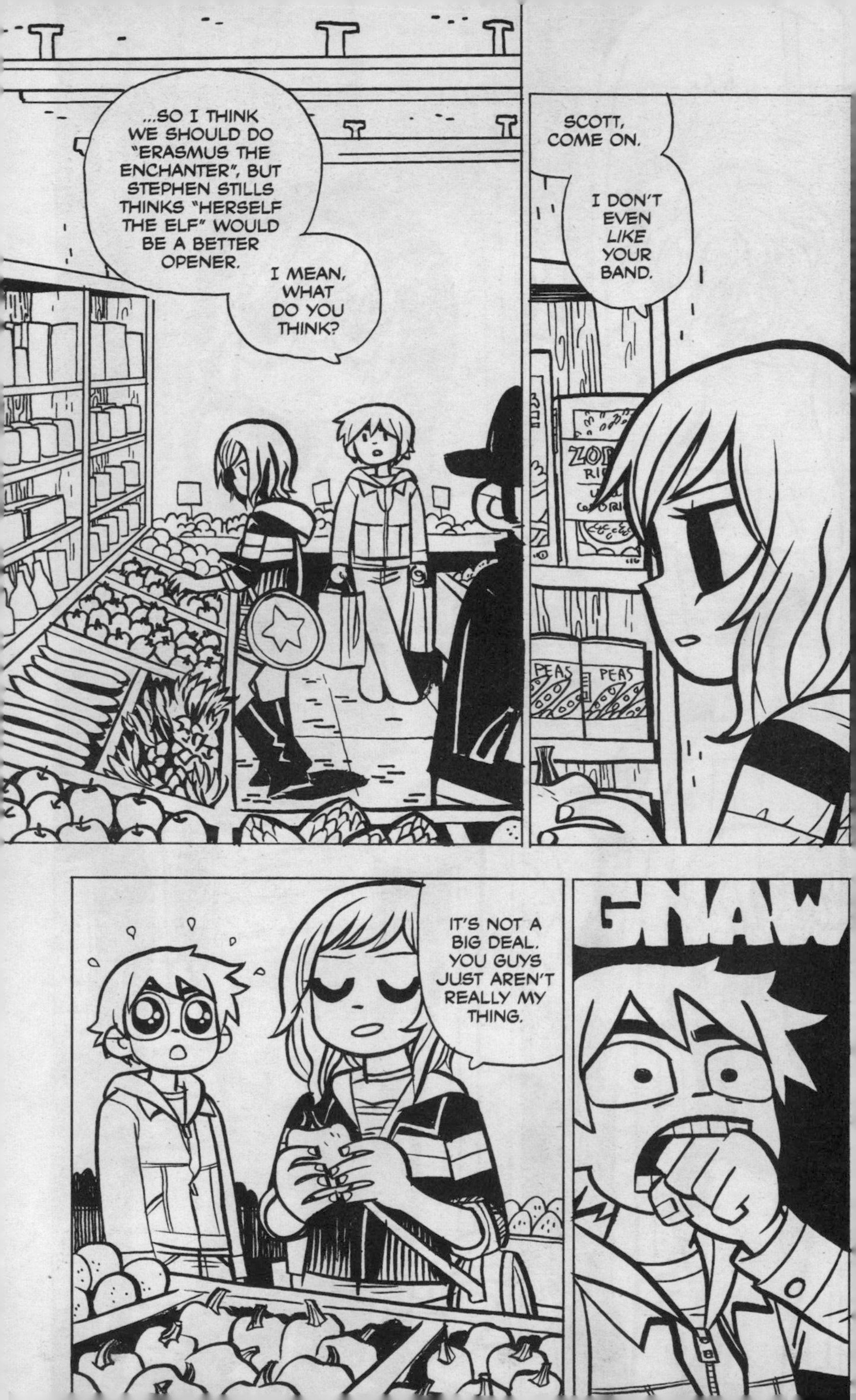
...SO I THINK WE SHOULD DO "ERASMUS THE ENCHANTER", BUT STEPHEN STILLS THINKS "HERSELF THE ELF" WOULD BE A BETTER OPENER.
I MEAN, WHAT DO YOU THINK?
SCOTT, COME ON.
I DON'T EVEN *LIKE* YOUR BAND.
PEAS
PEAS
IT'S NOT A BIG DEAL. YOU GUYS JUST AREN'T REALLY MY THING.
GNAW

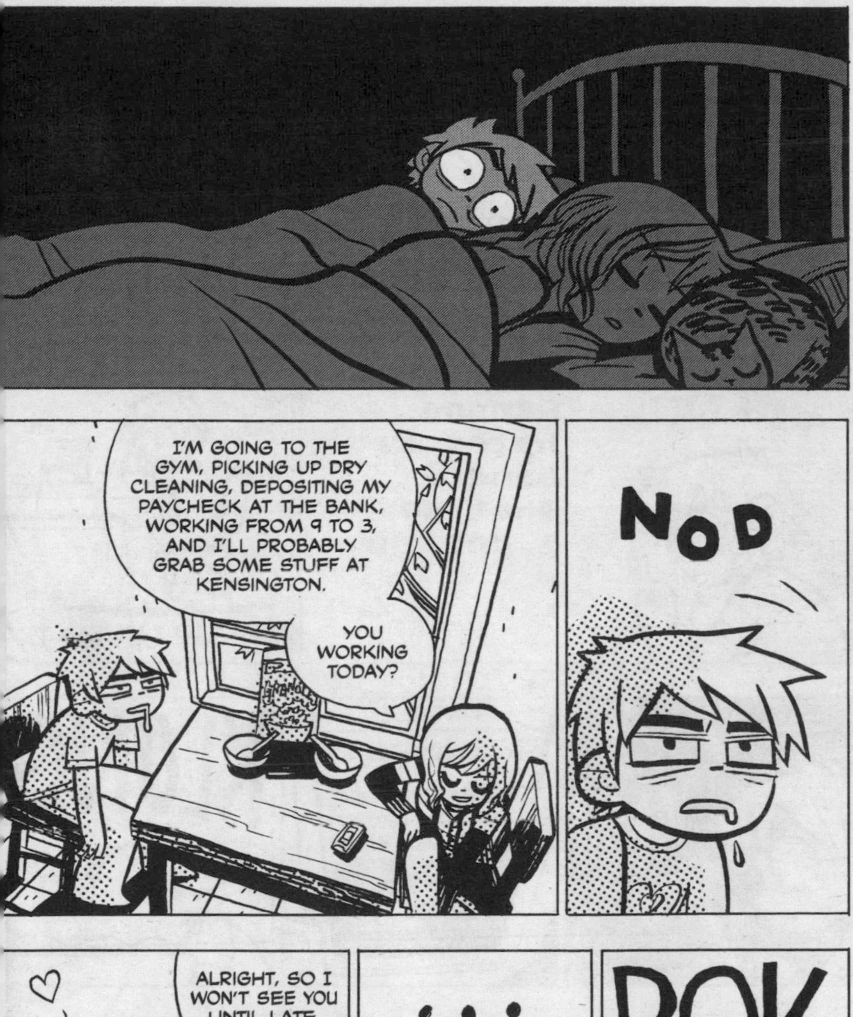
I'M GOING TO THE GYM, PICKING UP DRY CLEANING, DEPOSITING MY PAYCHECK AT THE BANK, WORKING FROM 9 TO 3, AND I'LL PROBABLY GRAB SOME STUFF AT KENSINGTON.
YOU WORKING TODAY?
NOD
ALRIGHT, SO I WON'T SEE YOU UNTIL LATE. LOVE YOU! BYE!
...
BOK

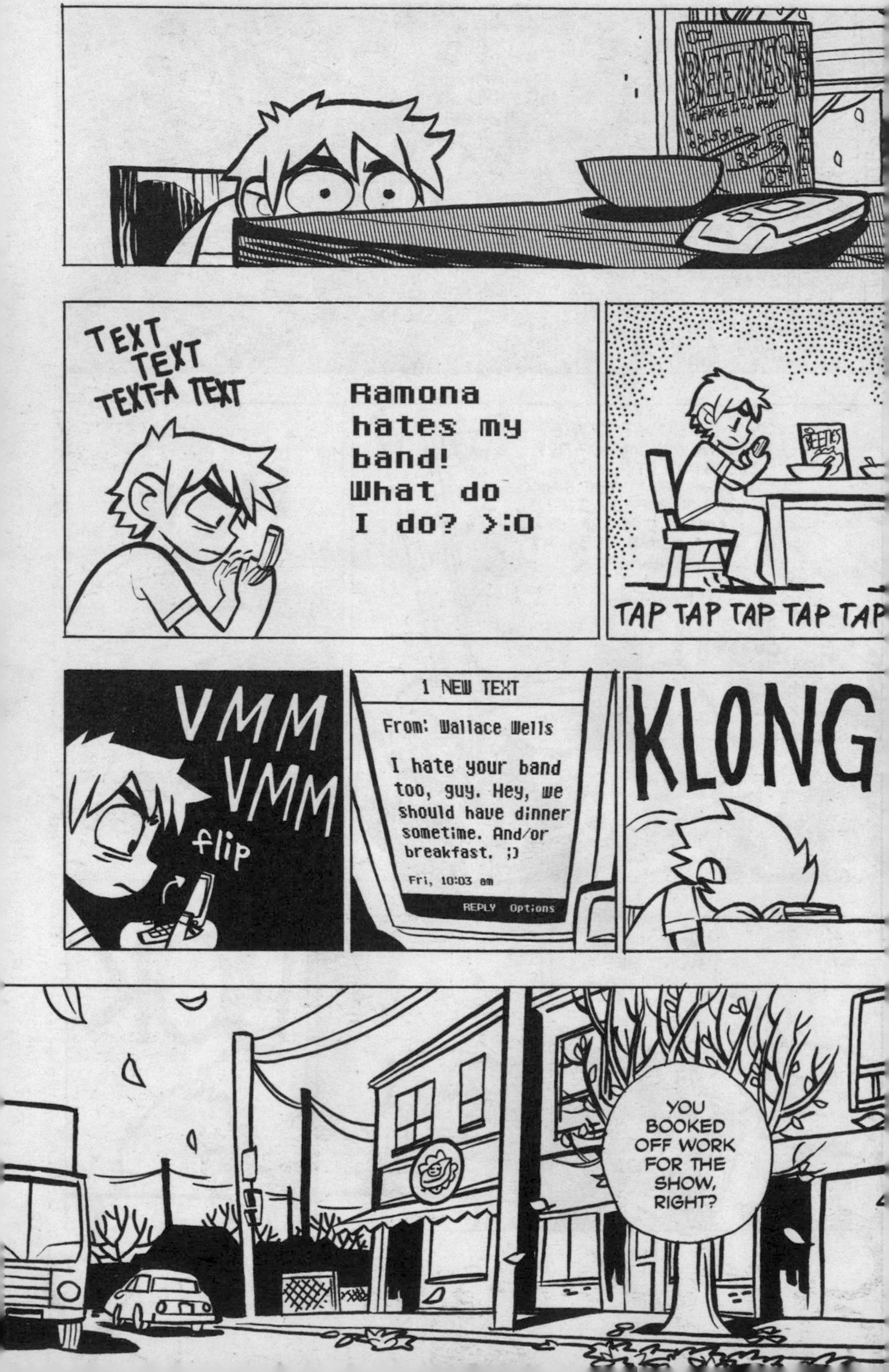
BEETIES
TEXT
TEXT
TEXT-A TEXT
Ramona hates my band! What do I do? >:O
TAP TAP TAP TAP TAP
VMM
VMM
flip
1 NEW TEXT
From: Wallace Wells
I hate your band too, guy. Hey, we should have dinner sometime. And/or breakfast. ;)
Fri, 10:03 am
REPLY Options
KLONG
YOU BOOKED OFF WORK FOR THE SHOW, RIGHT?

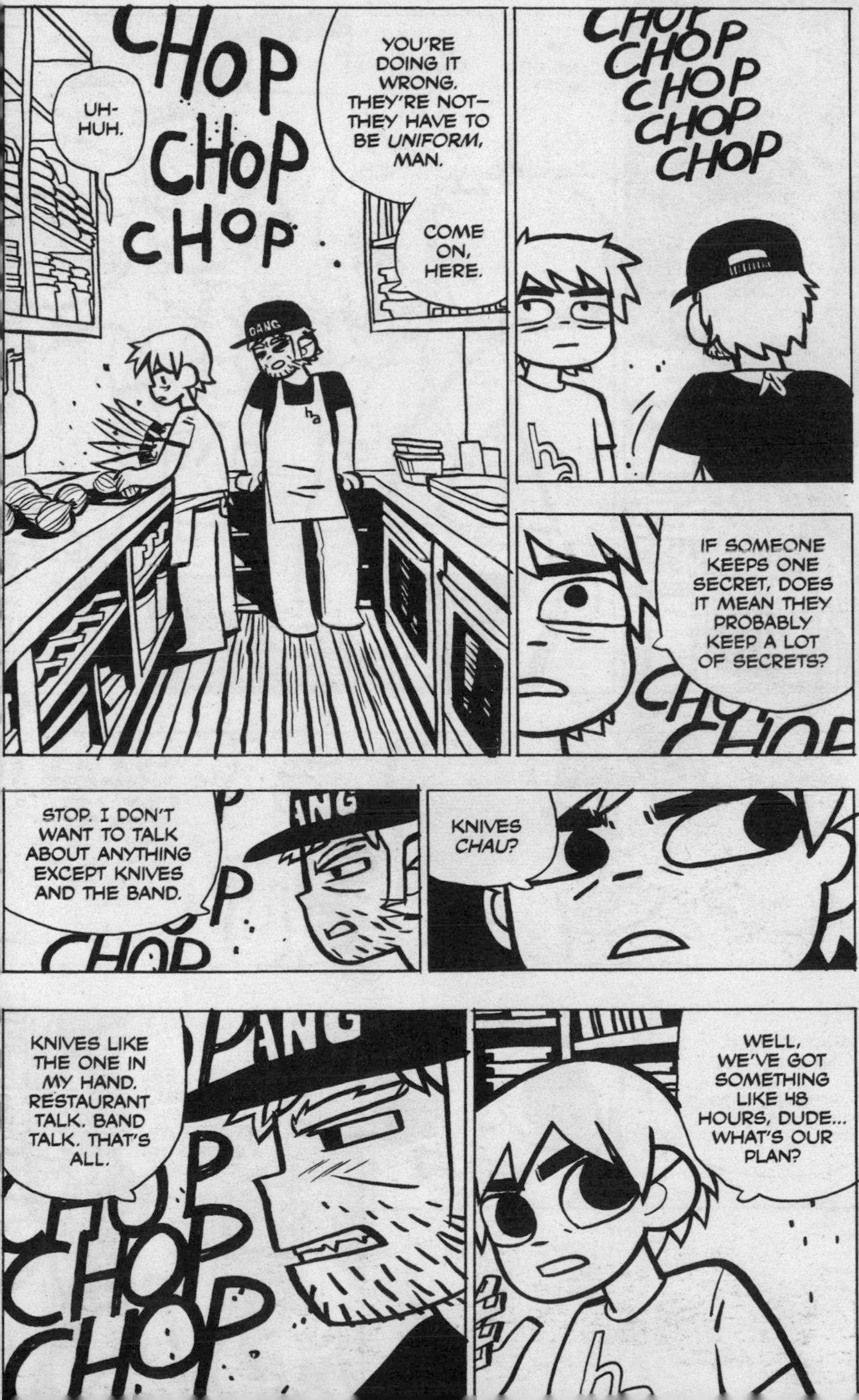
CHOP CHOP CHOP
UH-HUH.
YOU'RE DOING IT WRONG. THEY'RE NOT— THEY HAVE TO BE *UNIFORM*, MAN.
COME ON, HERE.
DANG
CHOP CHOP CHOP CHOP CHOP
IF SOMEONE KEEPS ONE SECRET, DOES IT MEAN THEY PROBABLY KEEP A LOT OF SECRETS?
STOP. I DON'T WANT TO TALK ABOUT ANYTHING EXCEPT KNIVES AND THE BAND.
KNIVES *CHAU*?
KNIVES LIKE THE ONE IN MY HAND. RESTAURANT TALK. BAND TALK. THAT'S ALL.
WELL, WE'VE GOT SOMETHING LIKE 48 HOURS, DUDE... WHAT'S OUR PLAN?

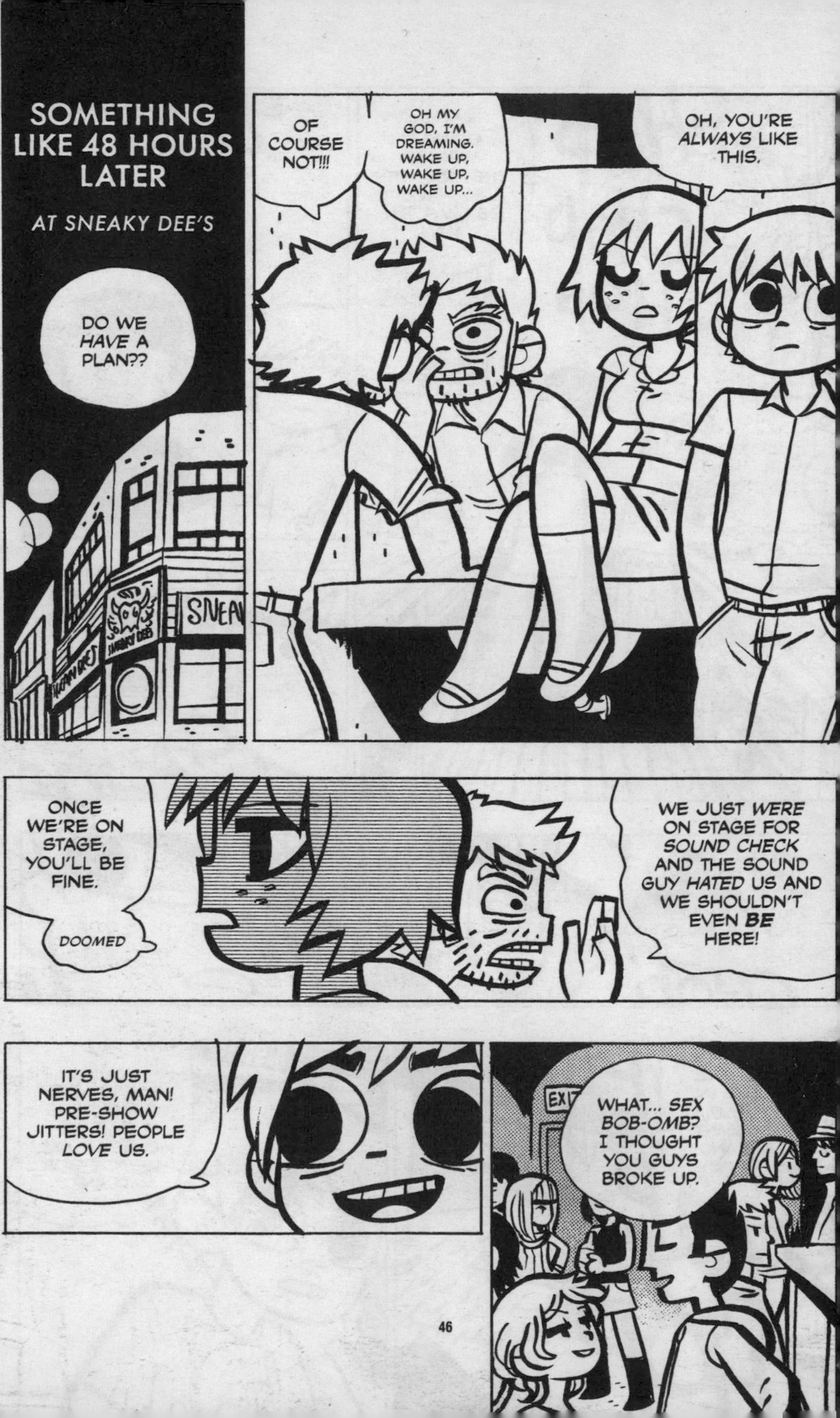
SOMETHING LIKE 48 HOURS LATER
AT SNEAKY DEE'S
DO WE *HAVE* A PLAN??
OF COURSE NOT!!!
OH MY GOD, I'M DREAMING. WAKE UP, WAKE UP, WAKE UP...
OH, YOU'RE *ALWAYS* LIKE THIS.
ONCE WE'RE ON STAGE, YOU'LL BE FINE.
DOOMED
WE JUST *WERE* ON STAGE FOR *SOUND CHECK* AND THE SOUND GUY *HATED* US AND WE SHOULDN'T EVEN ***BE*** HERE!
IT'S JUST NERVES, MAN! PRE-SHOW JITTERS! PEOPLE *LOVE* US.
WHAT... *SEX BOB-OMB?* I THOUGHT YOU GUYS BROKE UP.

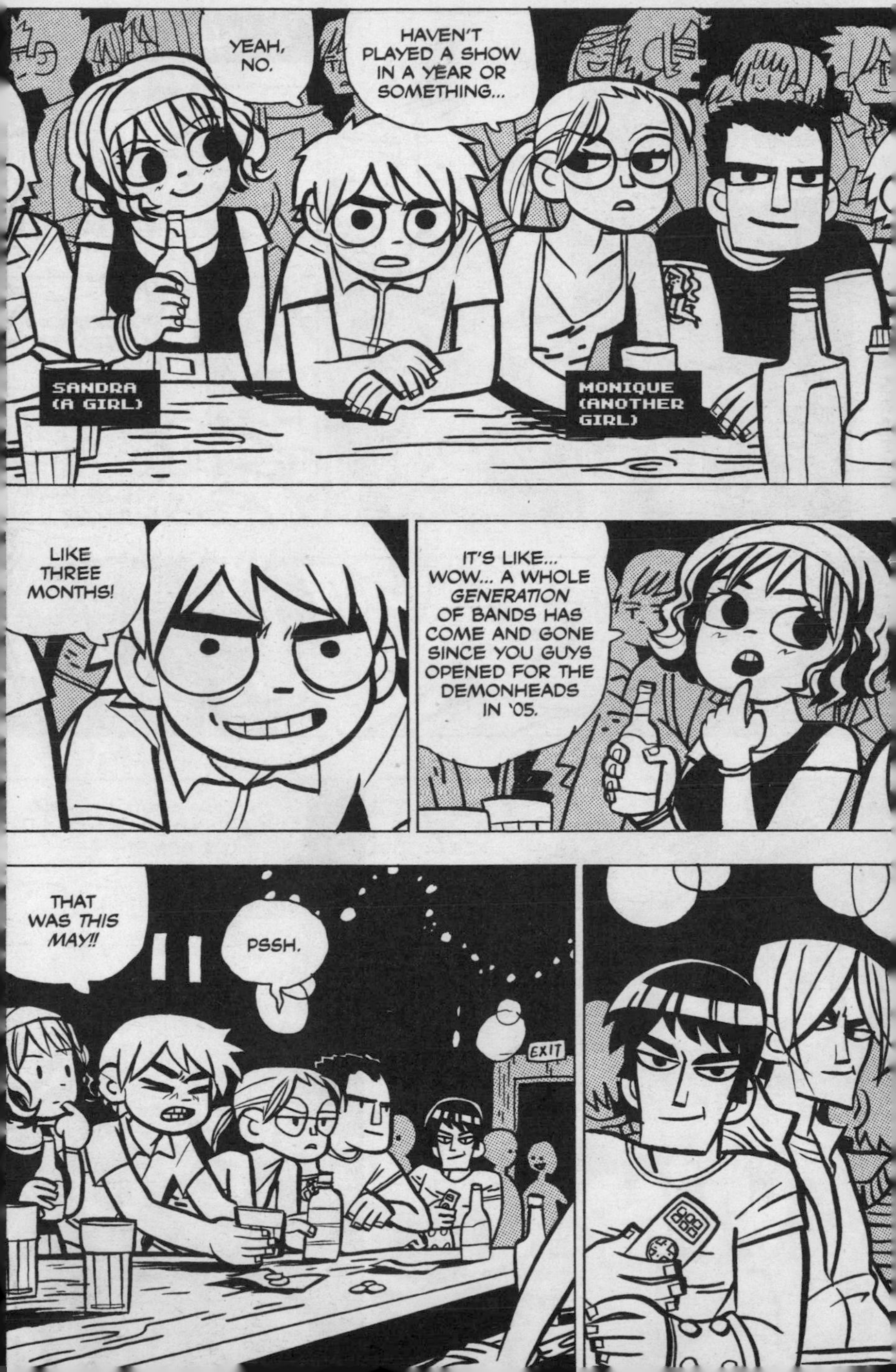
YEAH, NO.
HAVEN'T PLAYED A SHOW IN A YEAR OR SOMETHING...
SANDRA (A GIRL)
MONIQUE (ANOTHER GIRL)
LIKE THREE MONTHS!
IT'S LIKE... WOW... A WHOLE *GENERATION* OF BANDS HAS COME AND GONE SINCE YOU GUYS OPENED FOR THE DEMONHEADS IN '05.
THAT WAS *THIS MAY!!*
PSSH.
EXIT

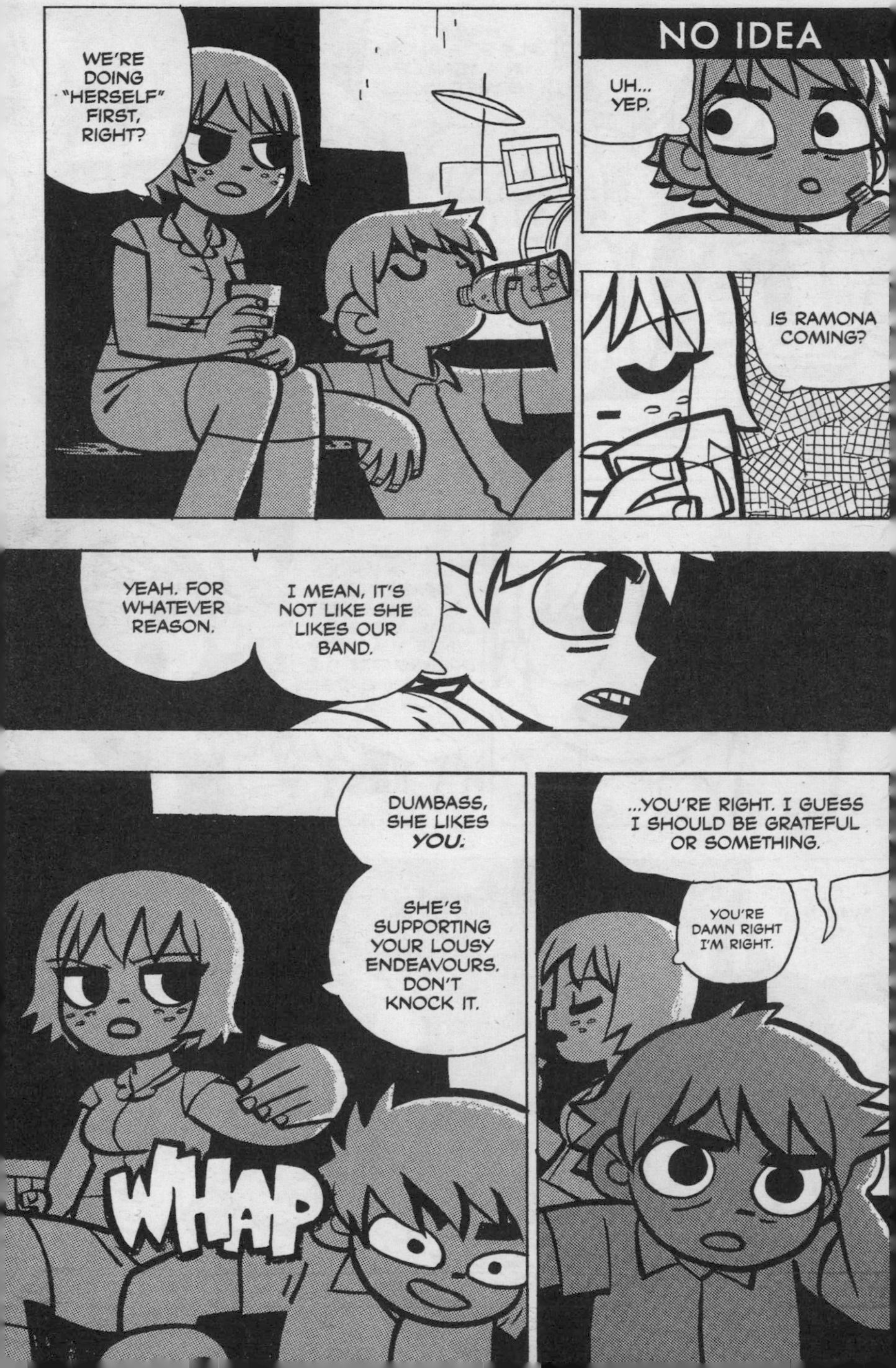
WE'RE DOING "HERSELF" FIRST, RIGHT?
NO IDEA
UH... YEP.
IS RAMONA COMING?
YEAH. FOR WHATEVER REASON.
I MEAN, IT'S NOT LIKE SHE LIKES OUR BAND.
DUMBASS, SHE LIKES YOU.
SHE'S SUPPORTING YOUR LOUSY ENDEAVOURS. DON'T KNOCK IT.
WHAP
...YOU'RE RIGHT. I GUESS I SHOULD BE GRATEFUL OR SOMETHING.
YOU'RE DAMN RIGHT I'M RIGHT.

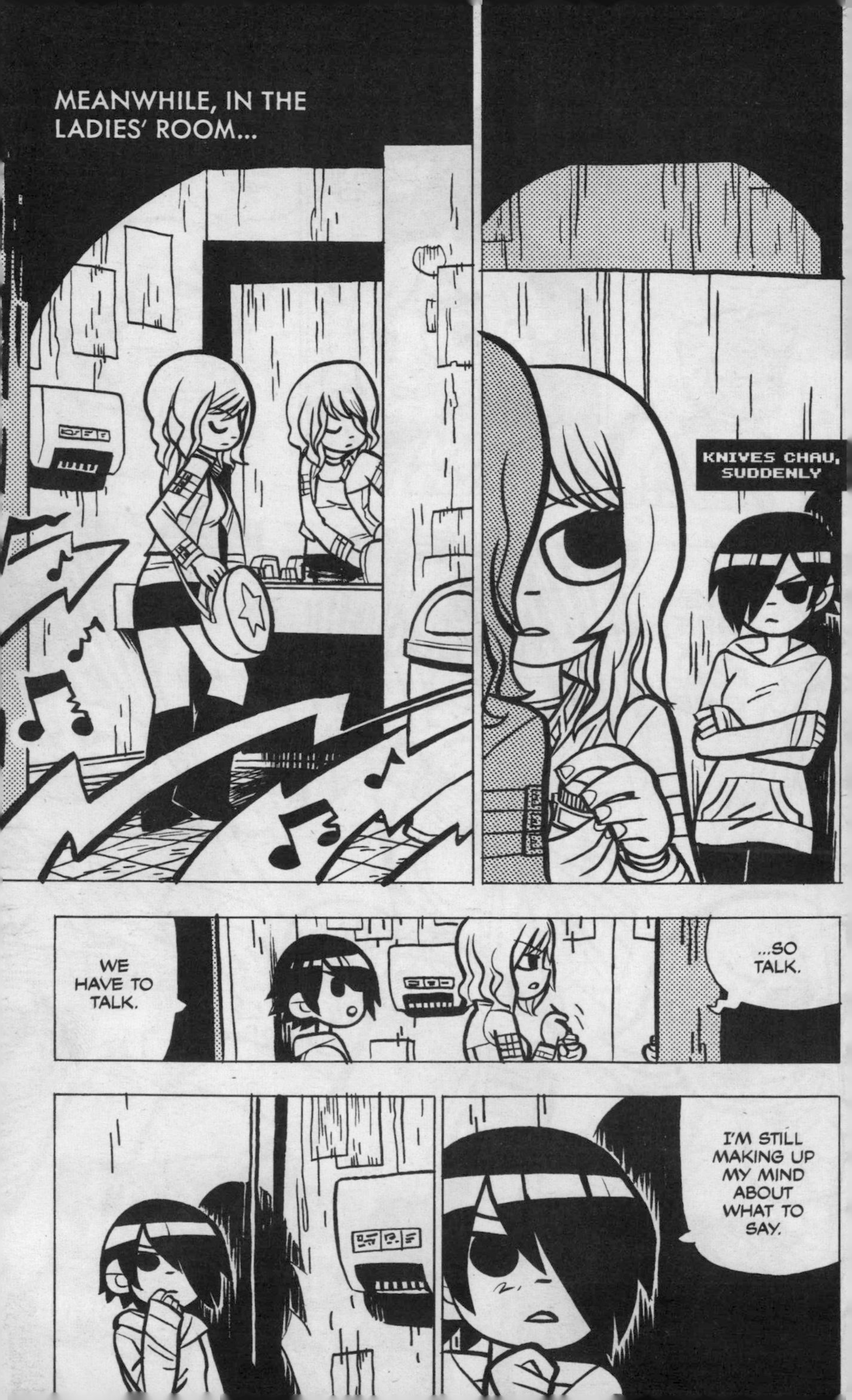
MEANWHILE, IN THE LADIES' ROOM...
KNIVES CHAU, SUDDENLY
WE HAVE TO TALK.
...SO TALK.
I'M STILL MAKING UP MY MIND ABOUT WHAT TO SAY.

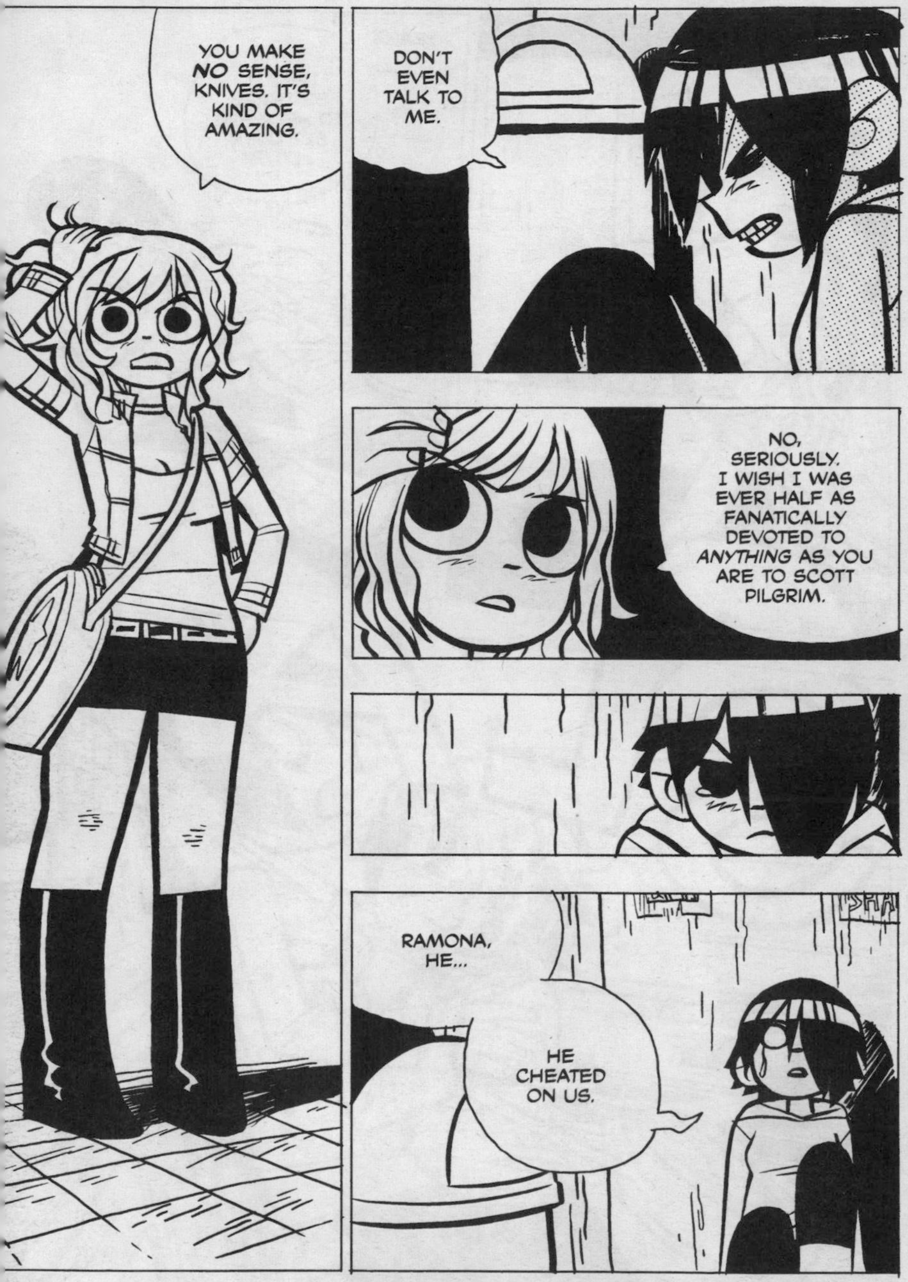

YOU MAKE *NO* SENSE, KNIVES. IT'S KIND OF AMAZING.
DON'T EVEN TALK TO ME.
NO, SERIOUSLY. I WISH I WAS EVER HALF AS FANATICALLY DEVOTED TO *ANYTHING* AS YOU ARE TO SCOTT PILGRIM.
RAMONA, HE...
HE CHEATED ON US.

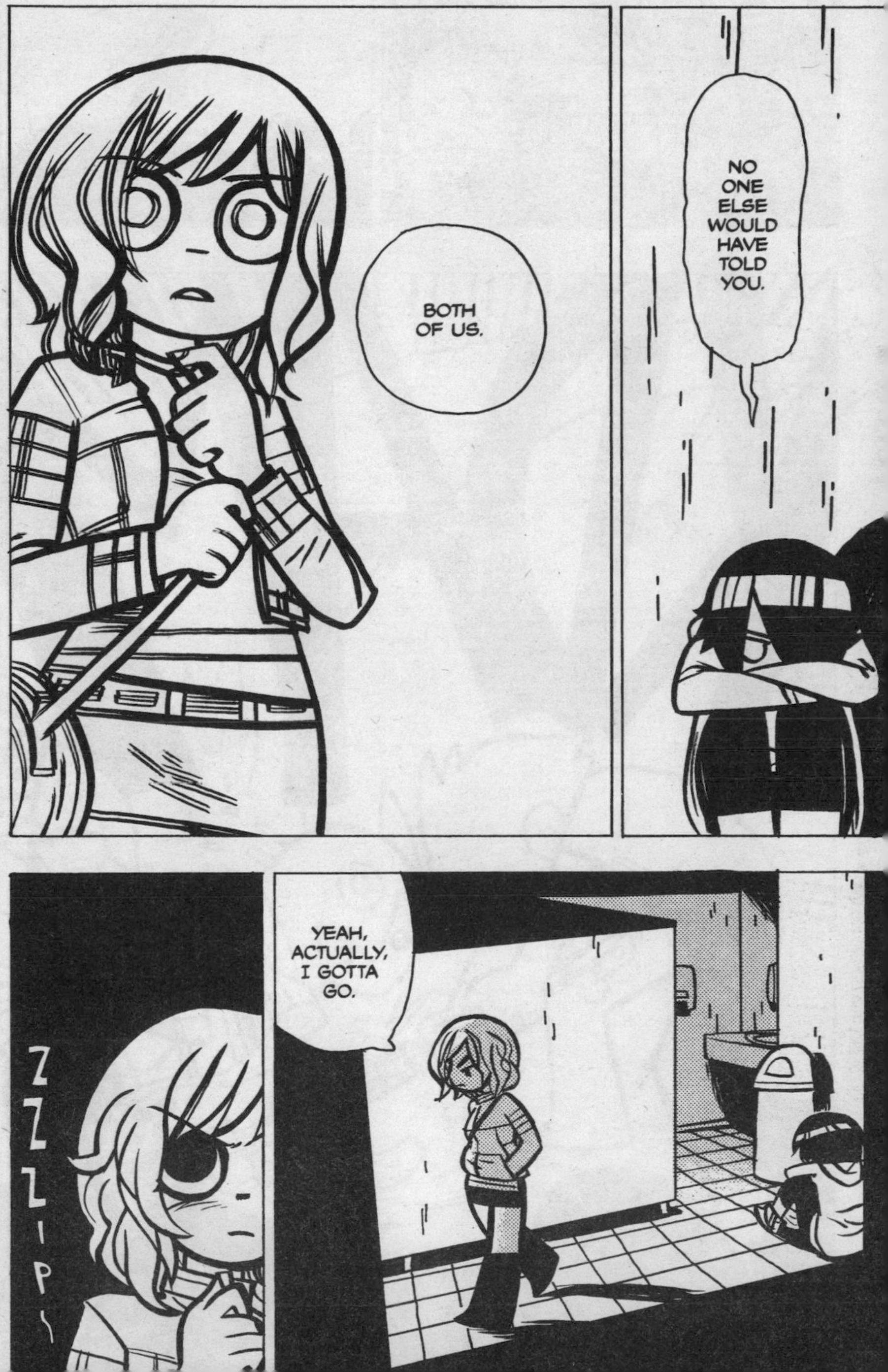
BOTH OF US.
NO ONE ELSE WOULD HAVE TOLD YOU.
ZZZIP
YEAH, ACTUALLY, I GOTTA GO.

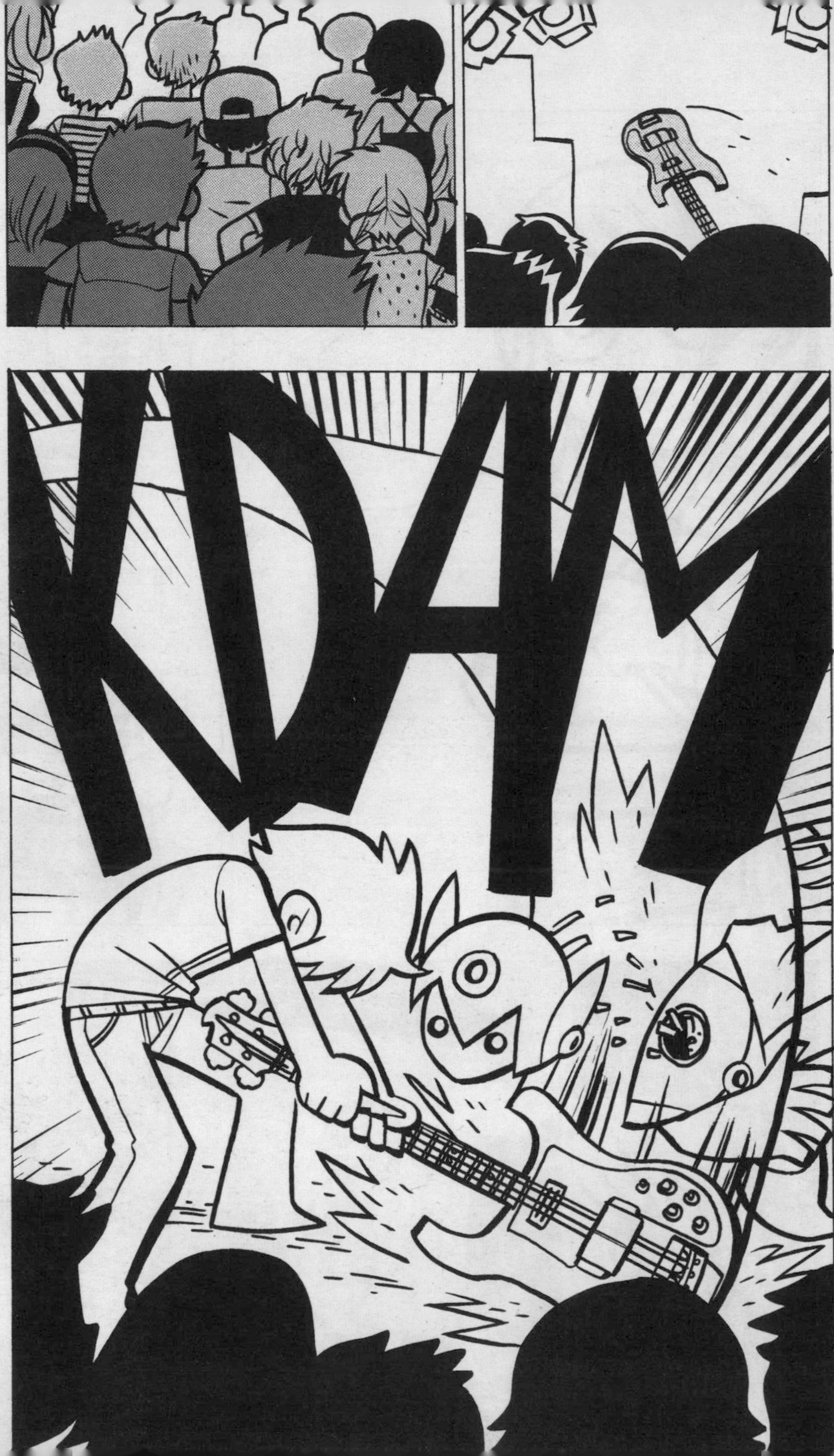
KDAM

WHAT THE HELL IS GOING ON HERE?

OH MAN! YOU MISSED ALL THE ACTION!

DID I?

YEAH, APPARENTLY THIS WHOLE GIG WAS A SETUP! THIS ROBOT WAS SUPPOSED TO KICK MY ASS.

A ROBOT SCOTT PILGRIM'S ASS WHILE U WATCH

HOW DID YOU GUYS NOT NOTICE THESE FLYERS?

SNEAKY DEE'S, NOVEMBER 11TH
ROBOTS PROVIDED BY
K&K KATA

SO DO WE FINISH OUR SET NOW, OR WHAT?

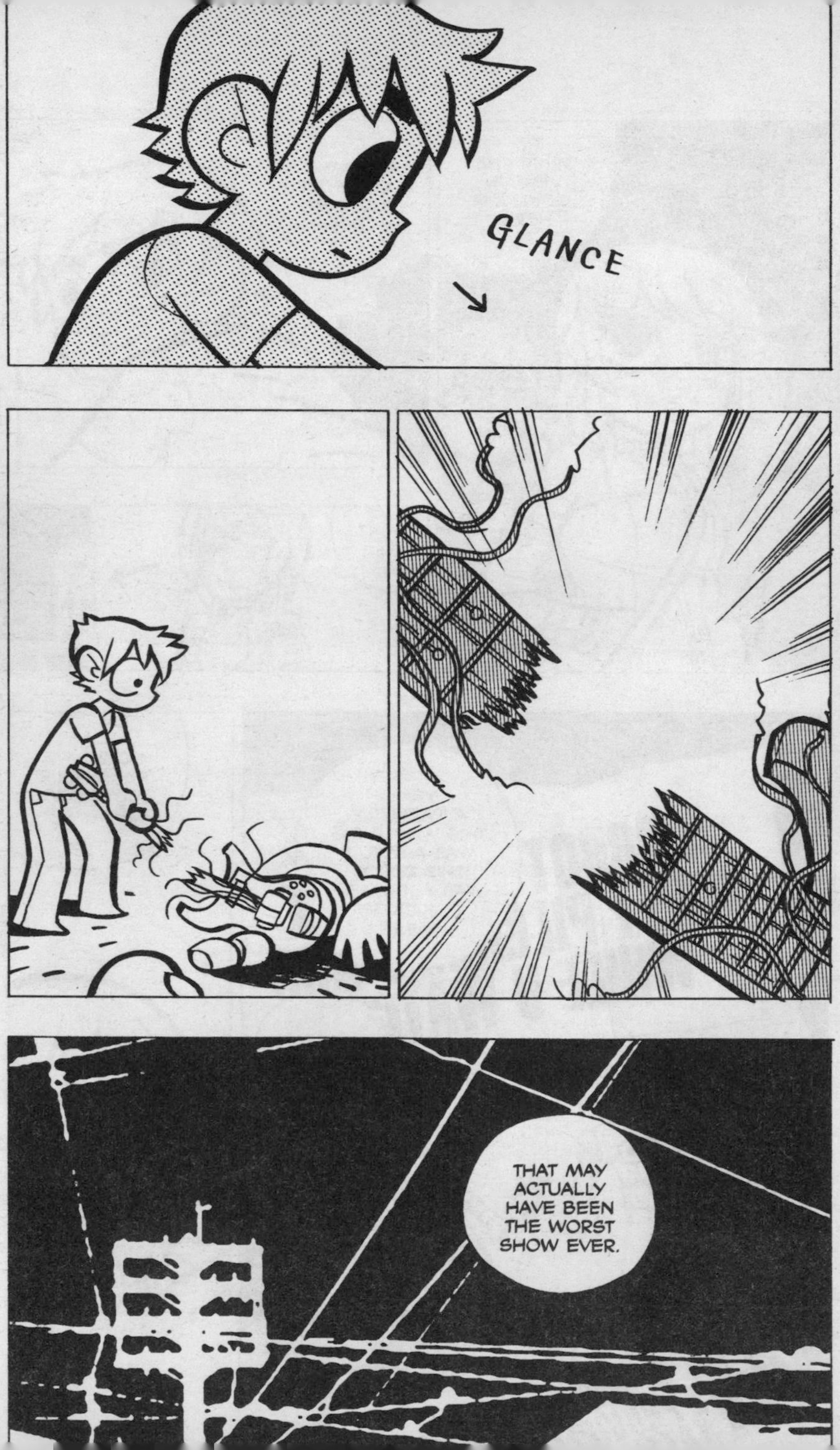
GLANCE
THAT MAY ACTUALLY HAVE BEEN THE WORST SHOW EVER.

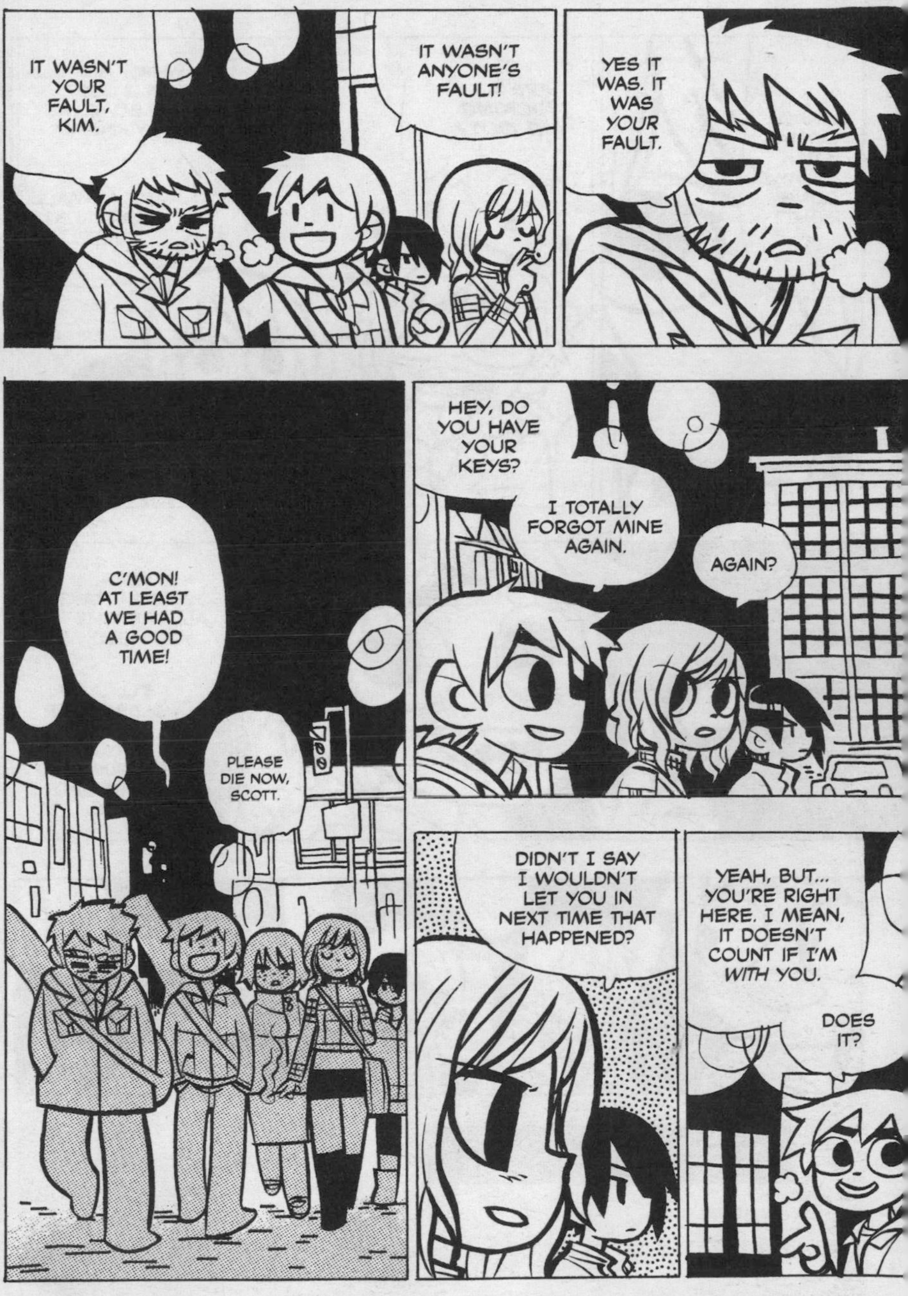
IT WASN'T YOUR FAULT, KIM.
IT WASN'T ANYONE'S FAULT!
YES IT WAS. IT WAS *YOUR* FAULT.
C'MON! AT LEAST WE HAD A GOOD TIME!
PLEASE DIE NOW, SCOTT.
HEY, DO YOU HAVE YOUR KEYS?
I TOTALLY FORGOT MINE AGAIN.
AGAIN?
DIDN'T I SAY I WOULDN'T LET YOU IN NEXT TIME THAT HAPPENED?
YEAH, BUT... YOU'RE RIGHT HERE. I MEAN, IT DOESN'T COUNT IF I'M *WITH* YOU.
DOES IT?

WELL, I'M SORRY THAT SHE KICKED YOU OUT.

WHAT? NO.

28

the GLOW

SHE JUST NEEDS SOME TIME ALONE OR WHATEVER.

IT'S A SMALL APARTMENT.

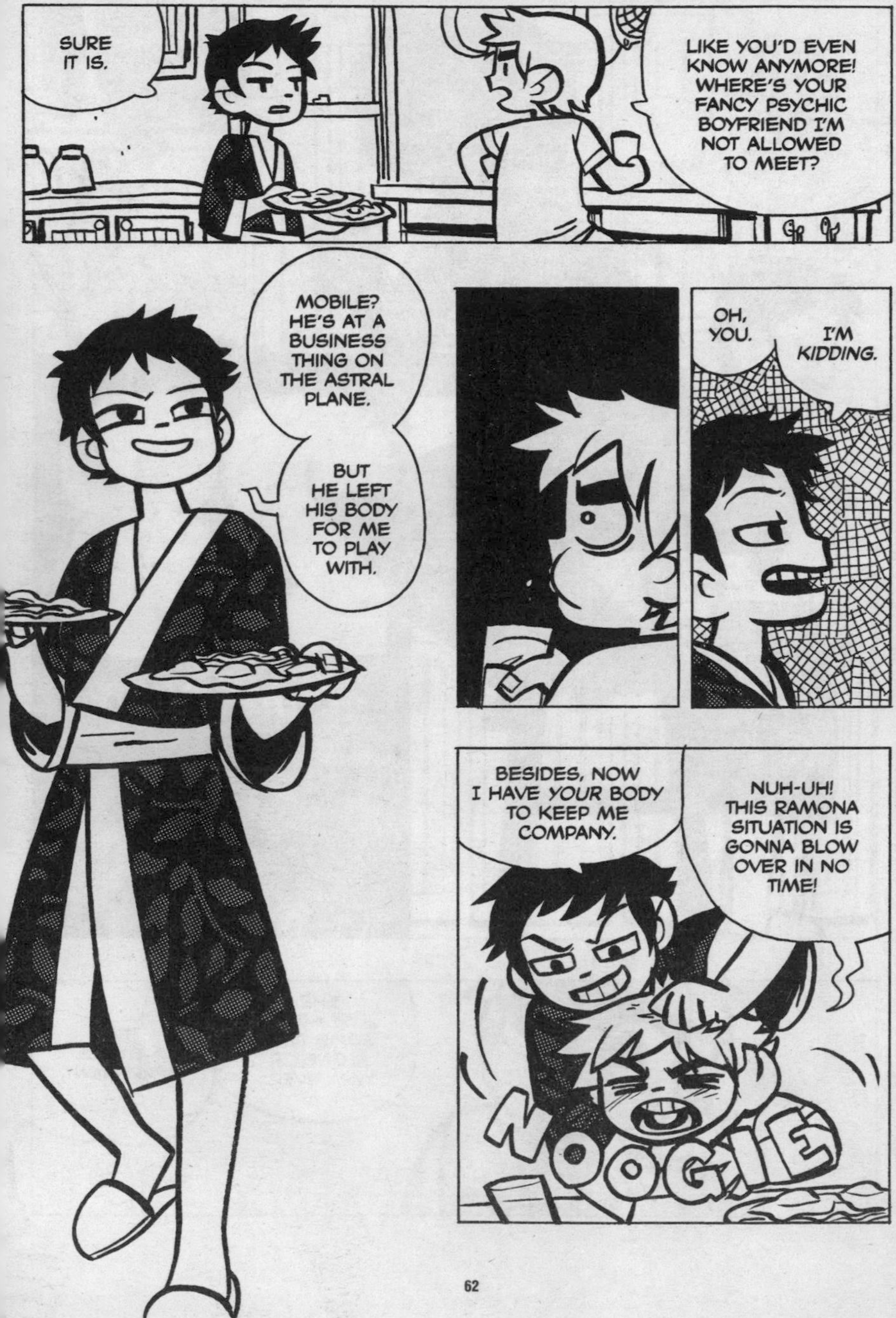
SURE IT IS.
LIKE YOU'D EVEN KNOW ANYMORE! WHERE'S YOUR FANCY PSYCHIC BOYFRIEND I'M NOT ALLOWED TO MEET?
MOBILE? HE'S AT A BUSINESS THING ON THE ASTRAL PLANE.
BUT HE LEFT HIS BODY FOR ME TO PLAY WITH.
OH, YOU.
I'M *KIDDING.*
BESIDES, NOW I HAVE *YOUR* BODY TO KEEP ME COMPANY.
NUH-UH! THIS RAMONA SITUATION IS GONNA BLOW OVER IN NO TIME!
NOOGIE

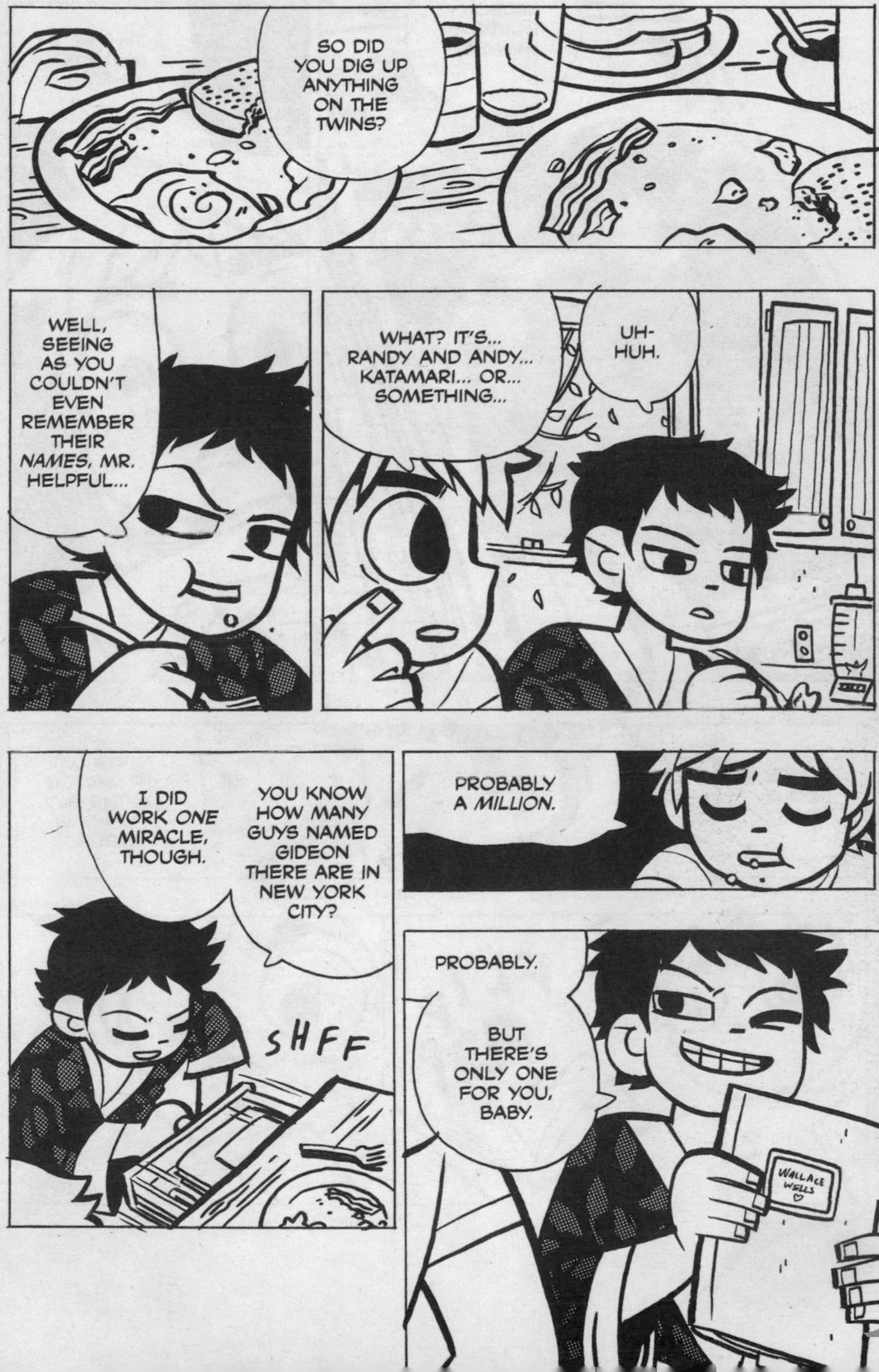
SO DID YOU DIG UP ANYTHING ON THE TWINS?
WELL, SEEING AS YOU COULDN'T EVEN REMEMBER THEIR *NAMES*, MR. HELPFUL...
WHAT? IT'S... RANDY AND ANDY... KATAMARI... OR... SOMETHING...
UH-HUH.
I DID WORK *ONE* MIRACLE, THOUGH.
YOU KNOW HOW MANY GUYS NAMED GIDEON THERE ARE IN NEW YORK CITY?
SHFF
PROBABLY A *MILLION.*
PROBABLY.
BUT THERE'S ONLY ONE FOR YOU, BABY.
WALLACE WELLS ♡

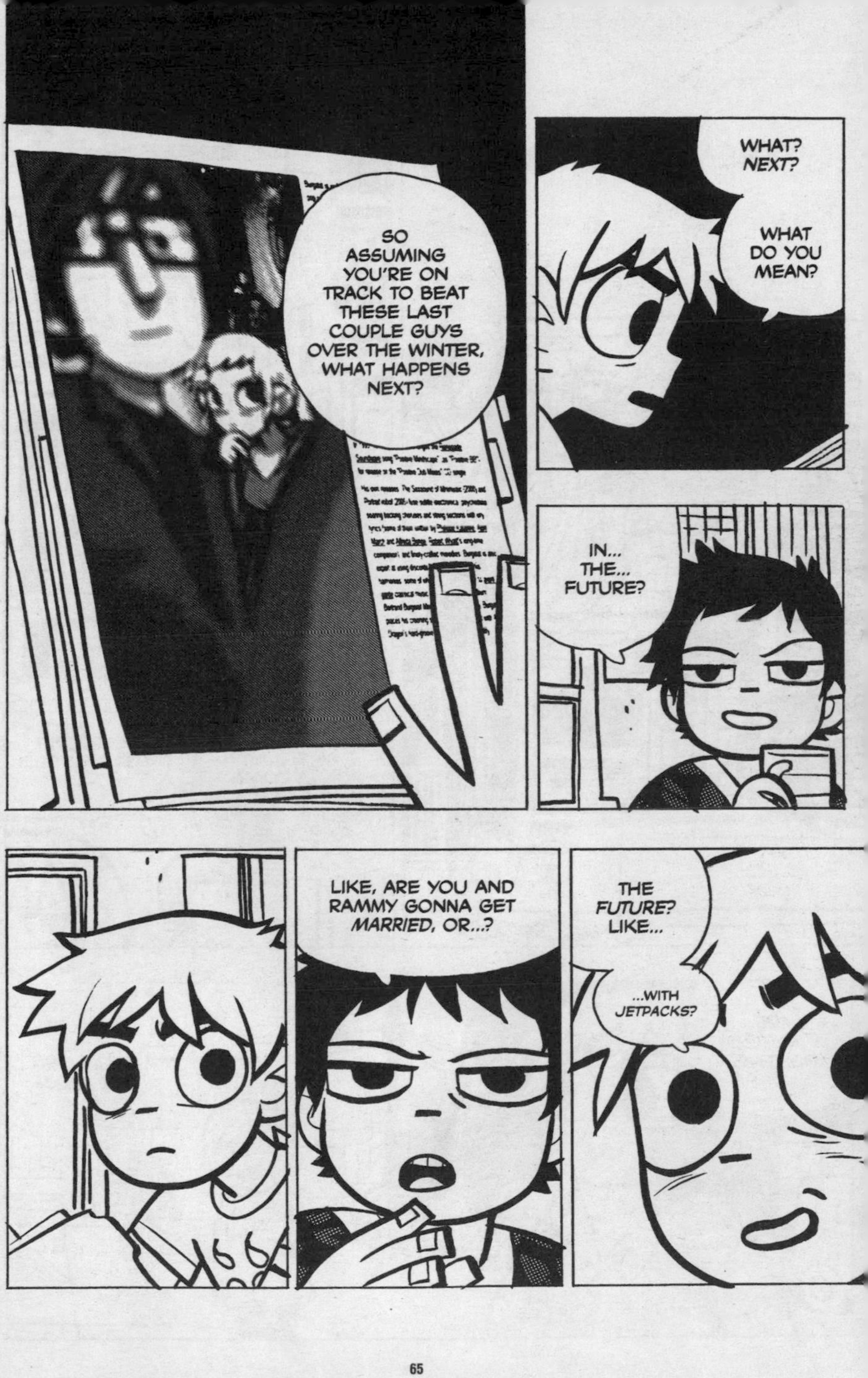
SO ASSUMING YOU'RE ON TRACK TO BEAT THESE LAST COUPLE GUYS OVER THE WINTER, WHAT HAPPENS NEXT?
WHAT? NEXT?
WHAT DO YOU MEAN?
IN... THE... FUTURE?
LIKE, ARE YOU AND RAMMY GONNA GET MARRIED, OR...?
THE FUTURE? LIKE...
...WITH JETPACKS?

THE VIDEO STORE

LET'S GO.

WHAT'S UP? I WAS JUST GONNA COME INSIDE FOR A MINUTE, SAY HI TO HOLLIE...

YOU DON'T NEED TO SEE HOLLIE.

ARE YOU GUYS FIGHTING?

WE'RE NOT *FIGHTING.* I JUST—

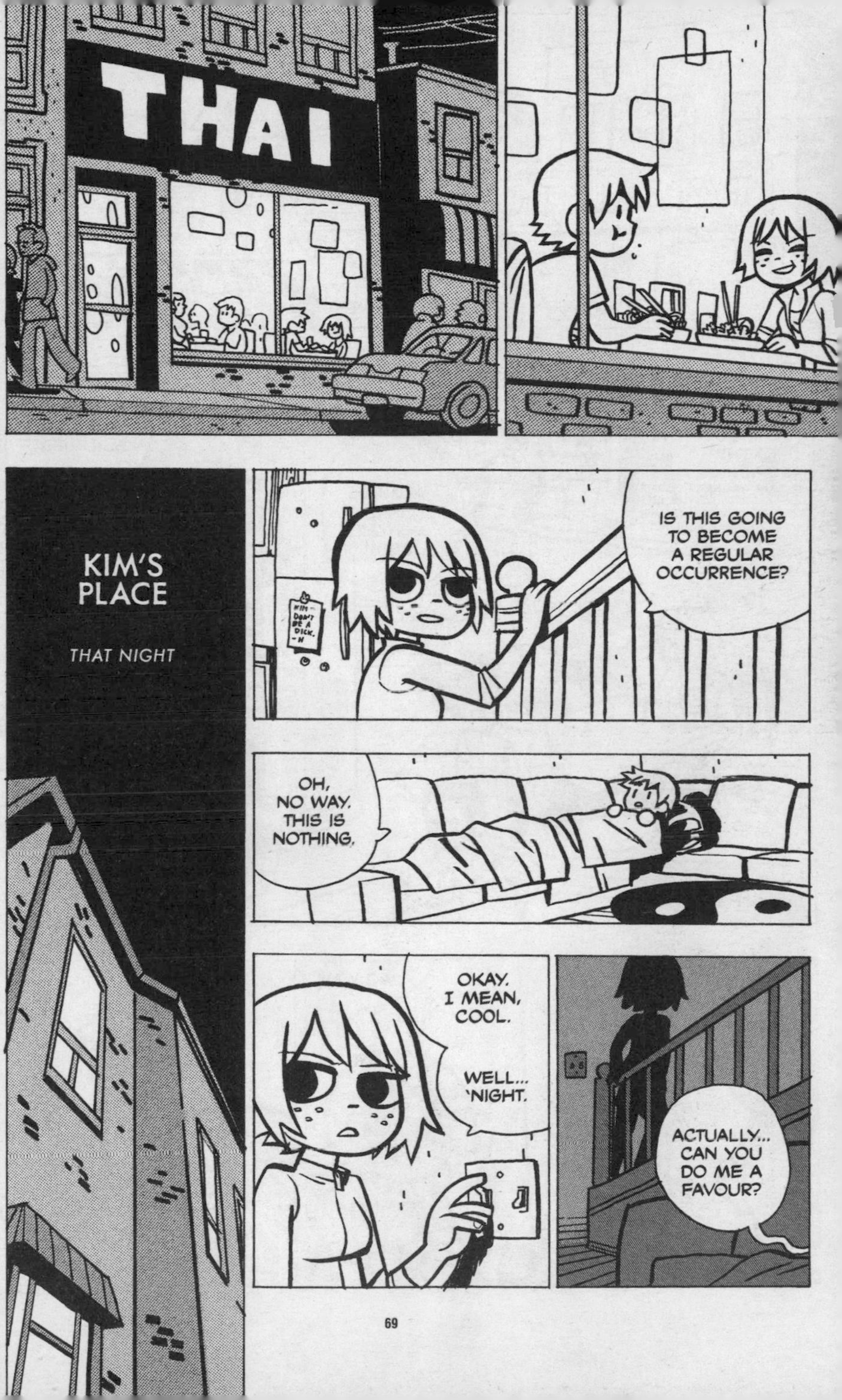
THAI
KIM'S PLACE
THAT NIGHT
IS THIS GOING TO BECOME A REGULAR OCCURRENCE?
OH, NO WAY. THIS IS NOTHING.
OKAY. I MEAN, COOL.
WELL... 'NIGHT.
ACTUALLY... CAN YOU DO ME A FAVOUR?

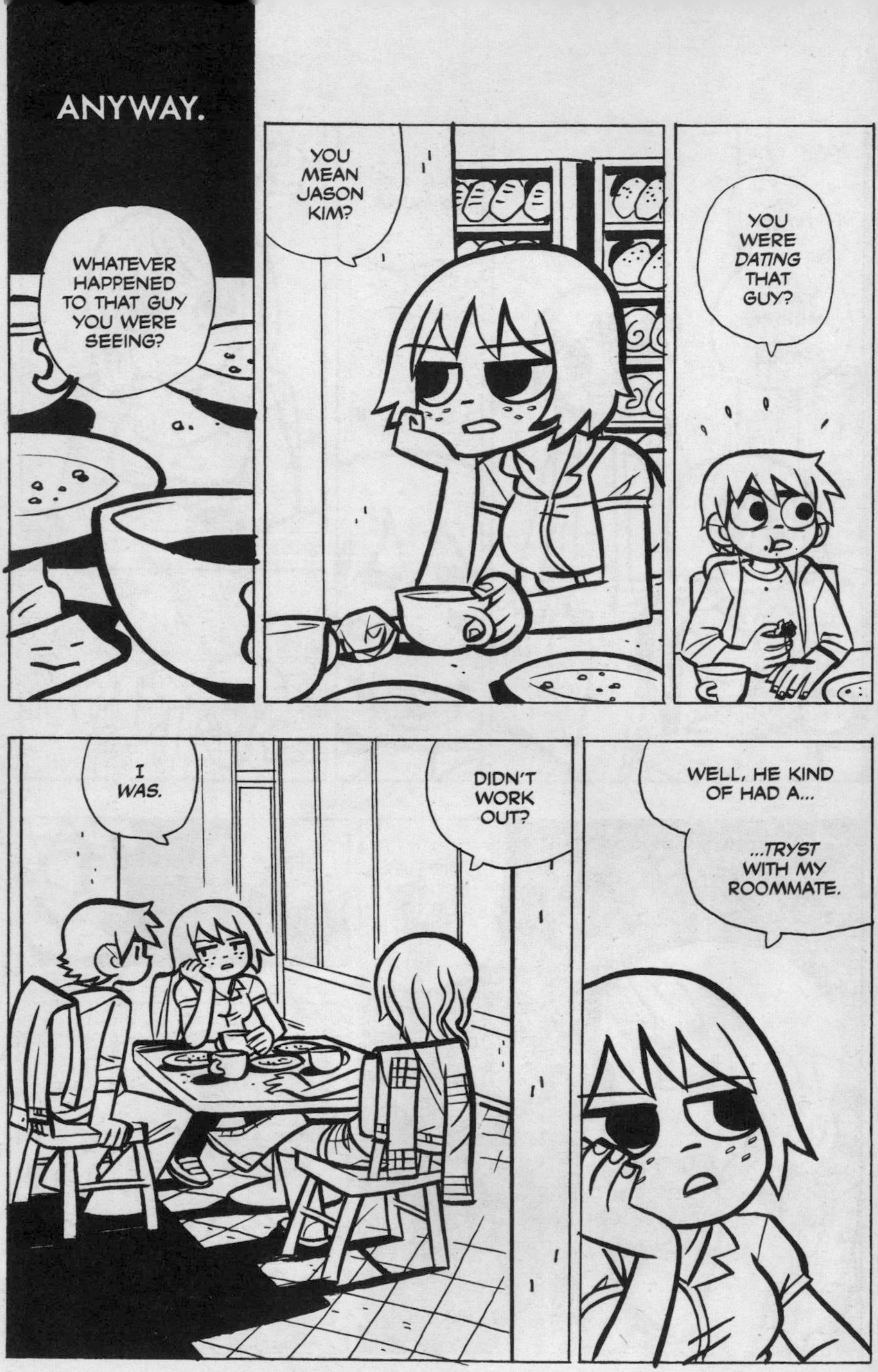
ANYWAY.
WHATEVER HAPPENED TO THAT GUY YOU WERE SEEING?
YOU MEAN JASON KIM?
YOU WERE *DATING* THAT GUY?
I *WAS.*
DIDN'T WORK OUT?
WELL, HE KIND OF HAD A...
...*TRYST* WITH MY ROOMMATE.

73

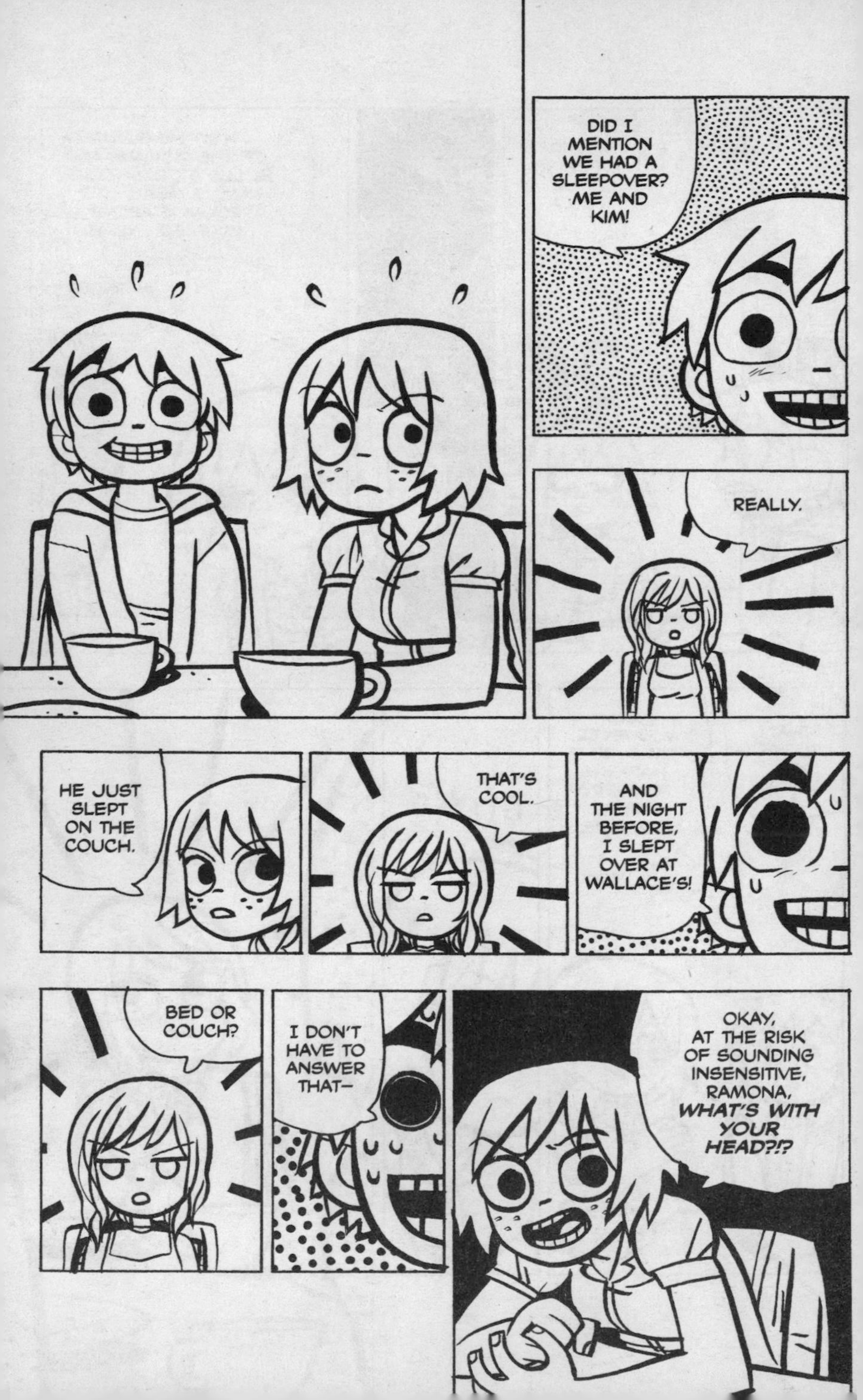
DID I MENTION WE HAD A SLEEPOVER? ME AND KIM!
REALLY.
HE JUST SLEPT ON THE COUCH.
THAT'S COOL.
AND THE NIGHT BEFORE, I SLEPT OVER AT WALLACE'S!
BED OR COUCH?
I DON'T HAVE TO ANSWER THAT–
OKAY, AT THE RISK OF SOUNDING INSENSITIVE, RAMONA, *WHAT'S WITH YOUR HEAD?!?*

75

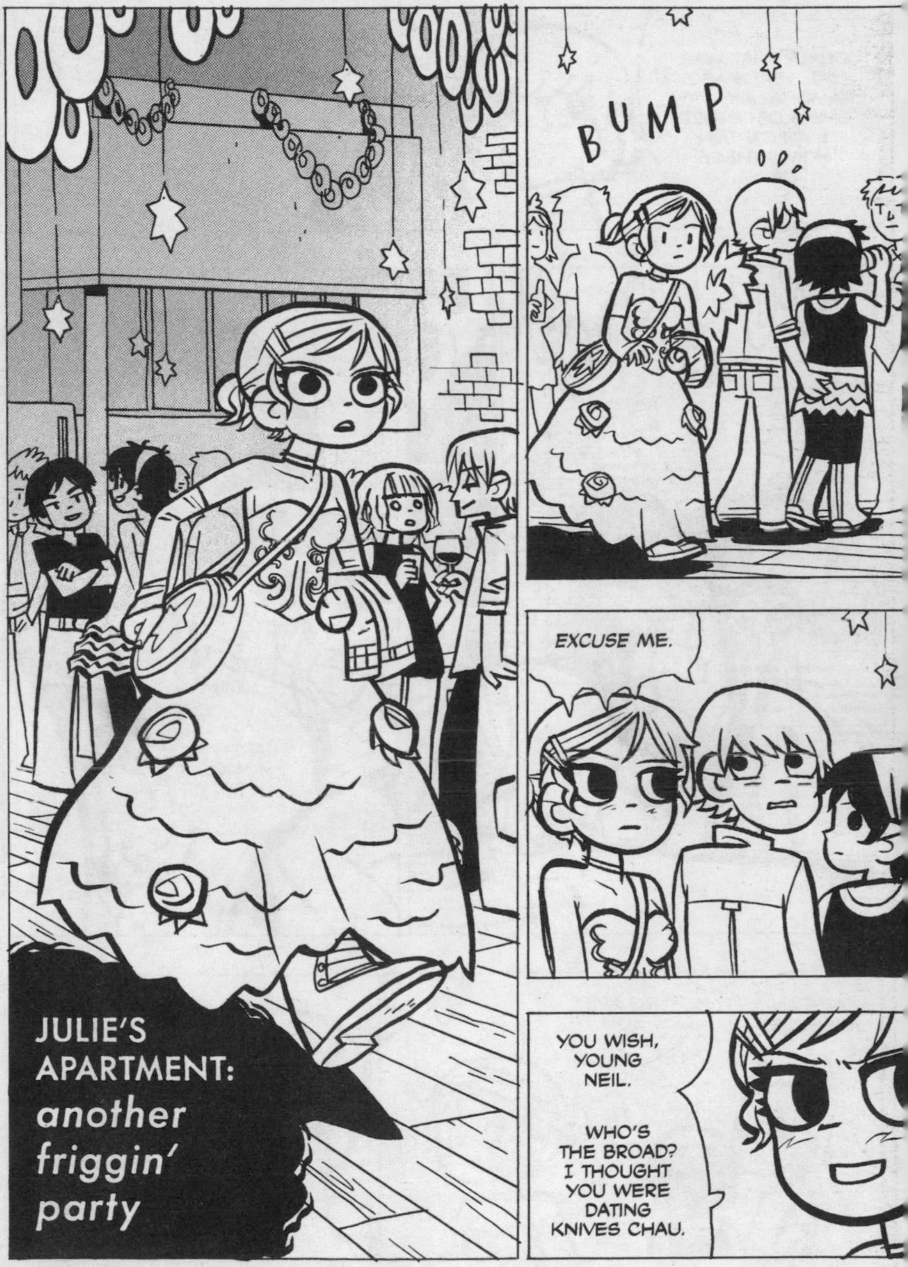
JULIE'S APARTMENT: another friggin' party
BUMP
EXCUSE ME.
YOU WISH, YOUNG NEIL.
WHO'S THE BROAD? I THOUGHT YOU WERE DATING KNIVES CHAU.

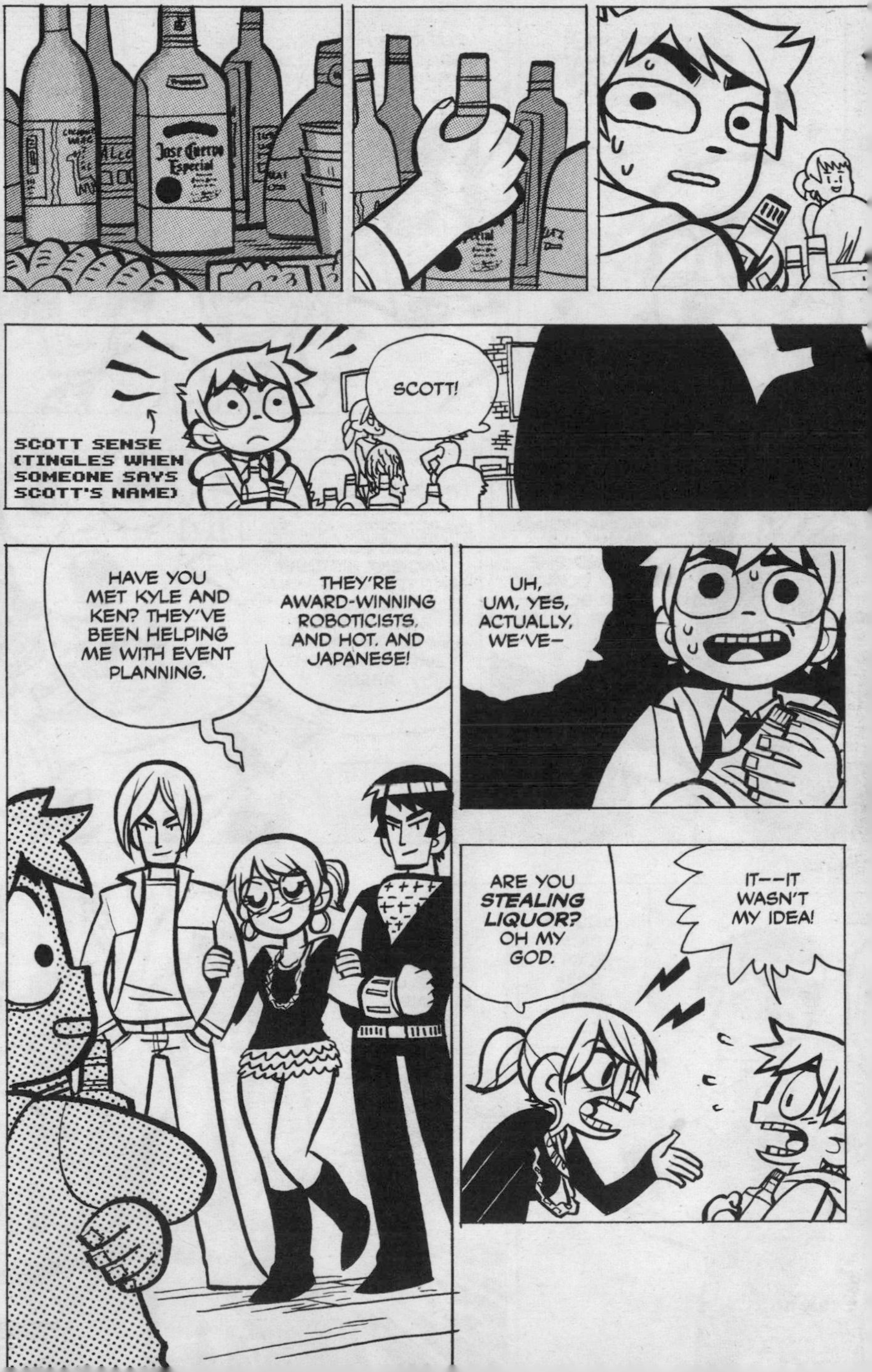
SCOTT!
SCOTT SENSE (TINGLES WHEN SOMEONE SAYS SCOTT'S NAME)
HAVE YOU MET KYLE AND KEN? THEY'VE BEEN HELPING ME WITH EVENT PLANNING.
THEY'RE AWARD-WINNING ROBOTICISTS, AND HOT, AND JAPANESE!
UH, UM, YES, ACTUALLY, WE'VE—
ARE YOU STEALING LIQUOR? OH MY GOD.
IT--IT WASN'T MY IDEA!

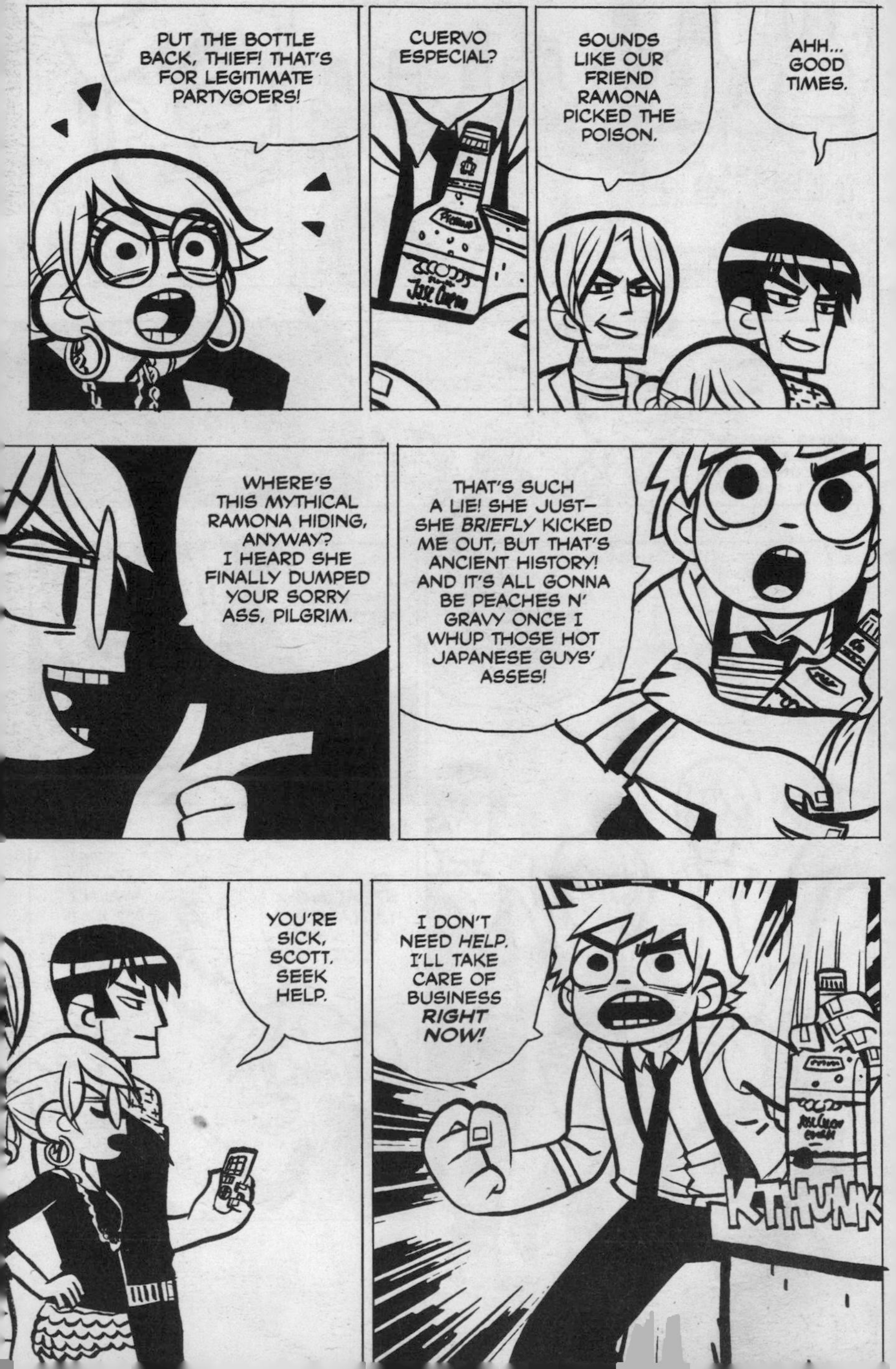
PUT THE BOTTLE BACK, THIEF! THAT'S FOR LEGITIMATE PARTYGOERS!
CUERVO ESPECIAL?
SOUNDS LIKE OUR FRIEND RAMONA PICKED THE POISON.
AHH... GOOD TIMES.
WHERE'S THIS MYTHICAL RAMONA HIDING, ANYWAY? I HEARD SHE FINALLY DUMPED YOUR SORRY ASS, PILGRIM.
THAT'S SUCH A LIE! SHE JUST— SHE *BRIEFLY* KICKED ME OUT, BUT THAT'S ANCIENT HISTORY! AND IT'S ALL GONNA BE PEACHES N' GRAVY ONCE I WHUP THOSE HOT JAPANESE GUYS' ASSES!
YOU'RE SICK, SCOTT. SEEK HELP.
I DON'T NEED *HELP*. I'LL TAKE CARE OF BUSINESS ***RIGHT NOW!***
KTHUNK

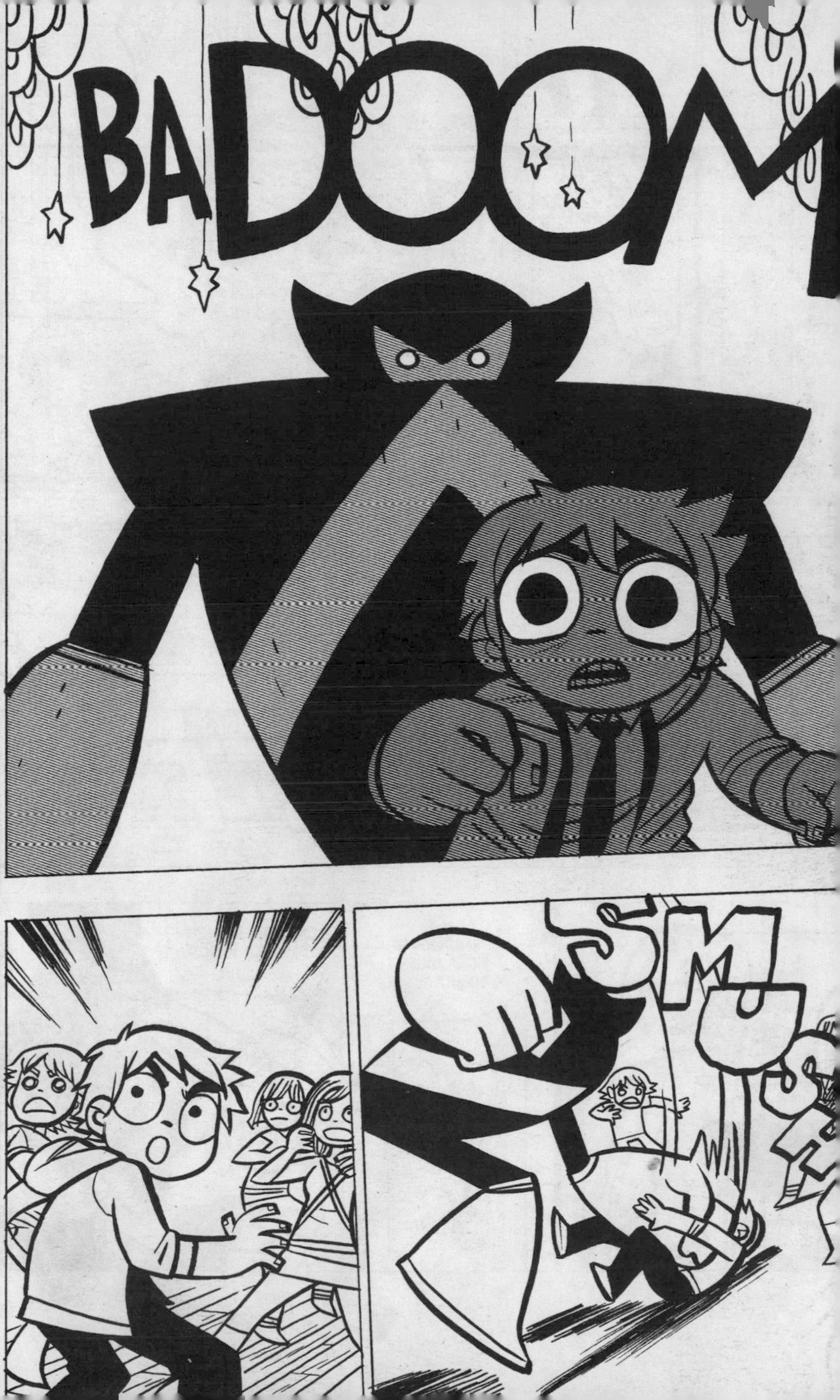
BADOOM
SMUS

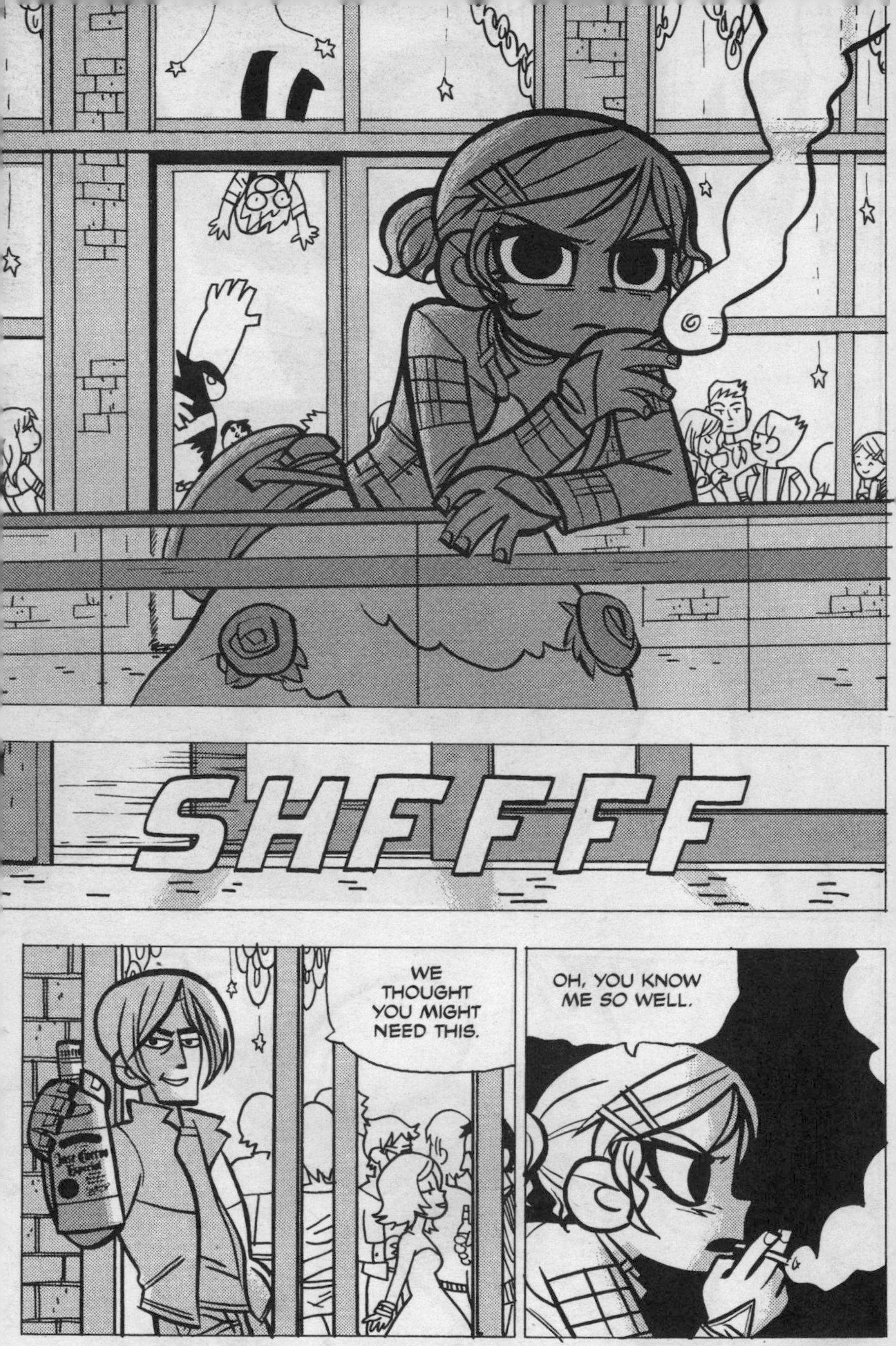
SHFFFF
WE THOUGHT YOU MIGHT NEED THIS.
OH, YOU KNOW ME SO WELL.

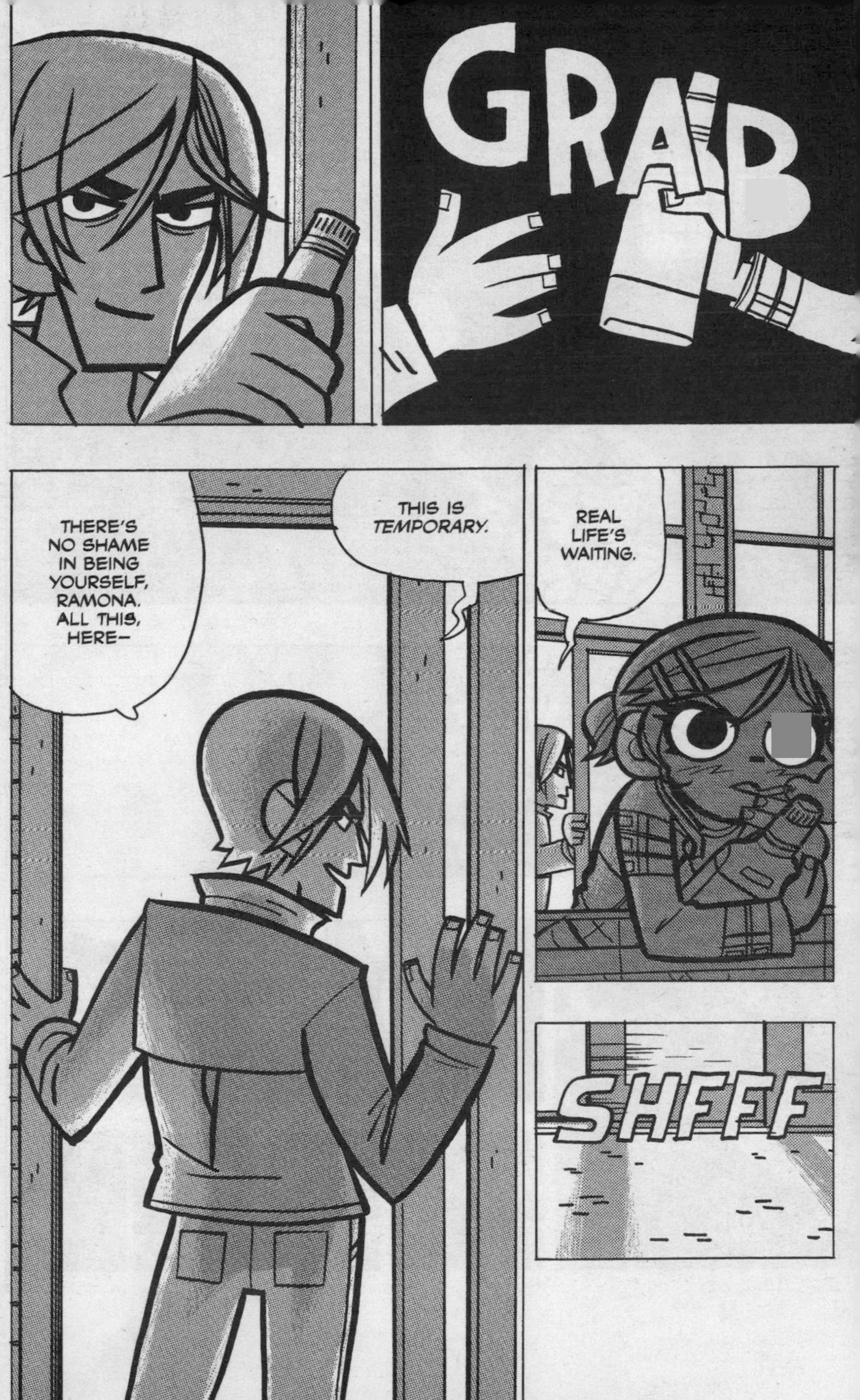
GRAB
THERE'S NO SHAME IN BEING YOURSELF, RAMONA. ALL THIS, HERE—
THIS IS *TEMPORARY.*
REAL LIFE'S WAITING.
SHFFF

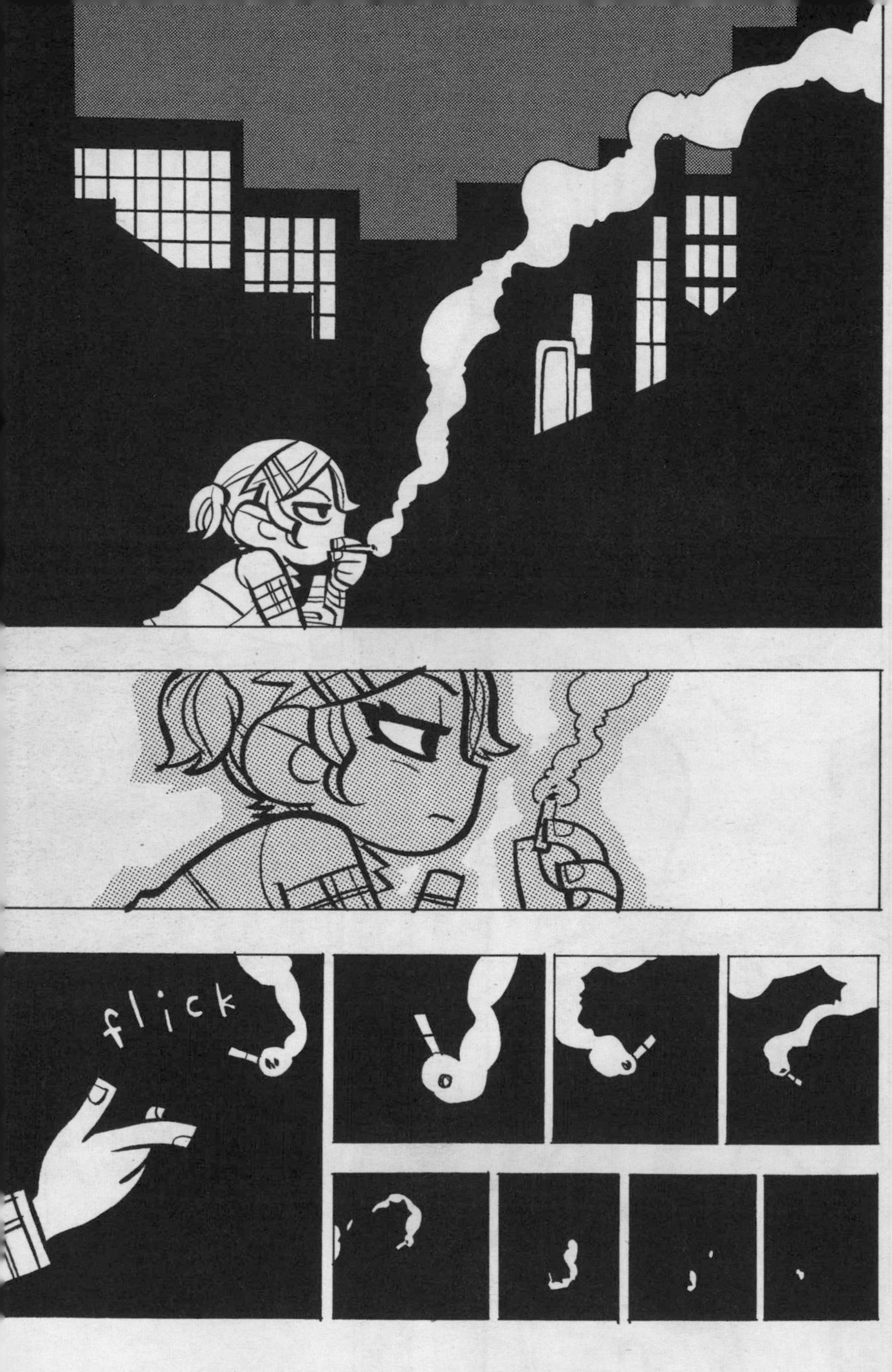
flick

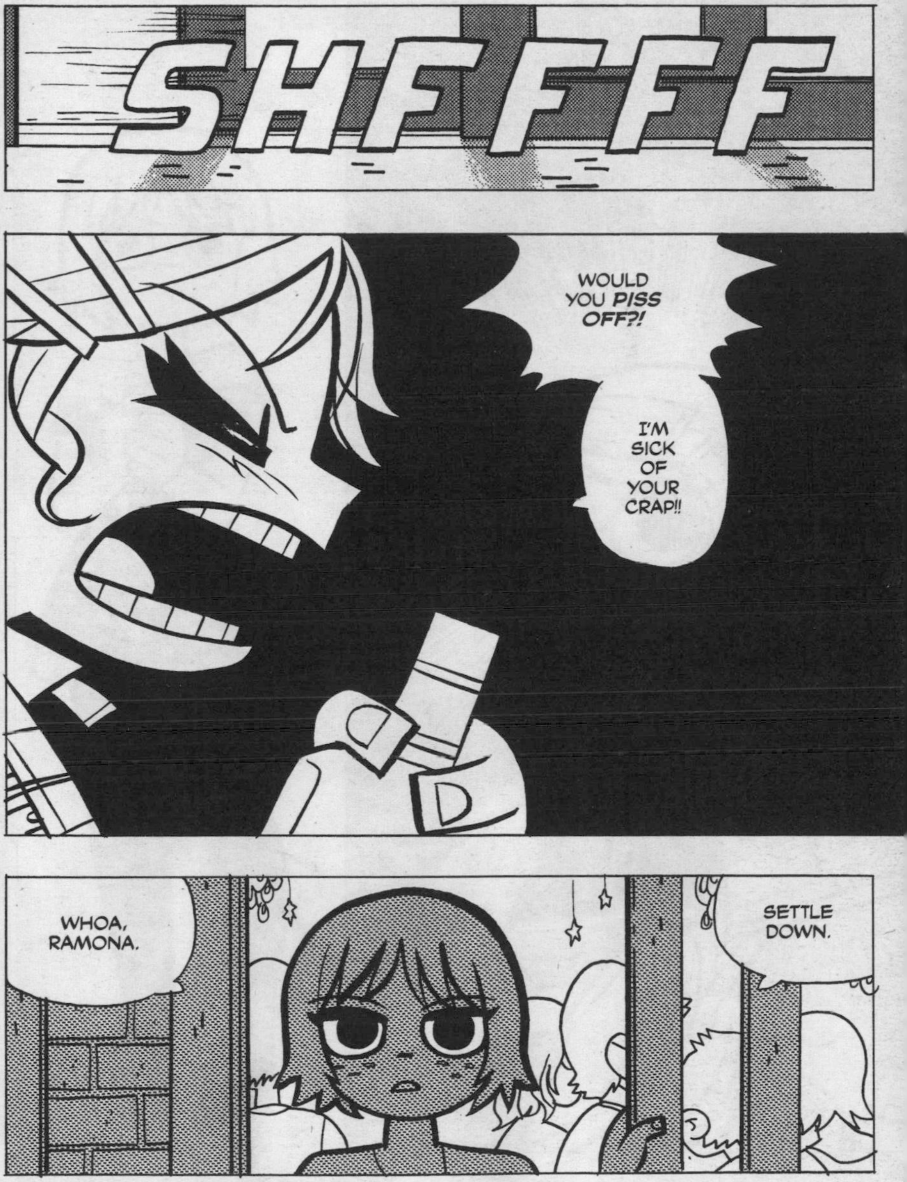
SHFFFF
WOULD YOU PISS OFF?!
I'M SICK OF YOUR CRAP!!
WHOA, RAMONA.
SETTLE DOWN.

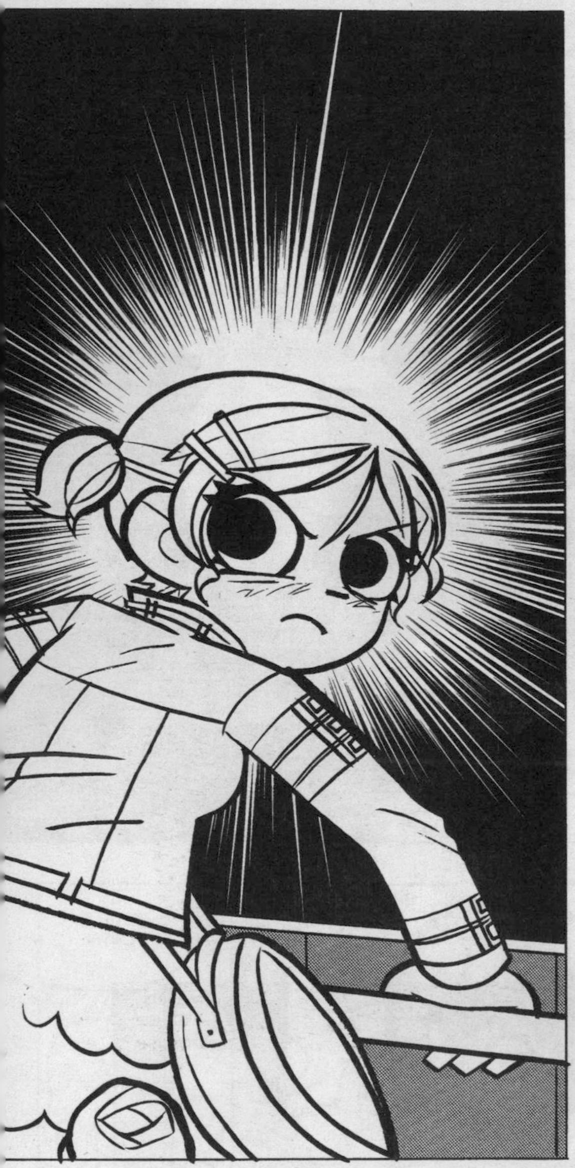

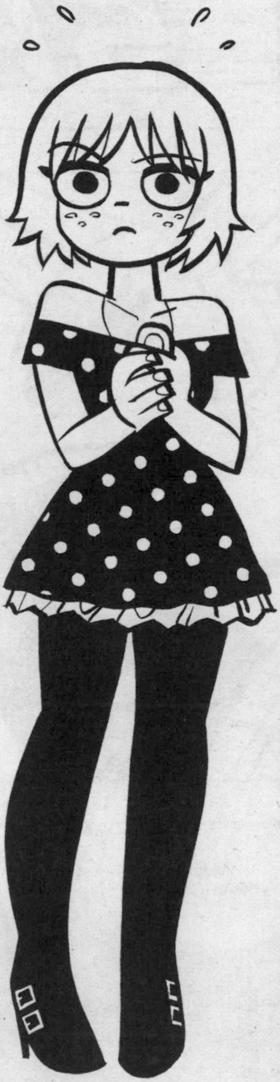

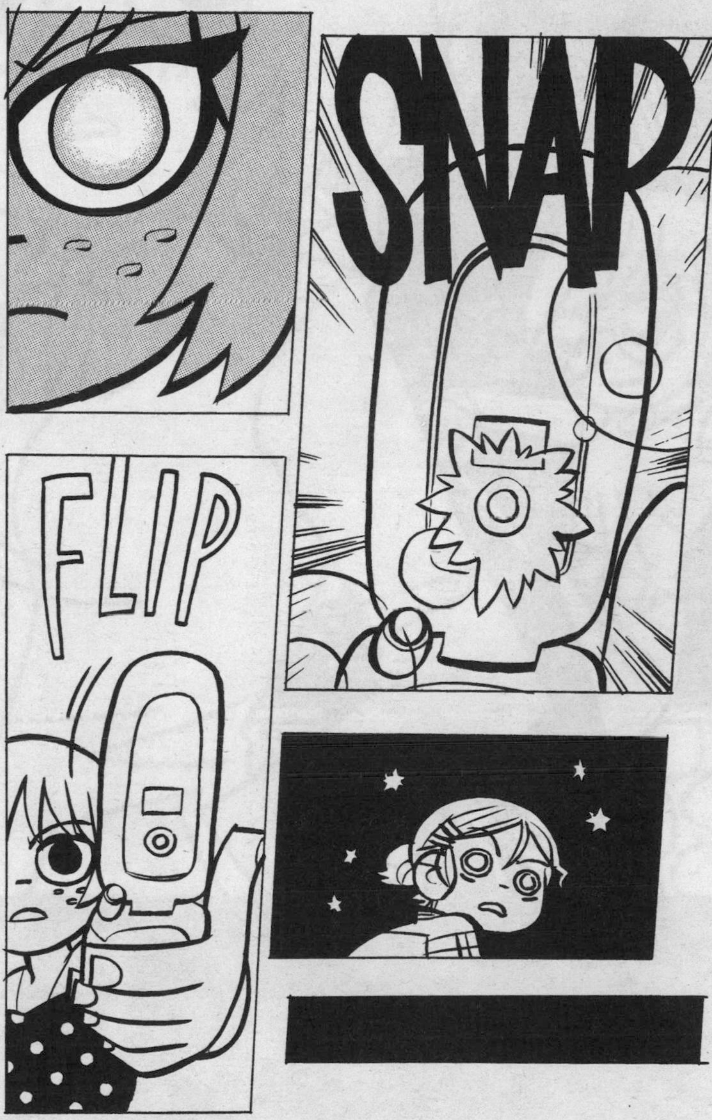
FLIP
SNAP

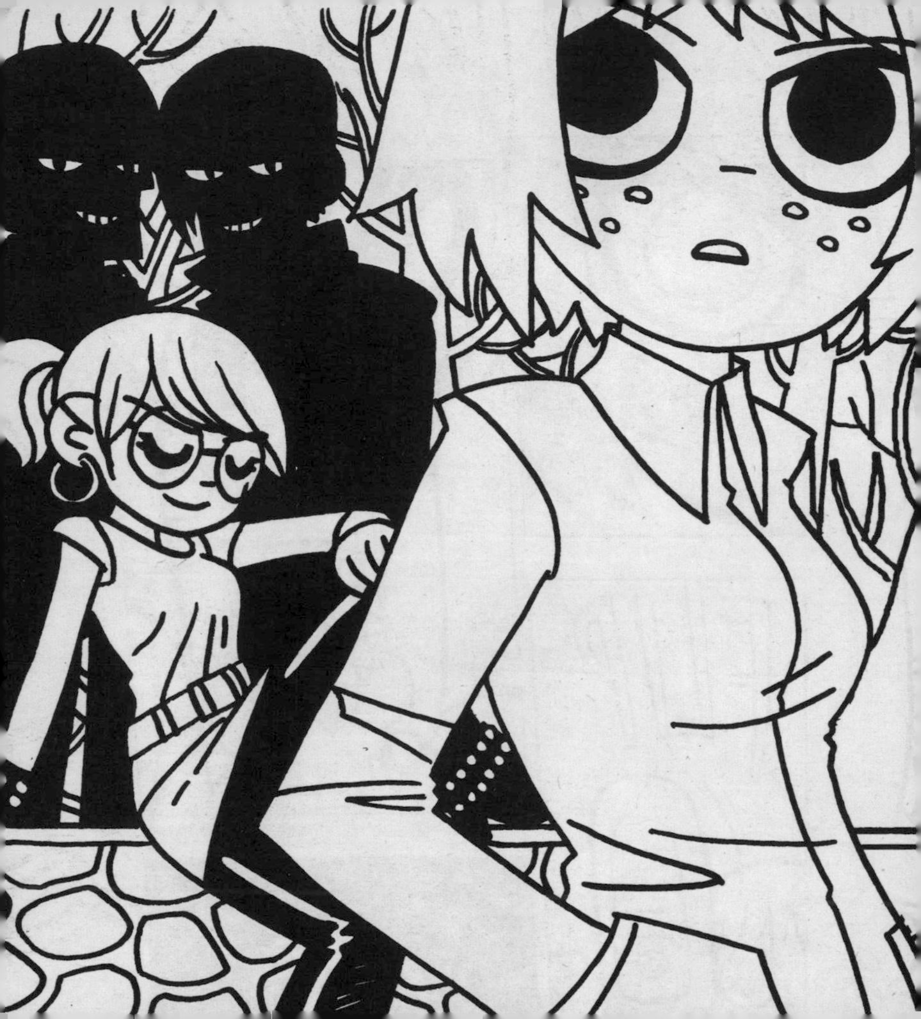

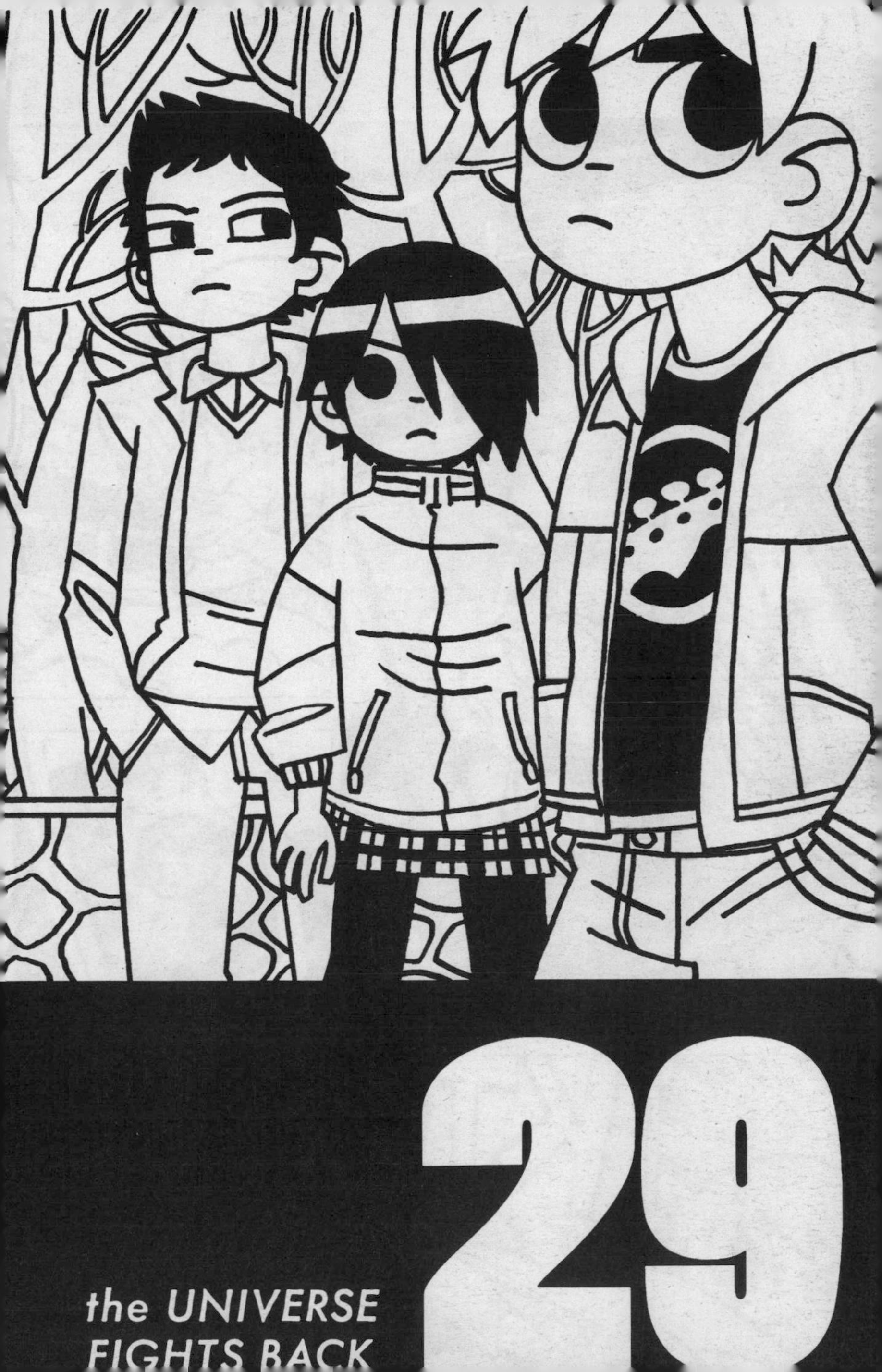

29

the UNIVERSE FIGHTS BACK

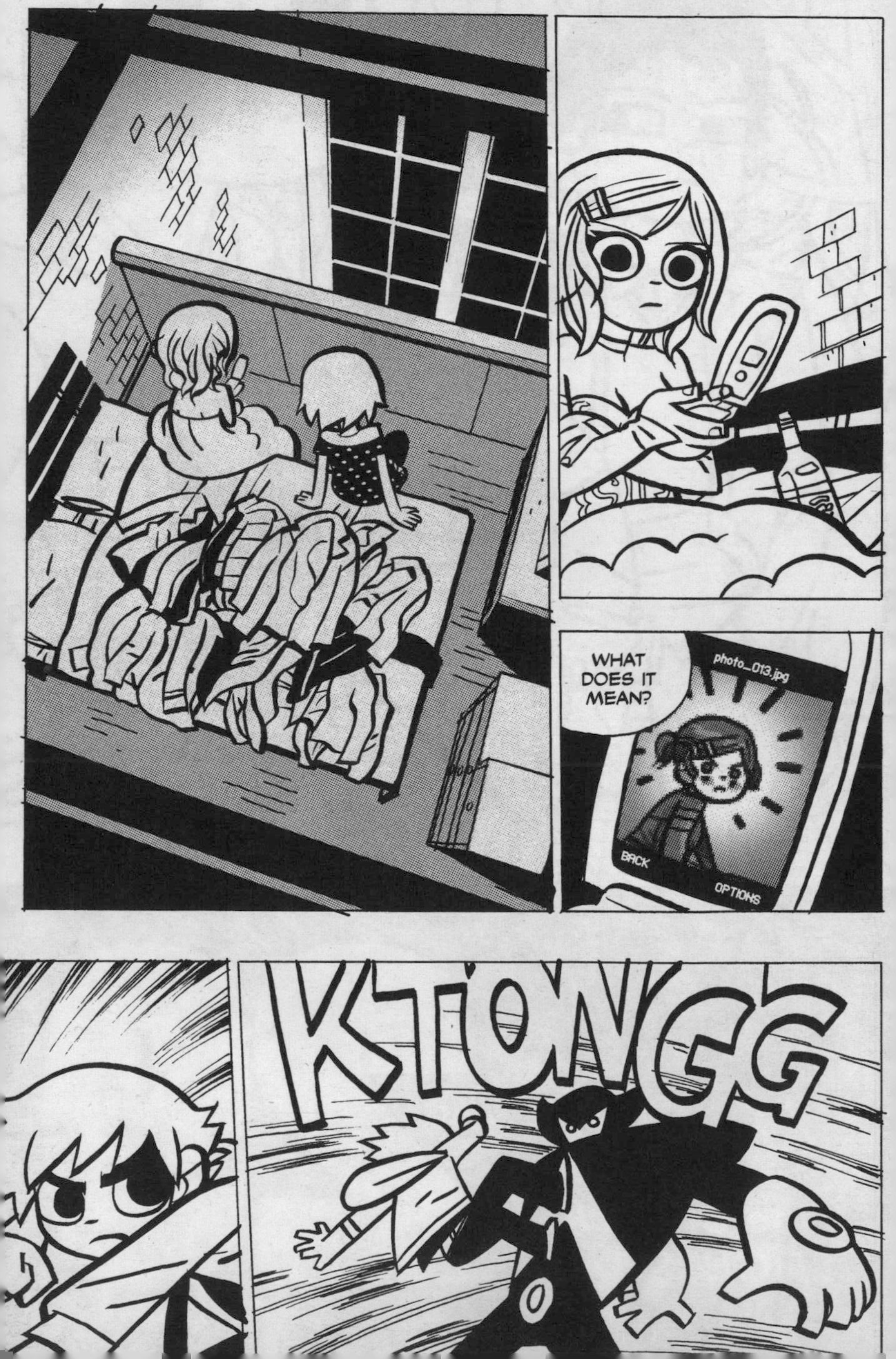
WHAT DOES IT MEAN?
photo_013.jpg
BACK
OPTIONS
KTONGG

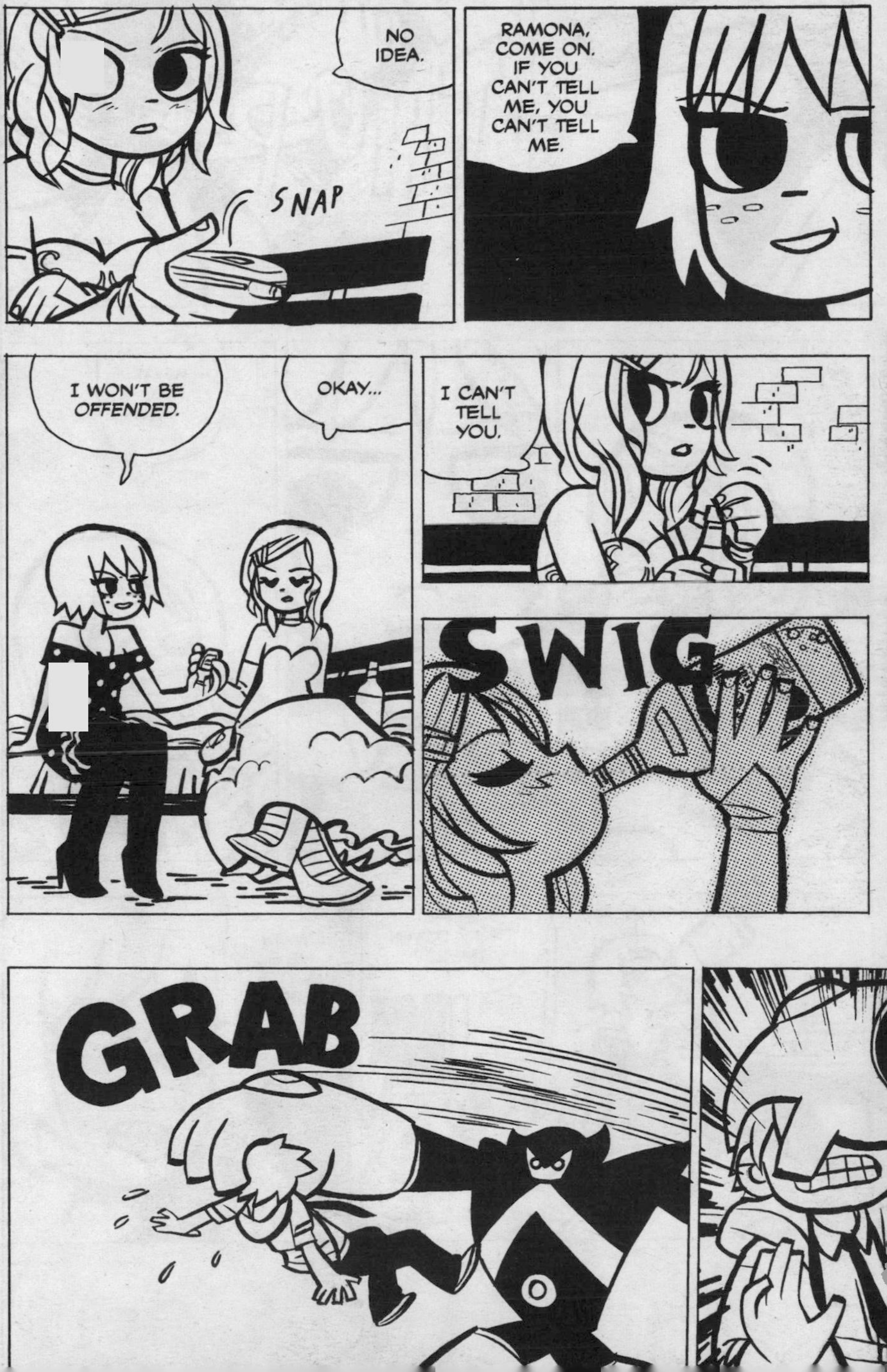

NO IDEA.
SNAP
RAMONA, COME ON. IF YOU CAN'T TELL ME, YOU CAN'T TELL ME.
I WON'T BE OFFENDED.
OKAY...
I CAN'T TELL YOU.
SWIG
GRAB

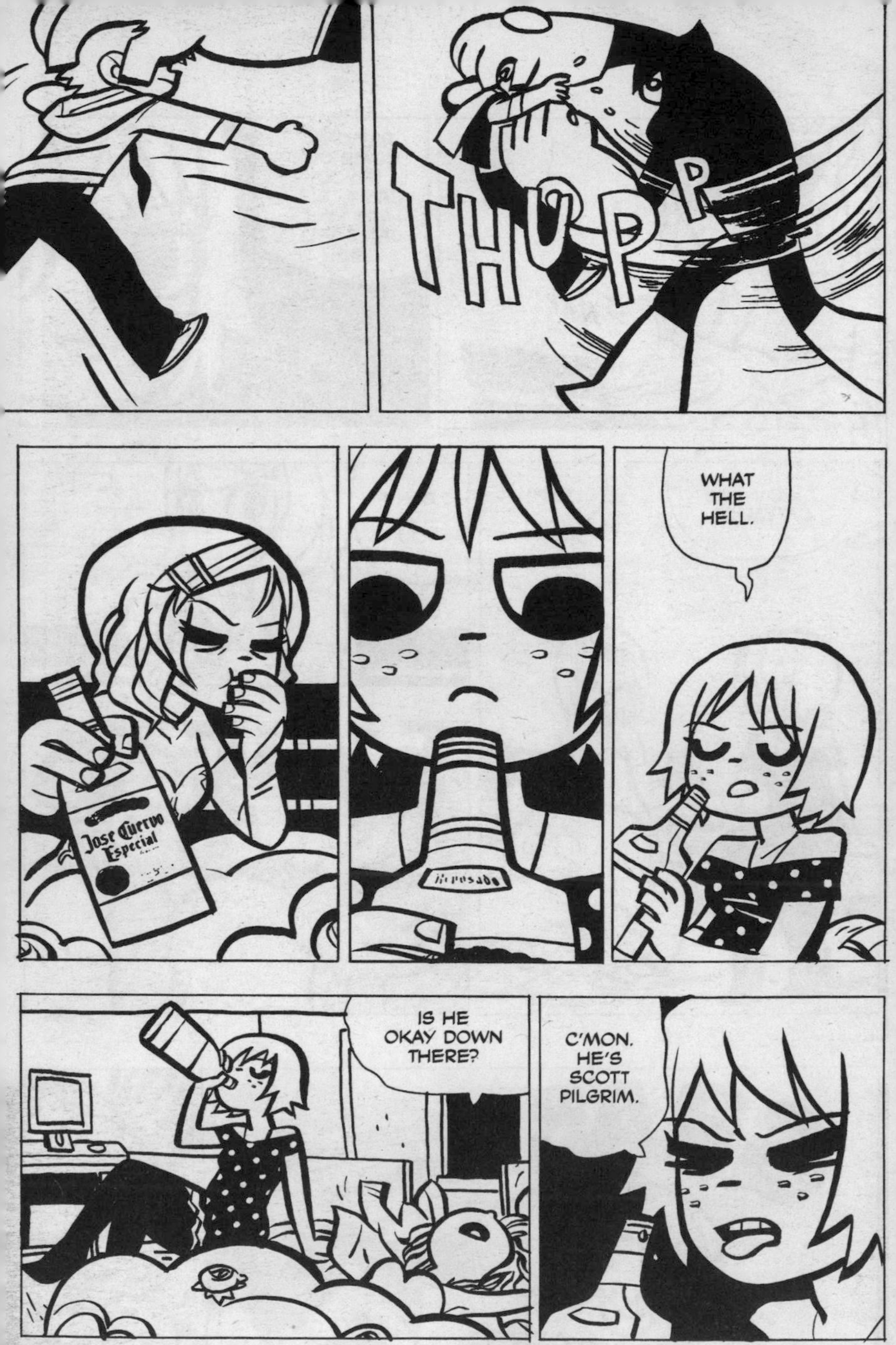
THUPP
Jose Cuervo
Especial
WHAT THE HELL.
IS HE OKAY DOWN THERE?
C'MON. HE'S SCOTT PILGRIM.

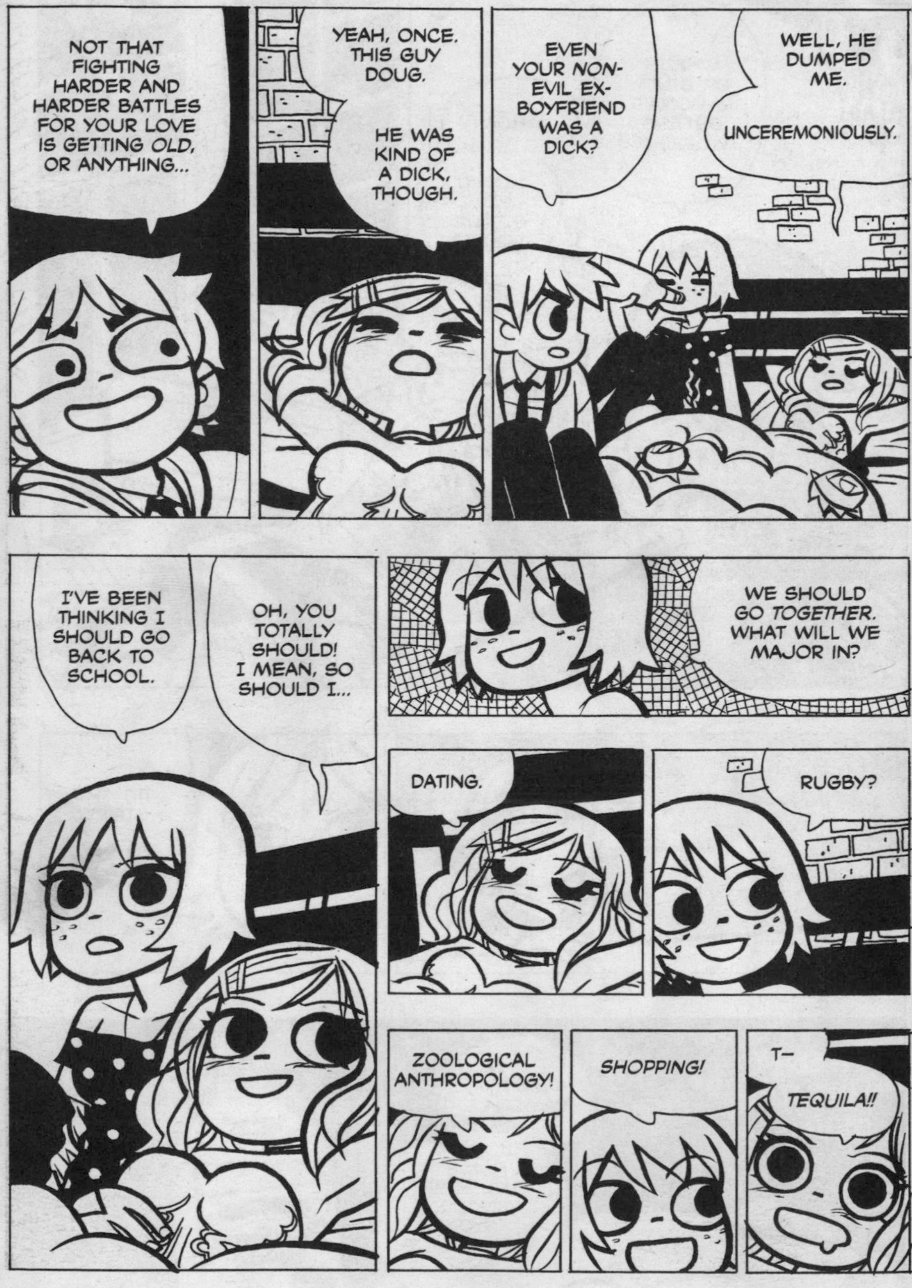
NOT THAT FIGHTING HARDER AND HARDER BATTLES FOR YOUR LOVE IS GETTING *OLD*, OR ANYTHING...
YEAH, ONCE. THIS GUY DOUG.
HE WAS KIND OF A DICK, THOUGH.
EVEN YOUR *NON*-EVIL EX-BOYFRIEND WAS A DICK?
WELL, HE DUMPED ME.
UNCEREMONIOUSLY.
I'VE BEEN THINKING I SHOULD GO BACK TO SCHOOL.
OH, YOU TOTALLY SHOULD! I MEAN, SO SHOULD I...
WE SHOULD GO *TOGETHER*. WHAT WILL WE MAJOR IN?
DATING.
RUGBY?
ZOOLOGICAL ANTHROPOLOGY!
SHOPPING!
T—
TEQUILA!!

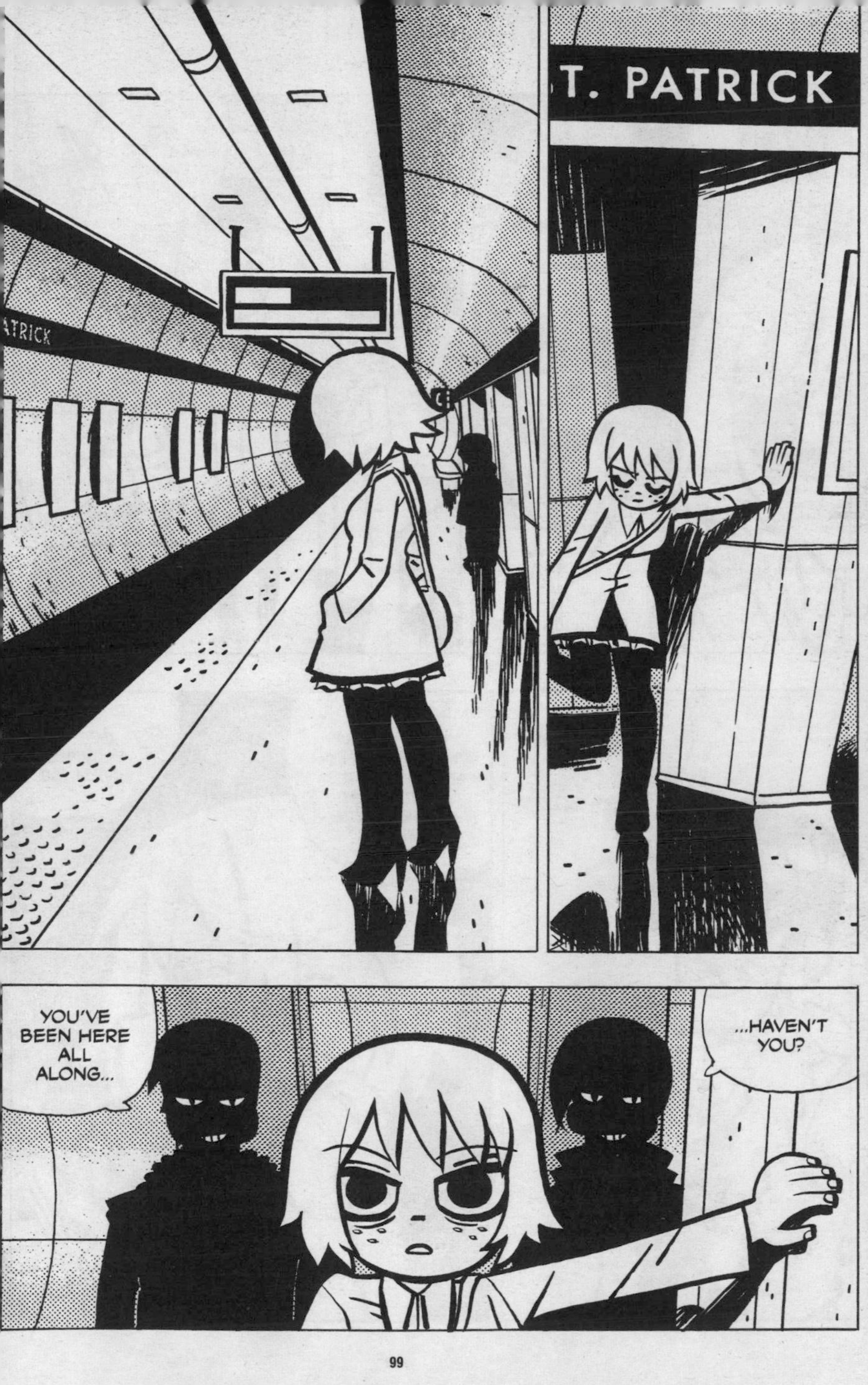
ATRICK
T. PATRICK
YOU'VE BEEN HERE ALL ALONG...
...HAVEN'T YOU?

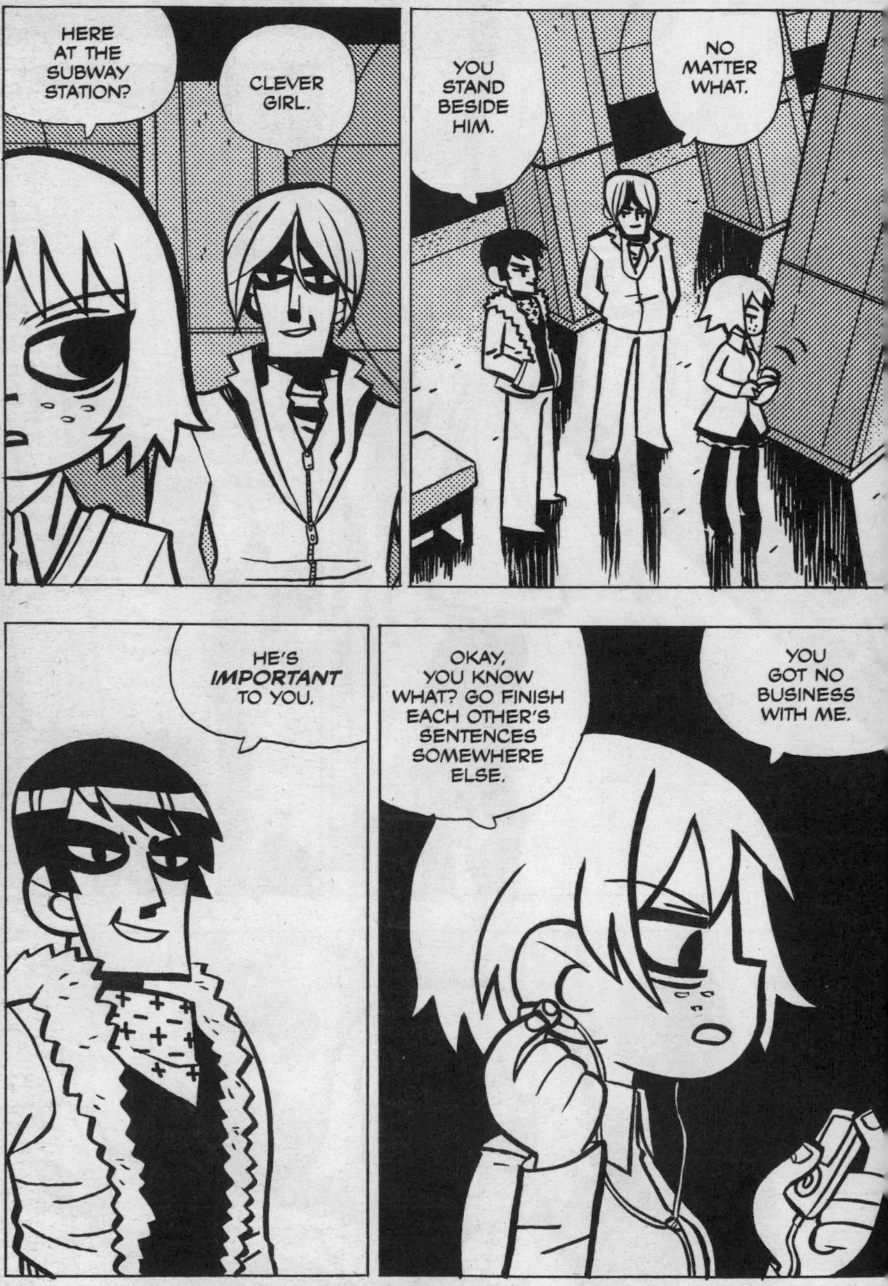
HERE AT THE SUBWAY STATION?
CLEVER GIRL.
YOU STAND BESIDE HIM.
NO MATTER WHAT.
HE'S *IMPORTANT* TO YOU.
OKAY, YOU KNOW WHAT? GO FINISH EACH OTHER'S SENTENCES SOMEWHERE ELSE.
YOU GOT NO BUSINESS WITH ME.

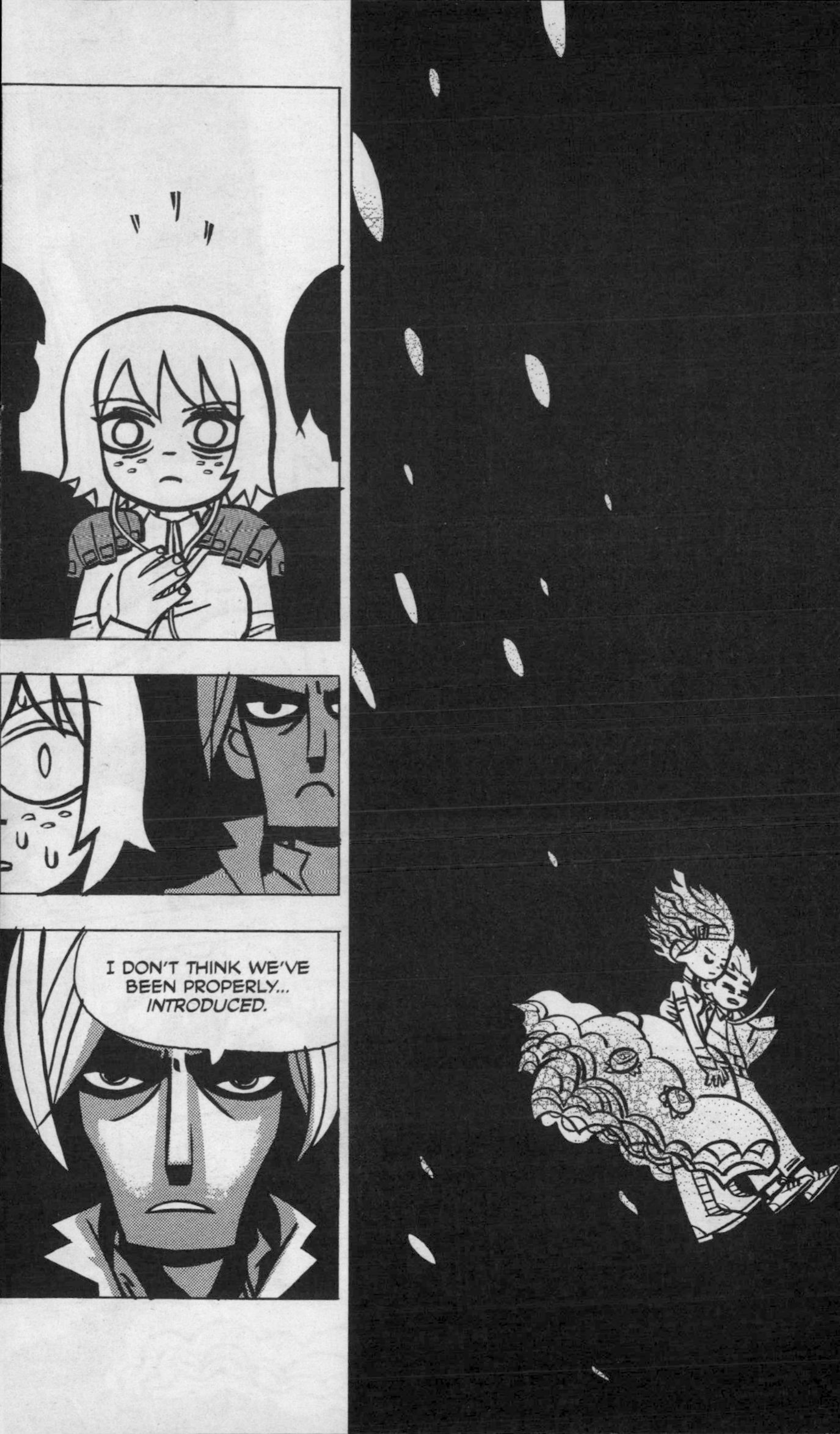
I DON'T THINK WE'VE BEEN PROPERLY... INTRODUCED.

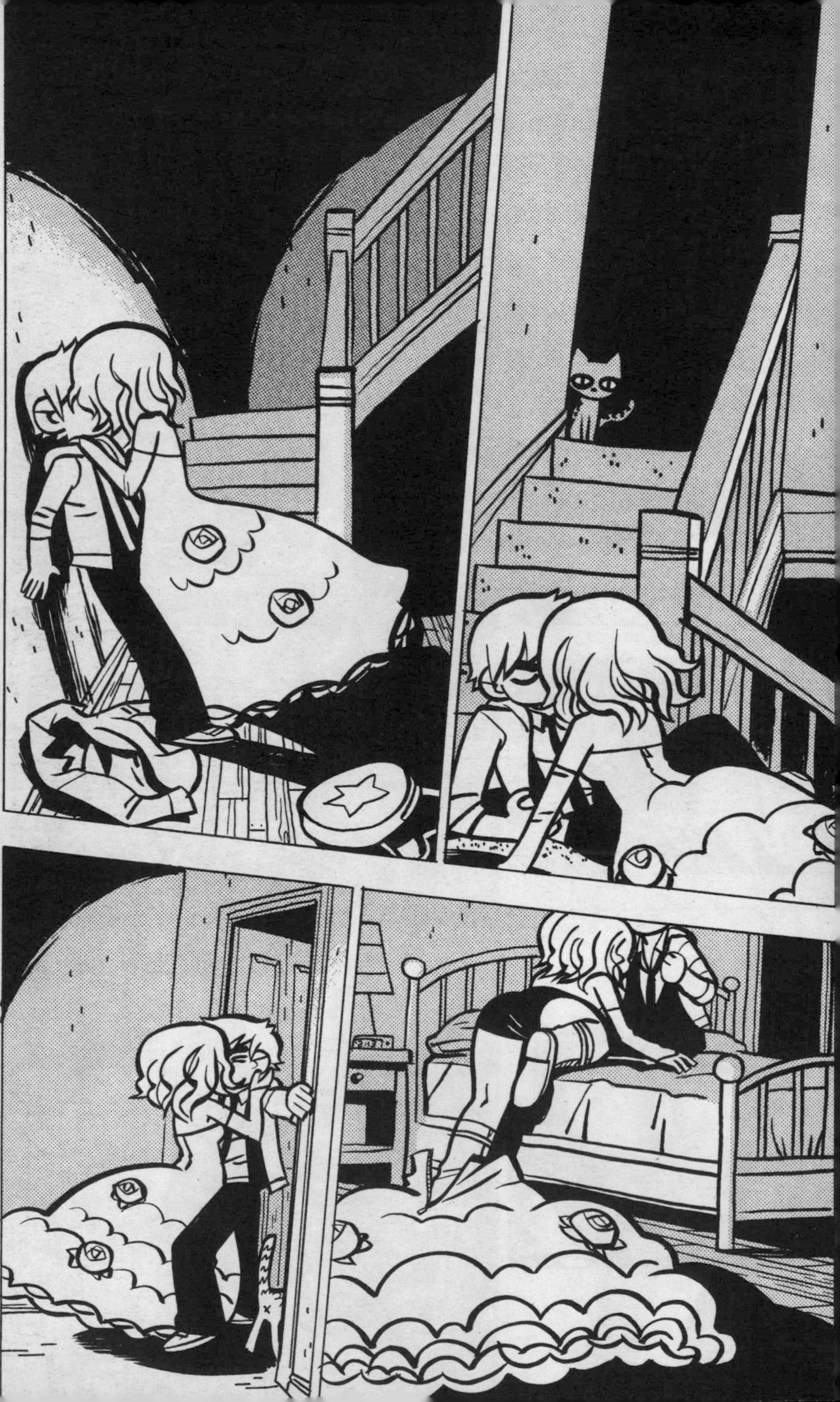

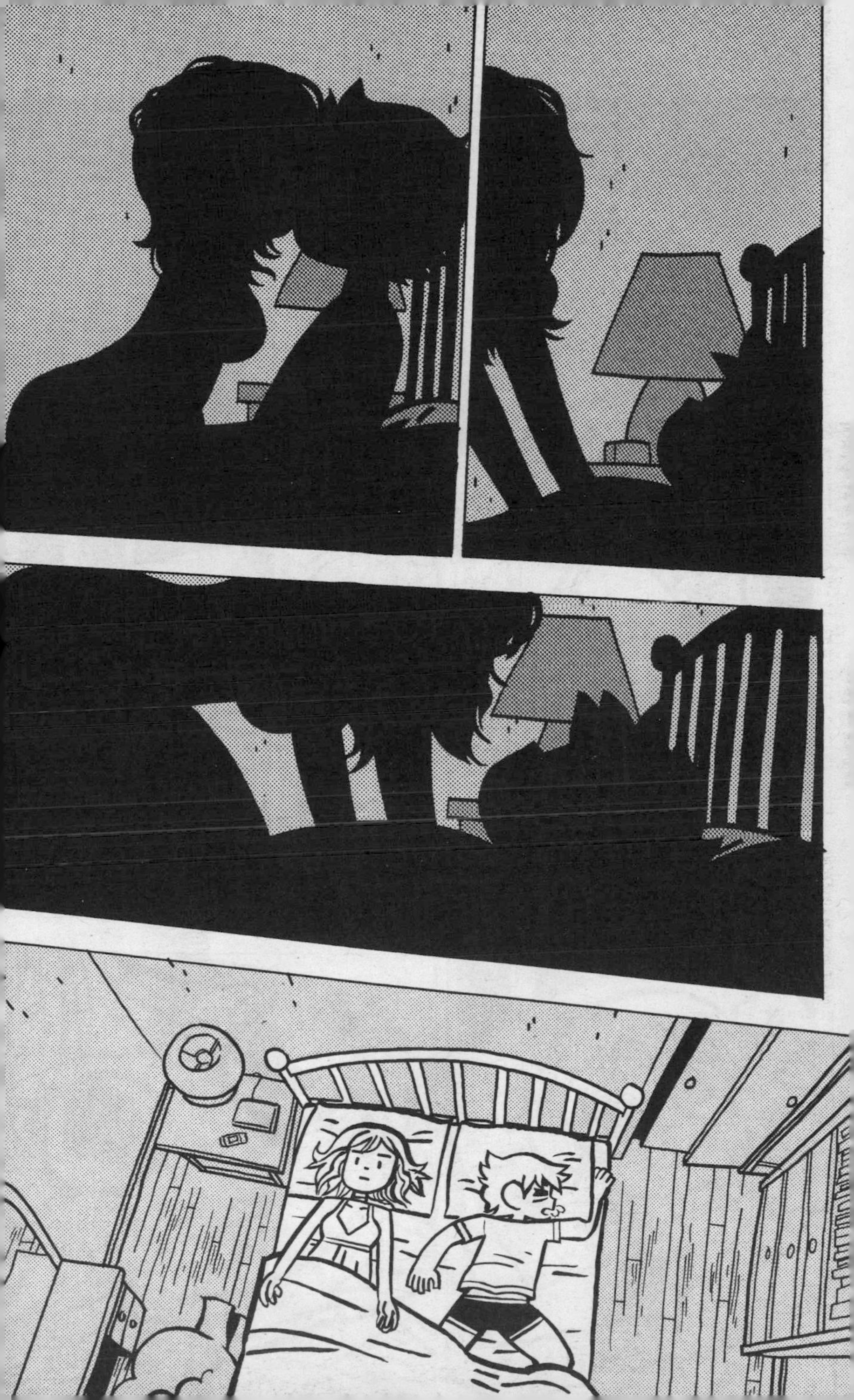

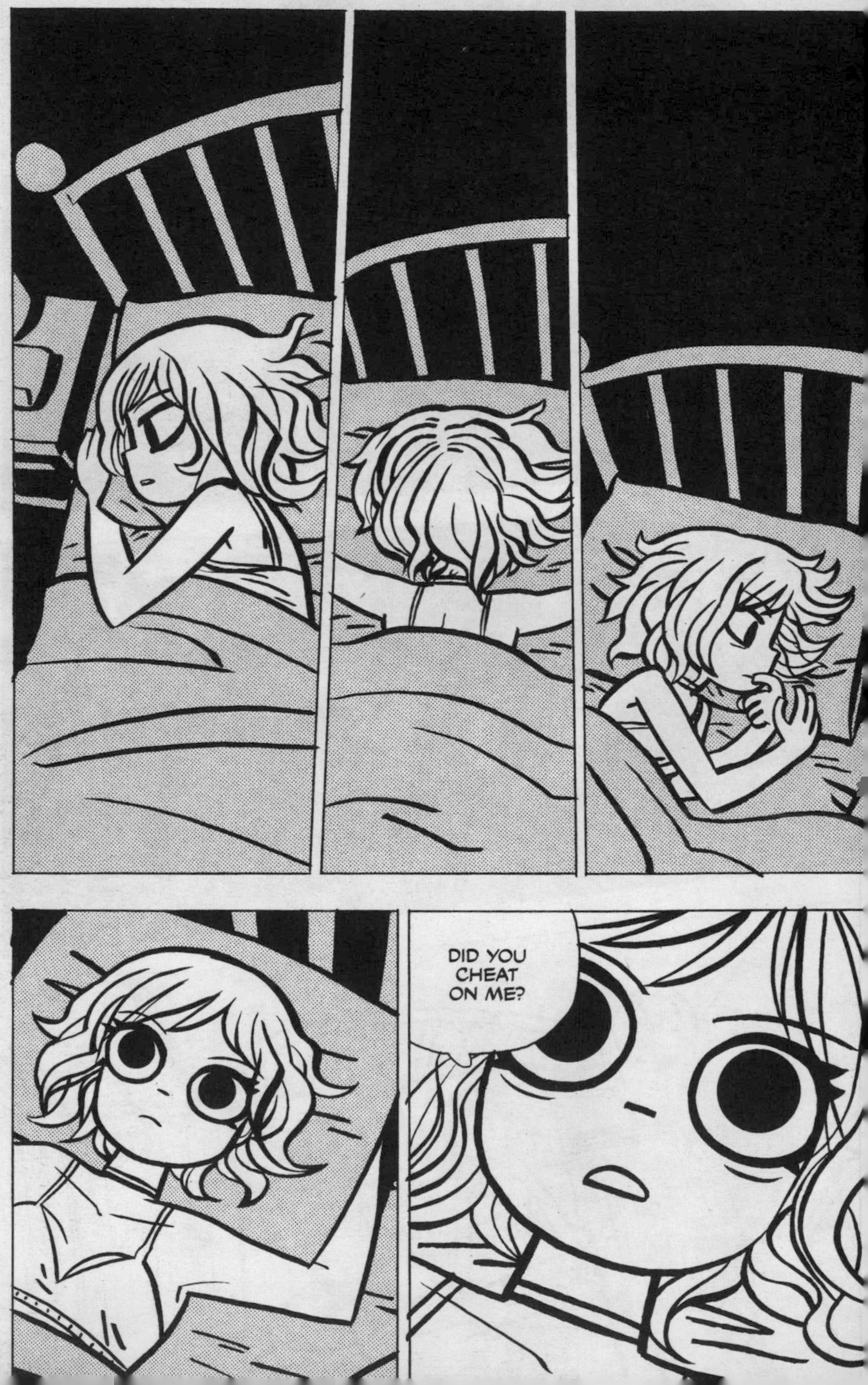
DID YOU CHEAT ON ME?

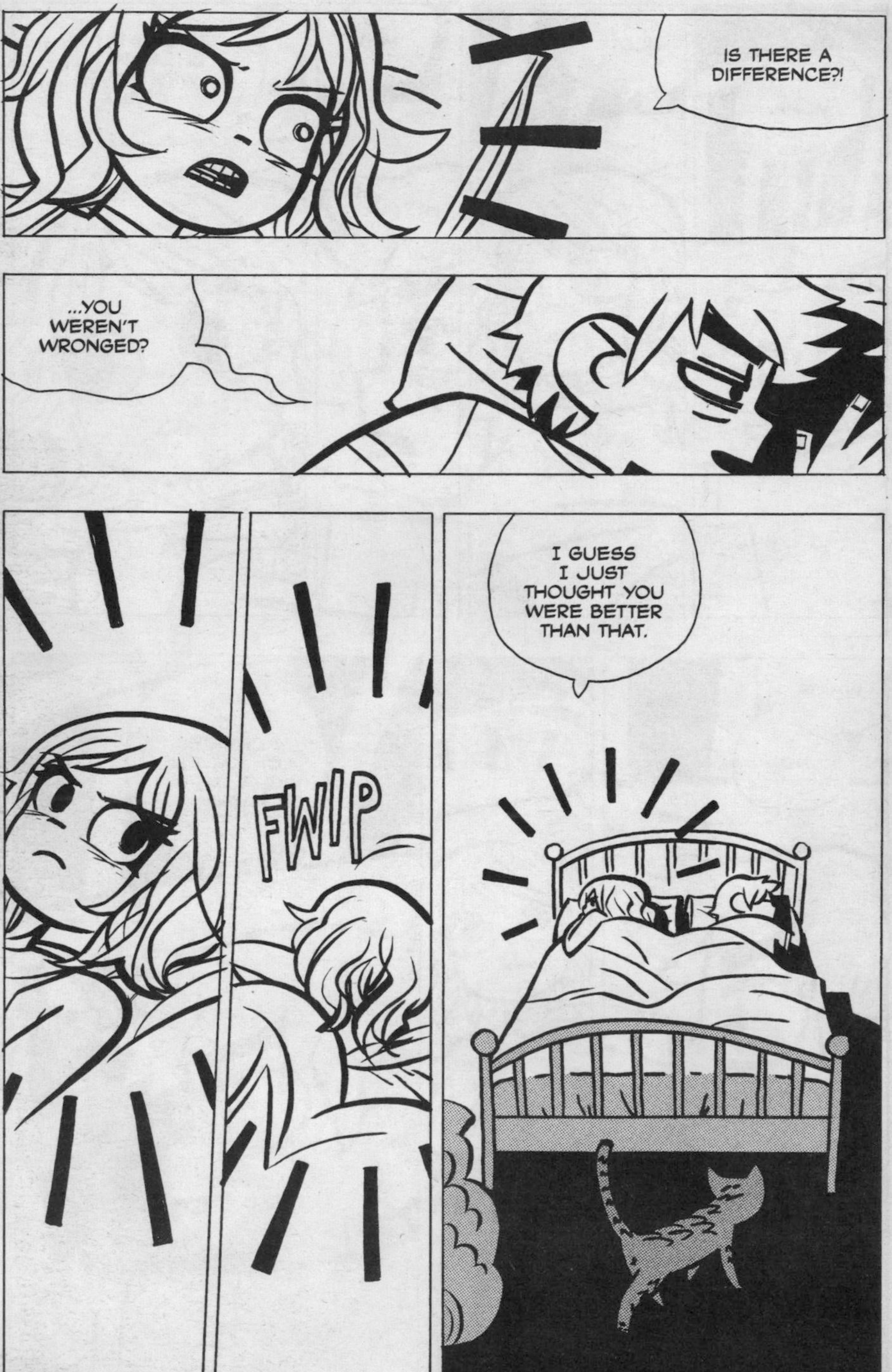
IS THERE A DIFFERENCE?!
...YOU WEREN'T WRONGED?
FWIP
I GUESS I JUST THOUGHT YOU WERE BETTER THAN THAT.

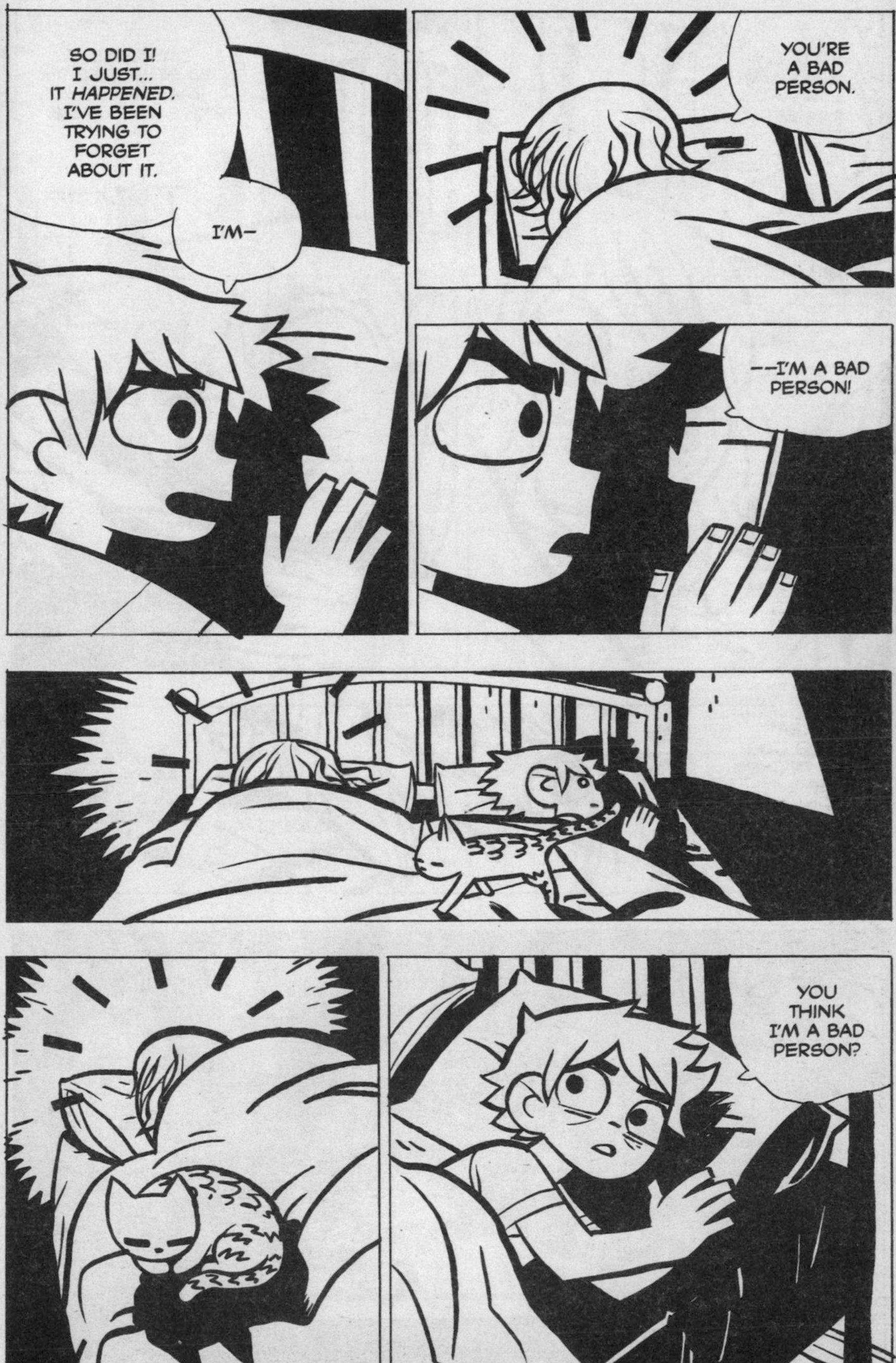
SO DID I! I JUST... IT *HAPPENED*. I'VE BEEN TRYING TO FORGET ABOUT IT.
I'M–
YOU'RE A BAD PERSON.
--I'M A BAD PERSON!
YOU THINK I'M A BAD PERSON?

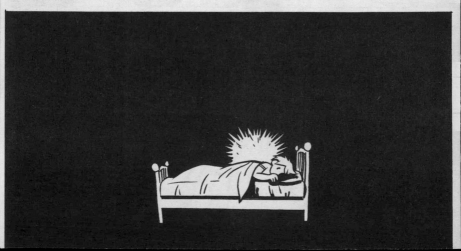

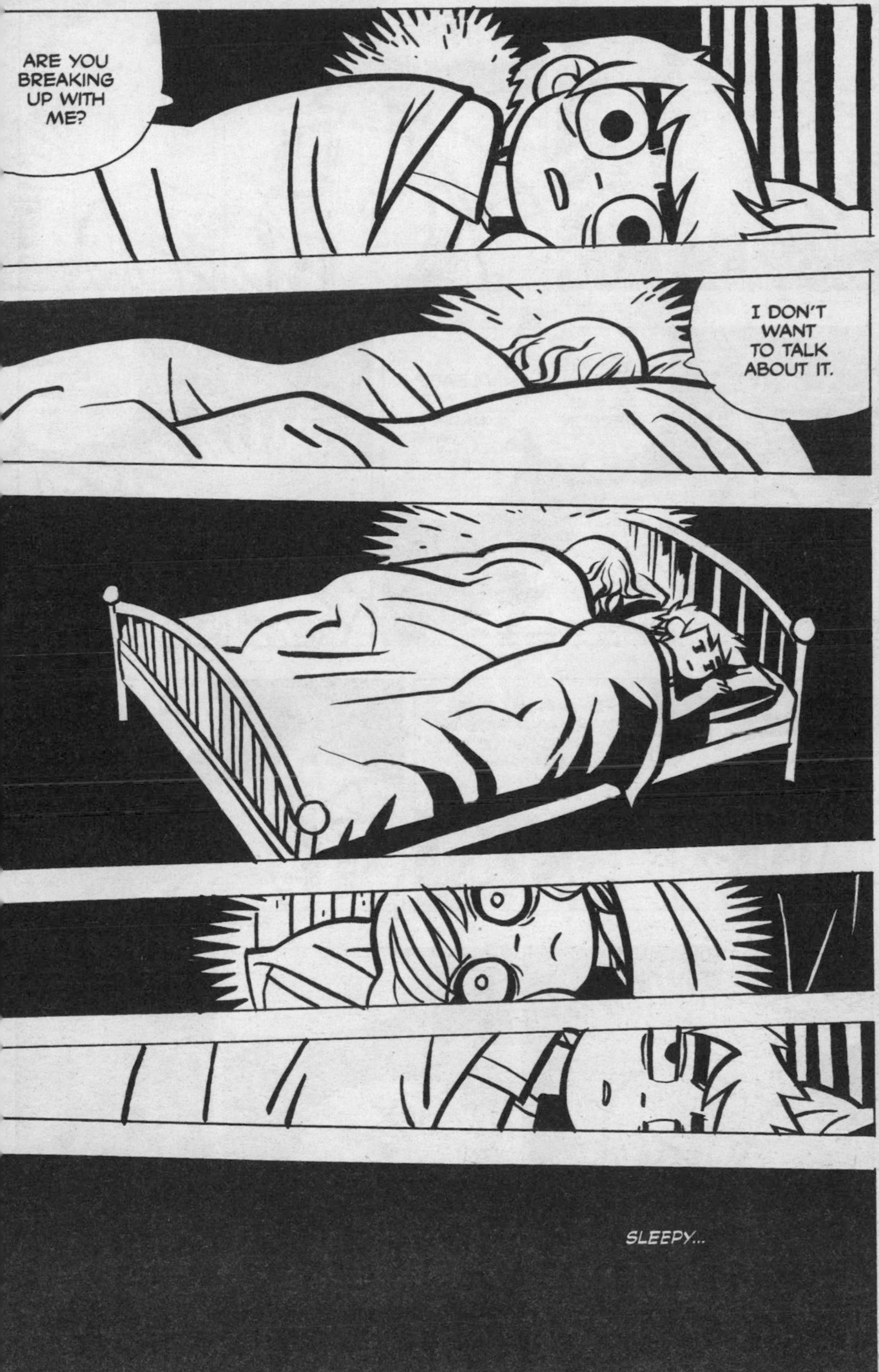
ARE YOU BREAKING UP WITH ME?
I DON'T WANT TO TALK ABOUT IT.
SLEEPY...

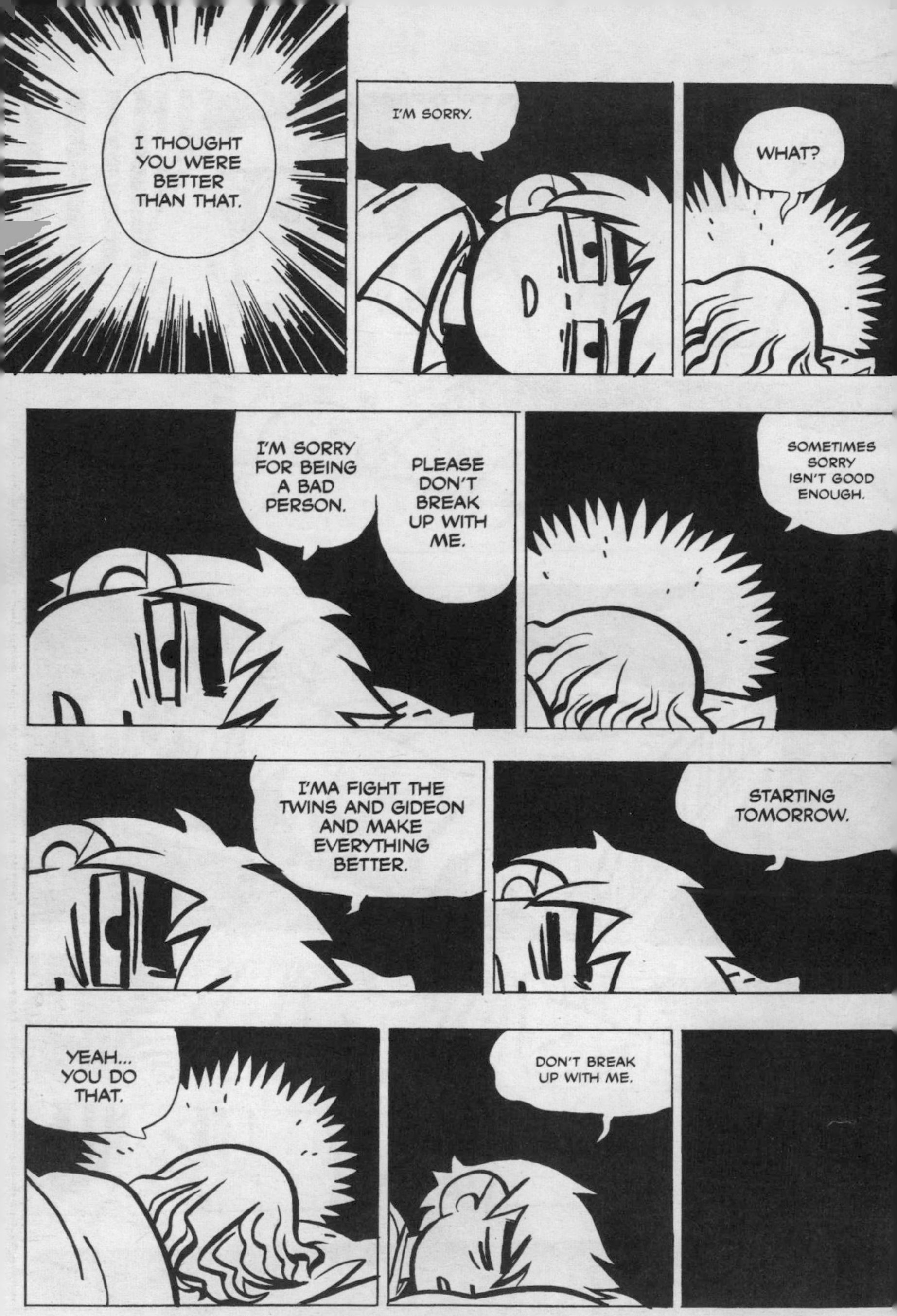
I THOUGHT YOU WERE BETTER THAN THAT.
I'M SORRY.
WHAT?
I'M SORRY FOR BEING A BAD PERSON.
PLEASE DON'T BREAK UP WITH ME.
SOMETIMES SORRY ISN'T GOOD ENOUGH.
I'MA FIGHT THE TWINS AND GIDEON AND MAKE EVERYTHING BETTER.
STARTING TOMORROW.
YEAH... YOU DO THAT.
DON'T BREAK UP WITH ME.

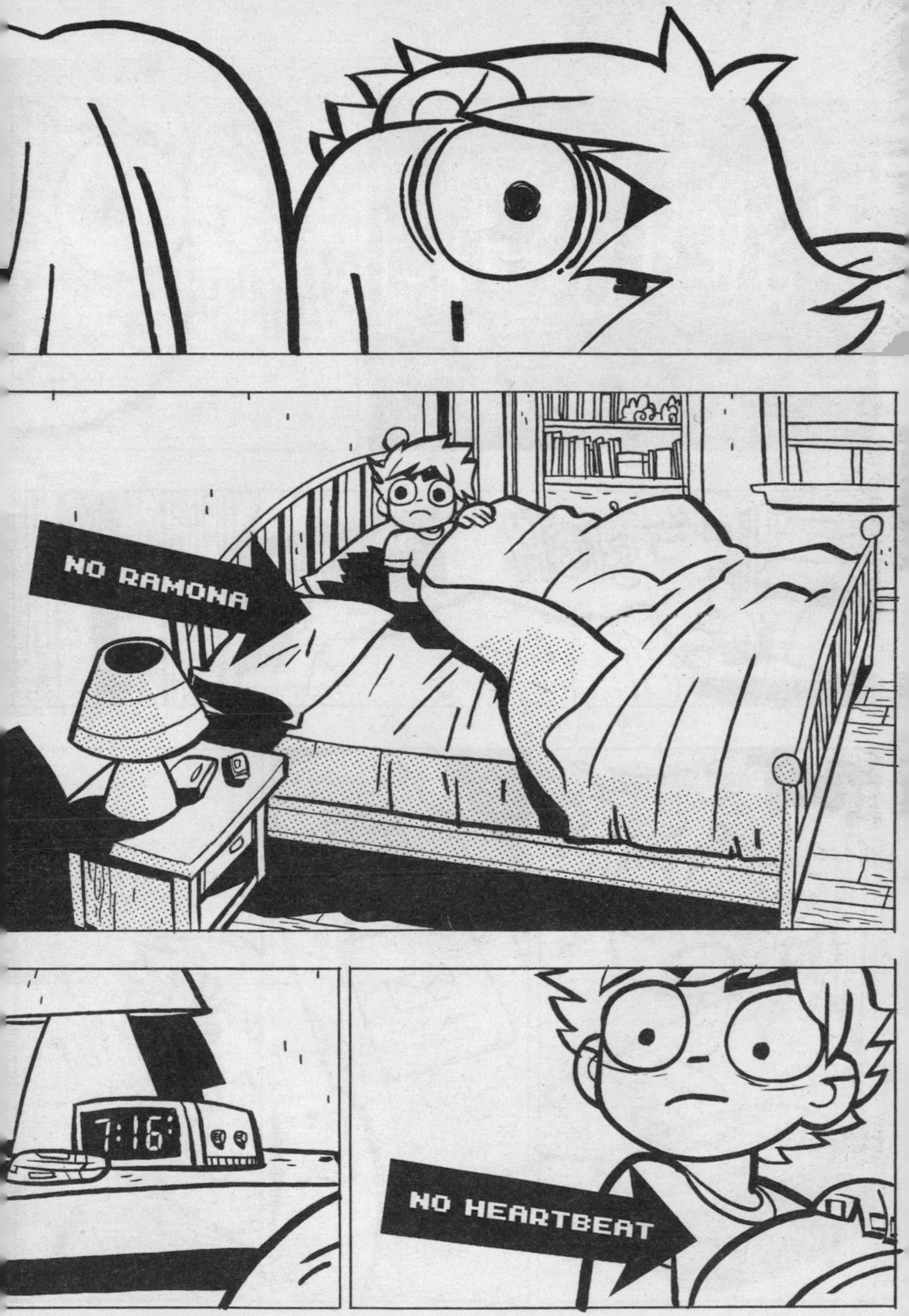
NO RAMONA
7:16
NO HEARTBEAT

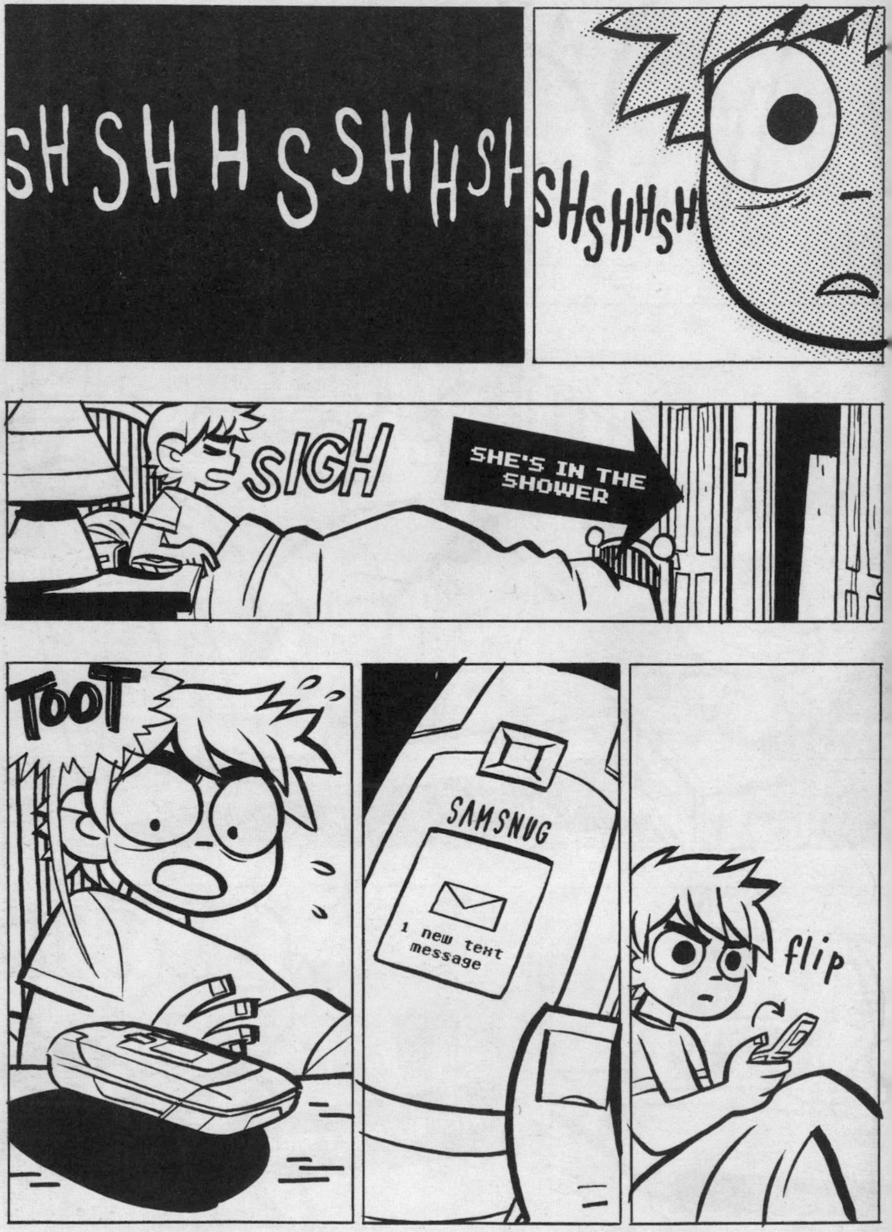
SHSHHSSHHSHSHSHHSH
SIGH
SHE'S IN THE SHOWER
TOOT
SAMSNUG
1 new text message
flip

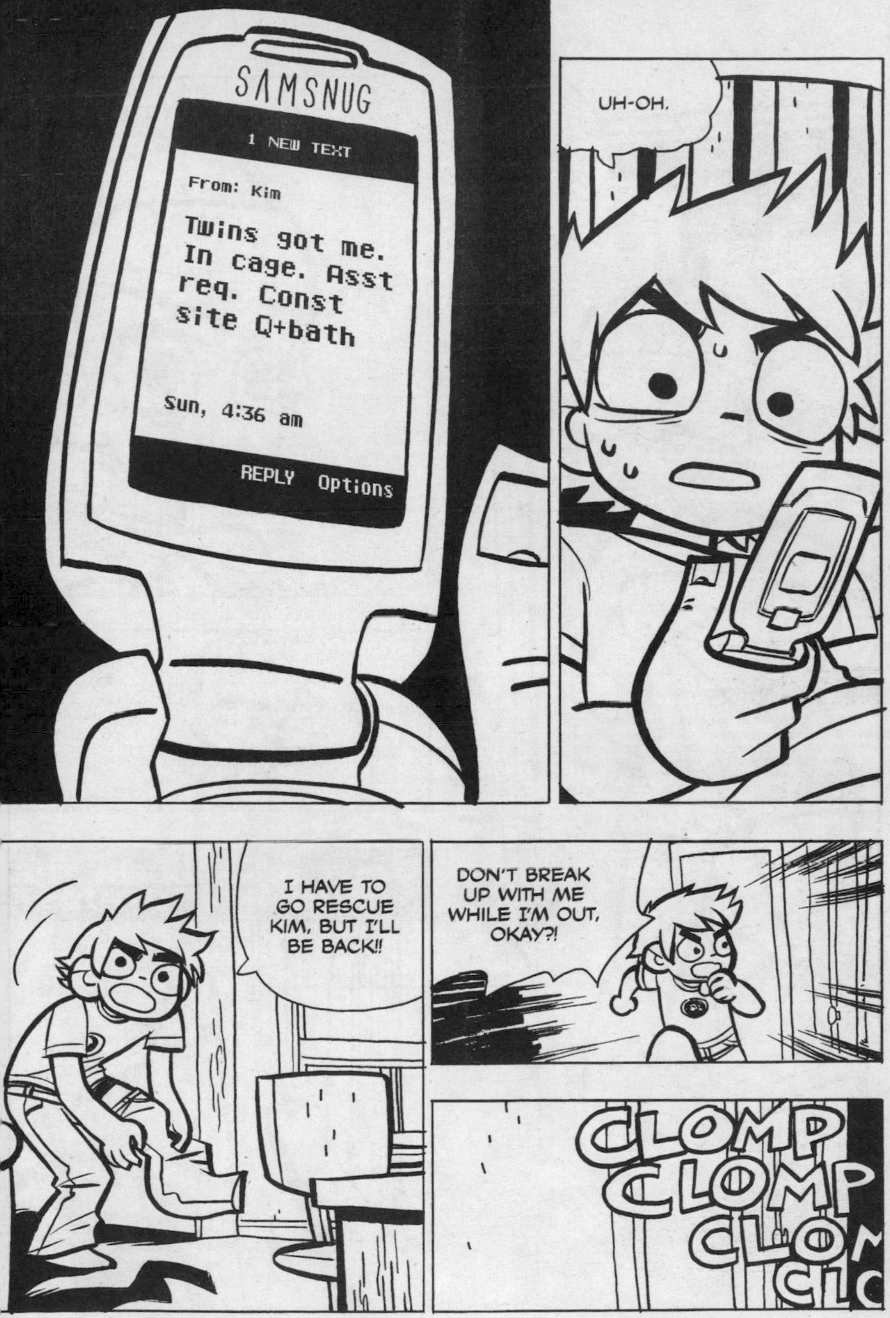
SAMSNUG
1 NEW TEXT
From: Kim
Twins got me. In cage. Asst req. Const site Q+bath
Sun, 4:36 am
REPLY Options
UH-OH.
I HAVE TO GO RESCUE KIM, BUT I'LL BE BACK!!
DON'T BREAK UP WITH ME WHILE I'M OUT, OKAY?!
CLOMP
CLOMP
CLOM
CLO

114

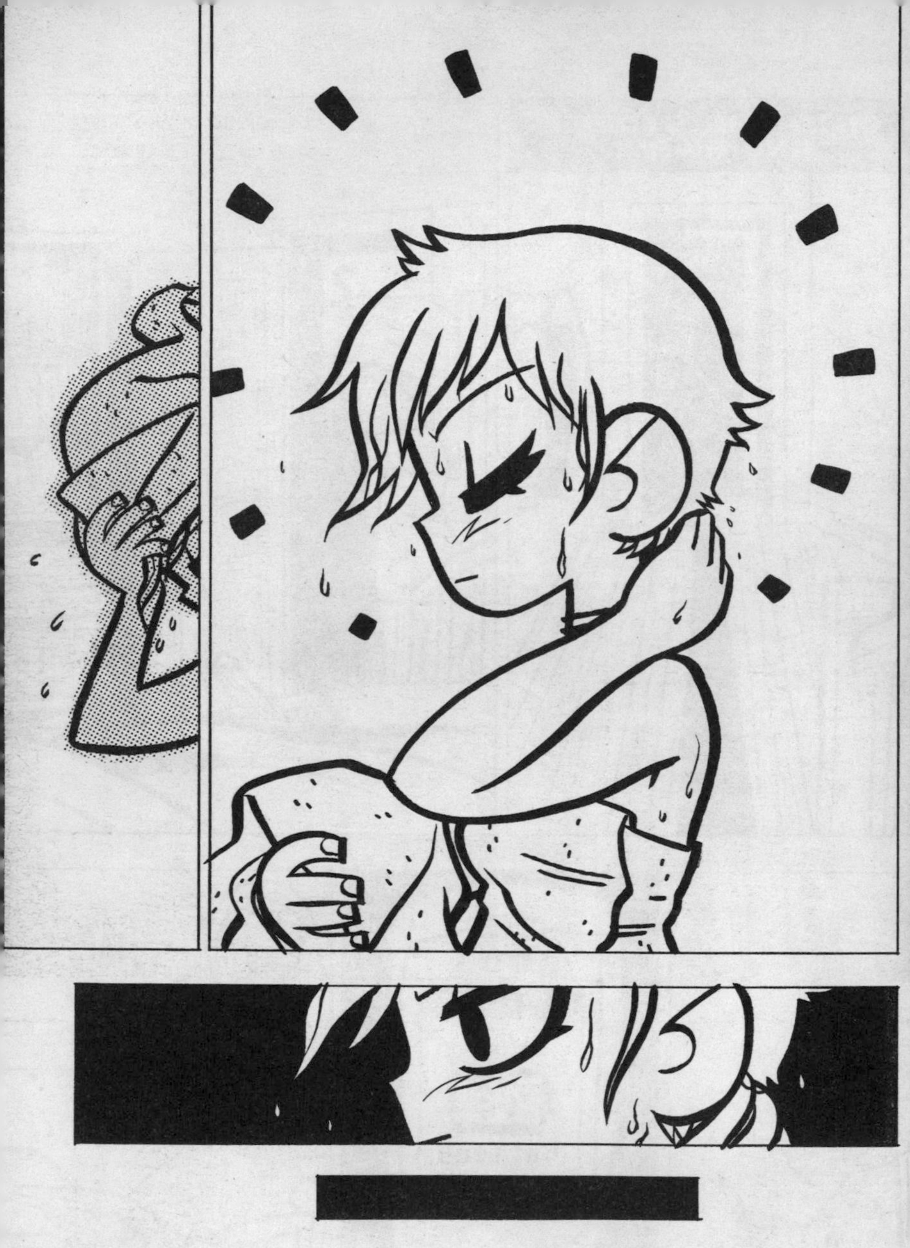

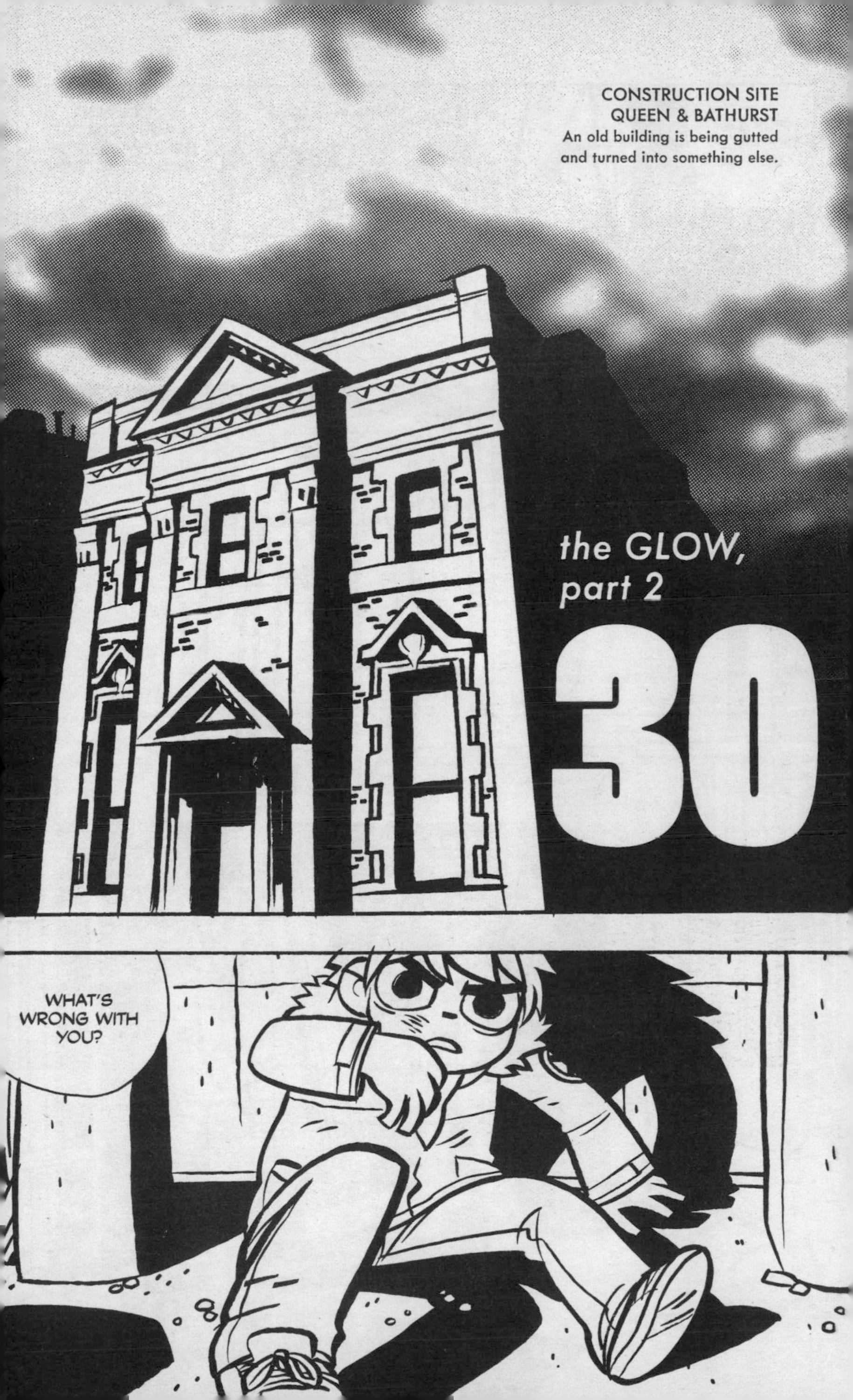
CONSTRUCTION SITE
QUEEN & BATHURST
An old building is being gutted and turned into something else.
the GLOW, part 2
30
WHAT'S WRONG WITH YOU?

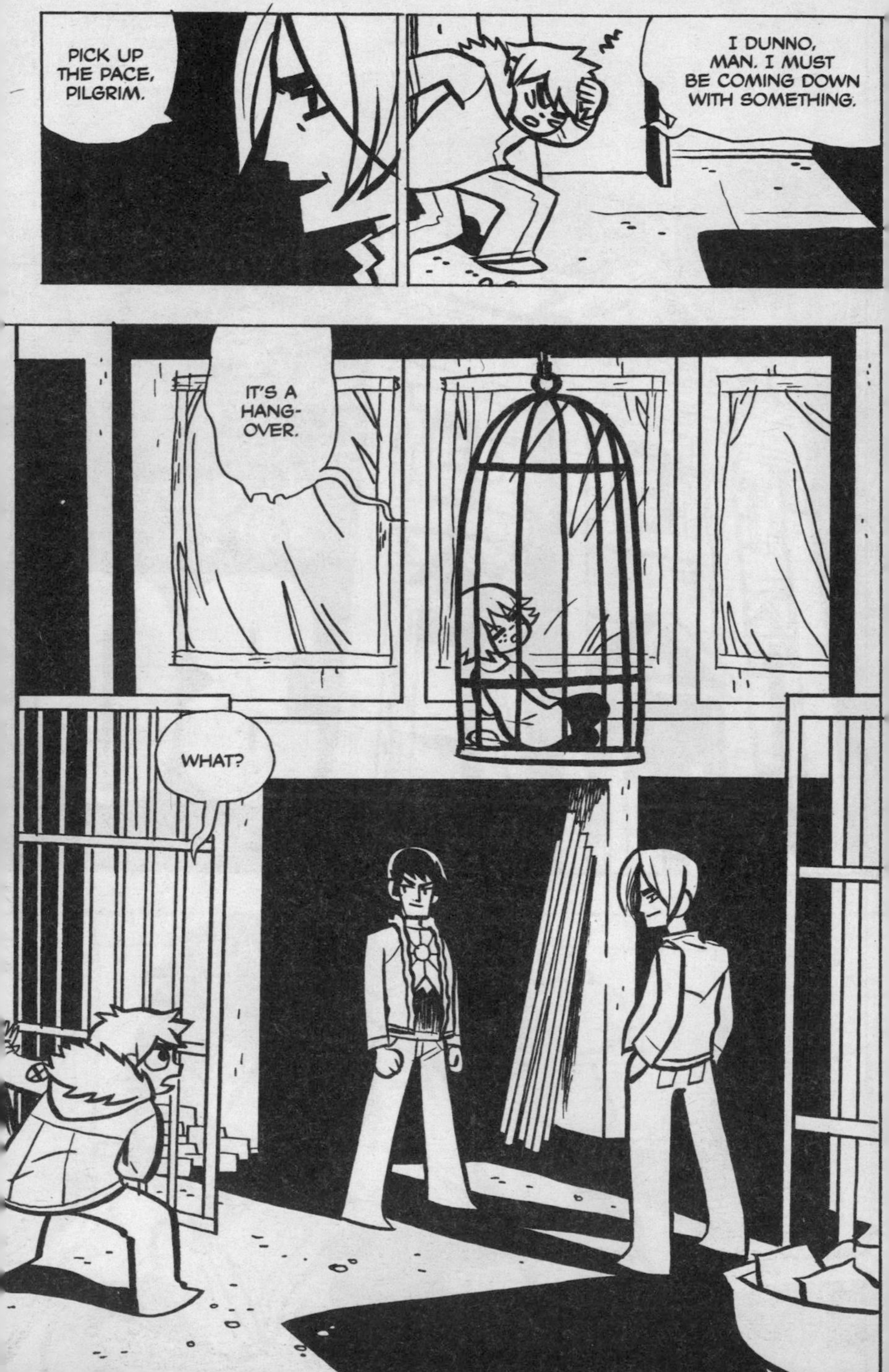
PICK UP THE PACE, PILGRIM.
I DUNNO, MAN. I MUST BE COMING DOWN WITH SOMETHING.
IT'S A HANG-OVER.
WHAT?

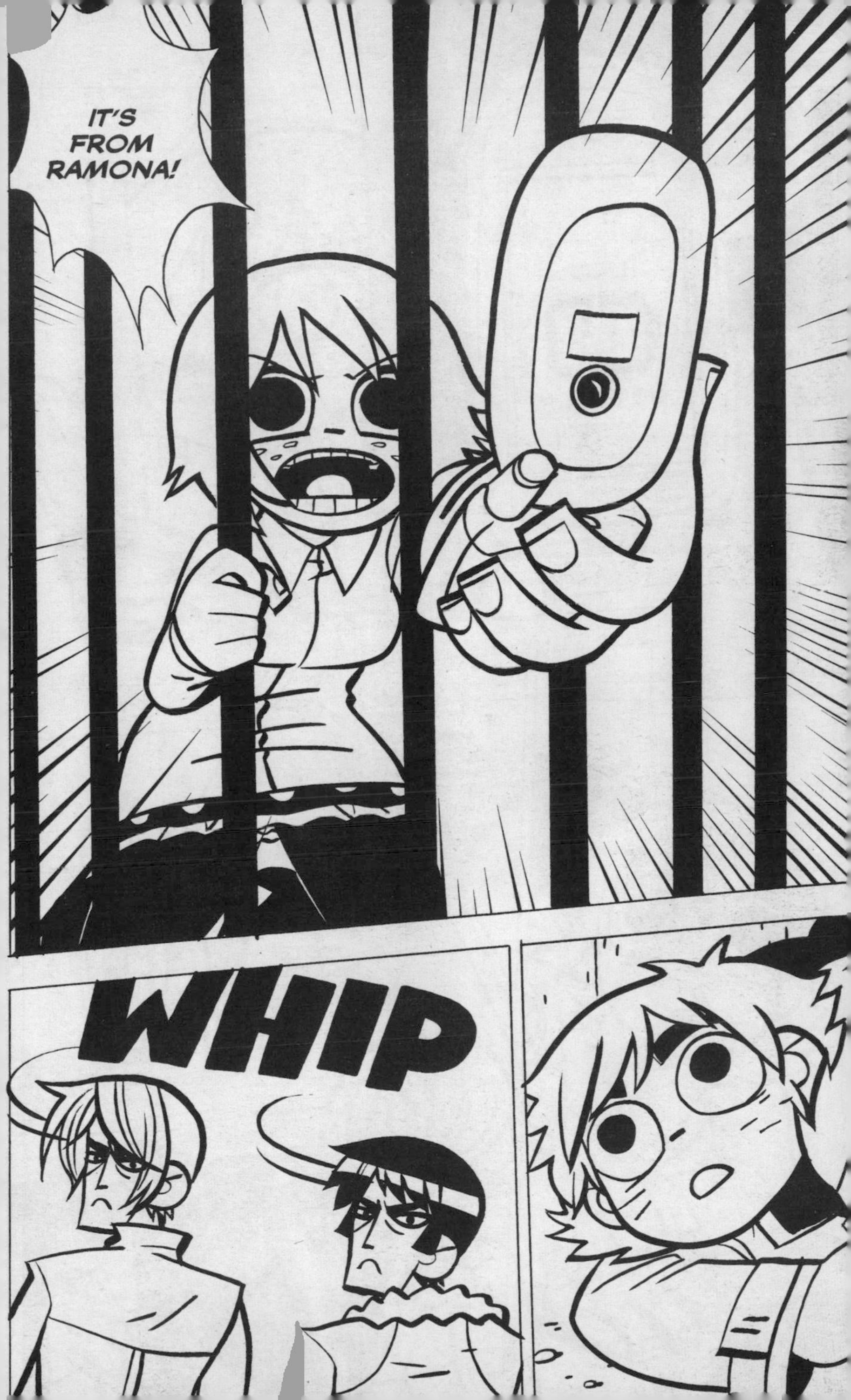
IT'S FROM RAMONA!
WHIP

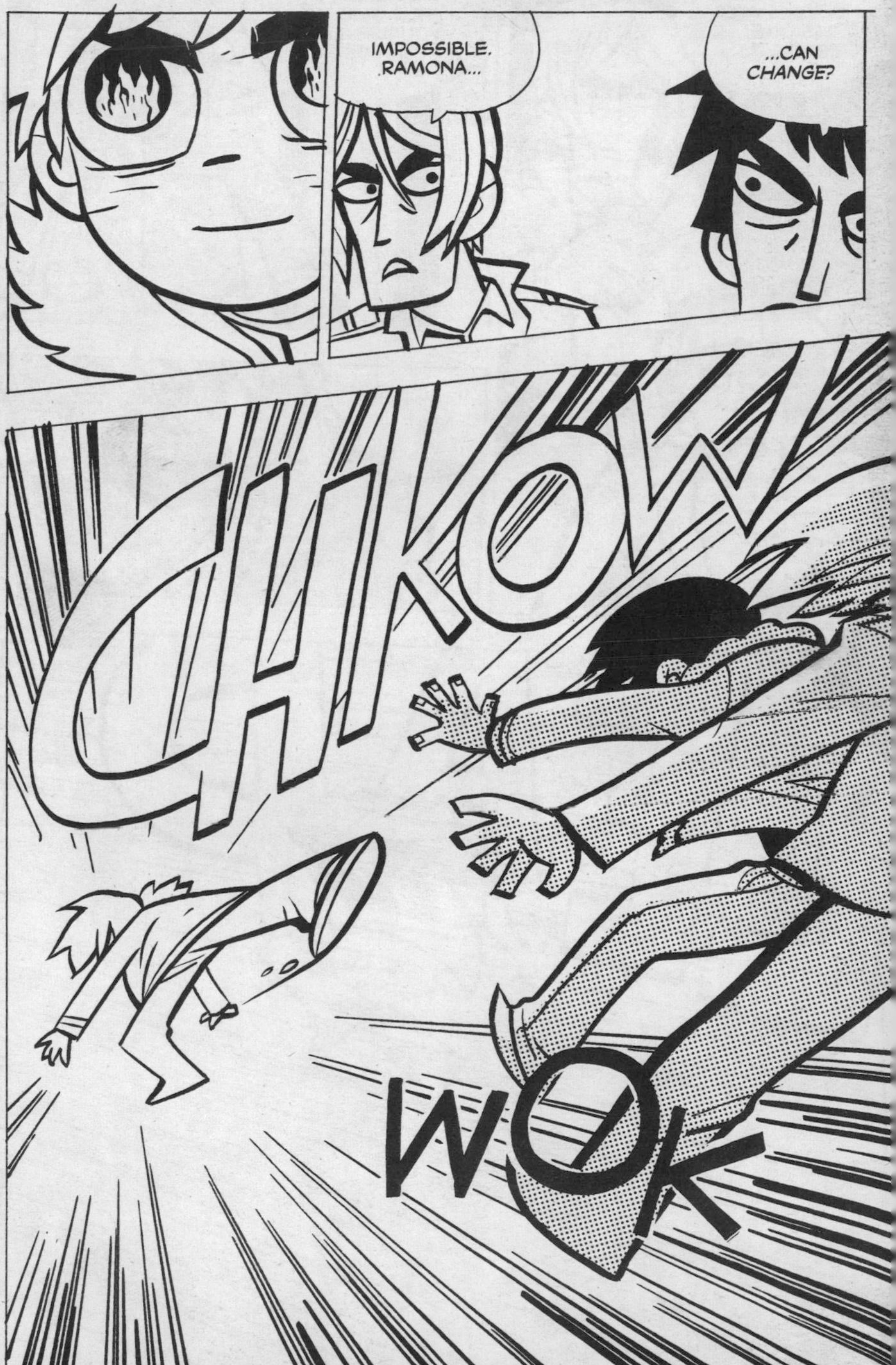

IMPOSSIBLE. RAMONA...
...CAN CHANGE?
CHKOW
WOK

After Scott solved the puzzle of the dangling cage...

WHATEVER. IT'S COOL.

I'M SORRY YOU HAD TO GET INVOLVED.

ARE YOU OKAY?

I AM SO READY TO HOP IN THE SHOWER.

WHAT ABOUT YOU? ARE *YOU* GONNA BE OKAY?

ONE MORE ASSHOLE TO GO, RIGHT? I SHOULD REALLY RUN HOME, THOUGH.

ME AND RAMONA, WE'RE—

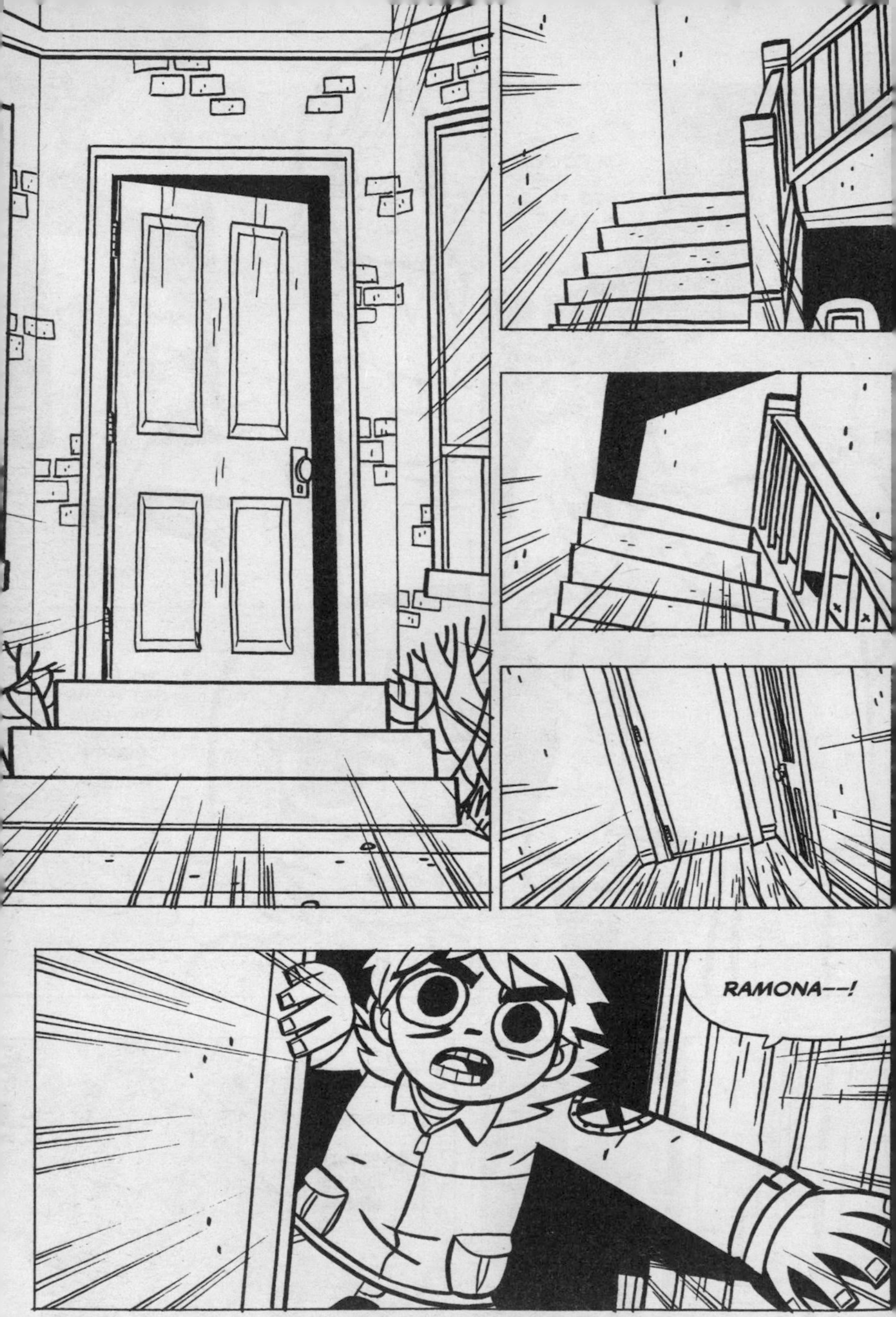
RAMONA--!

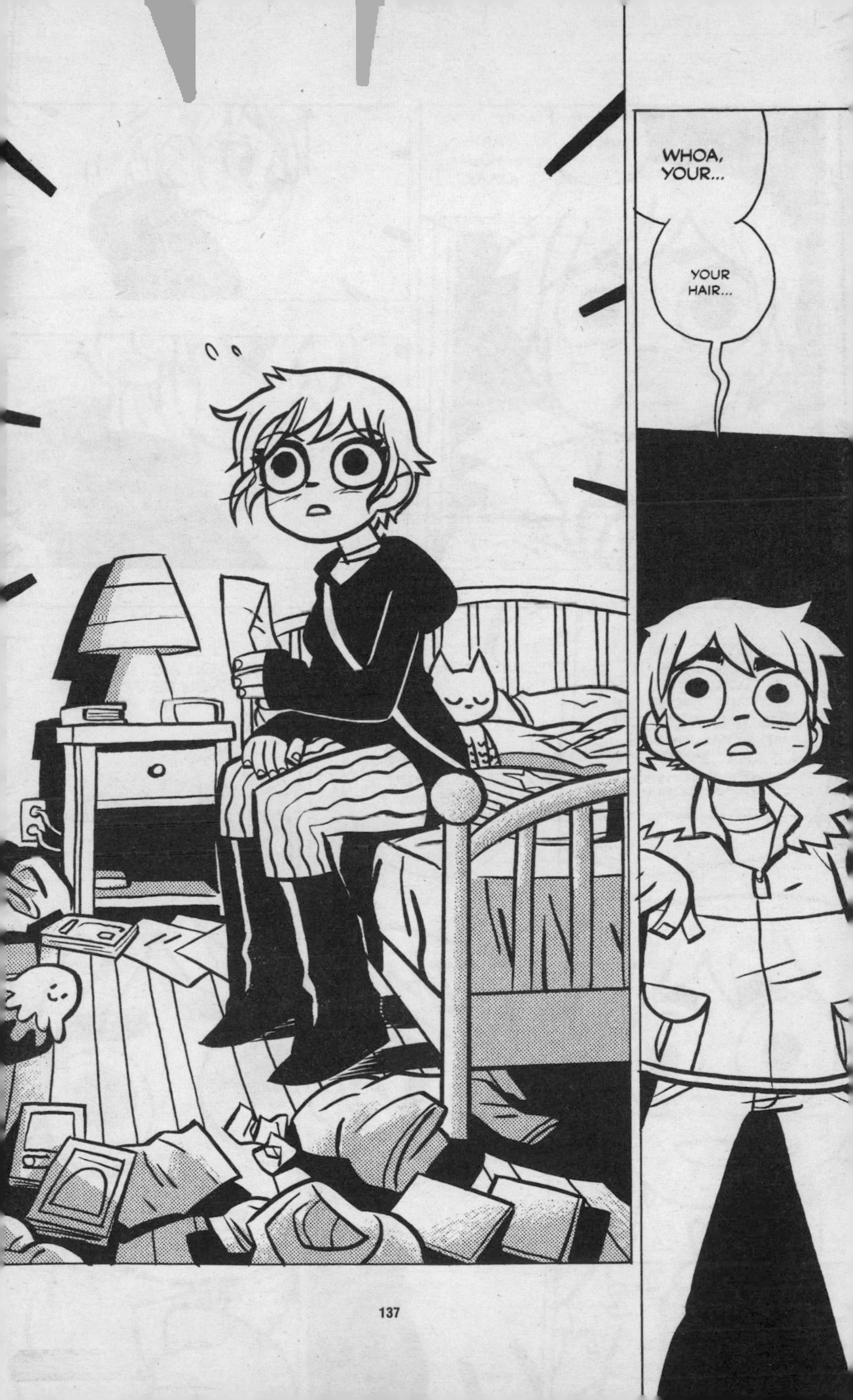
WHOA, YOUR...
YOUR HAIR...

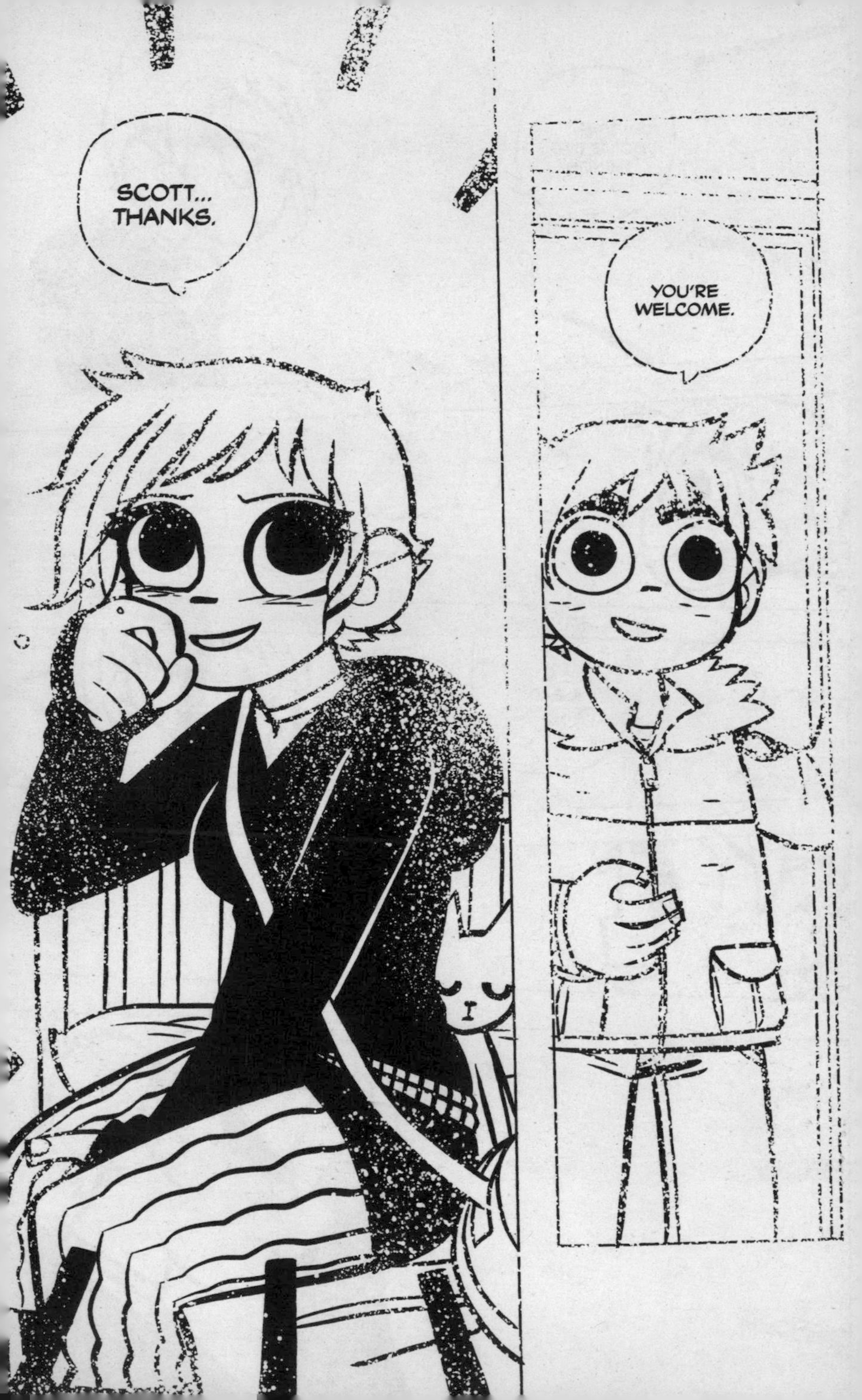
SCOTT... THANKS.
YOU'RE WELCOME.

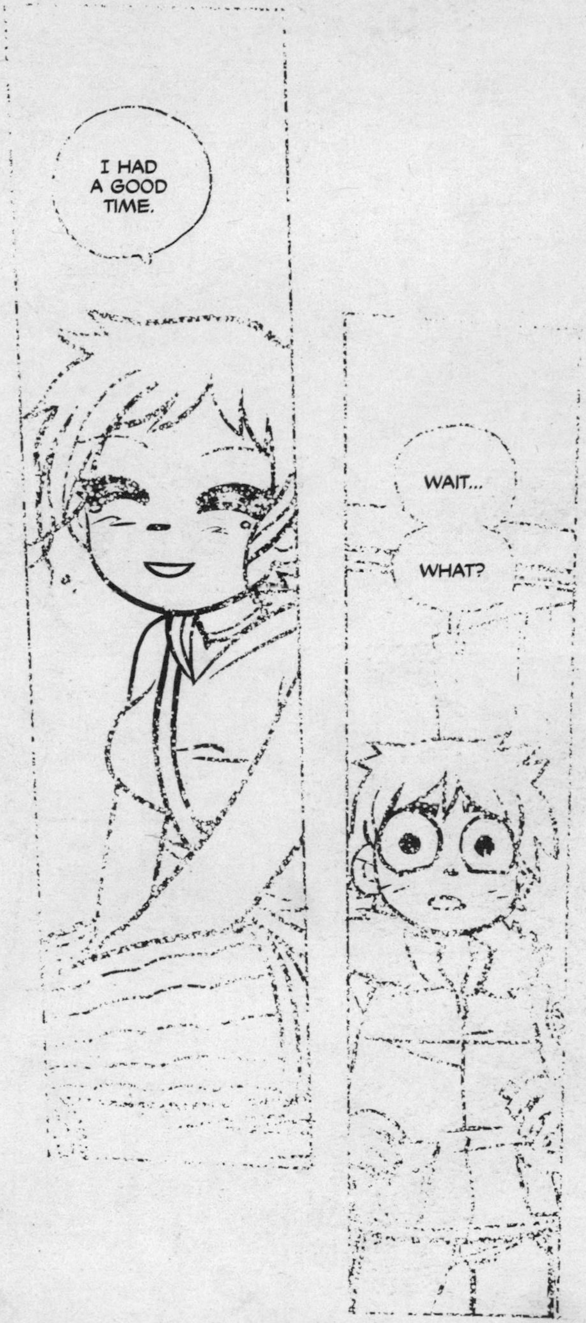
I HAD A GOOD TIME.
WAIT...
WHAT?

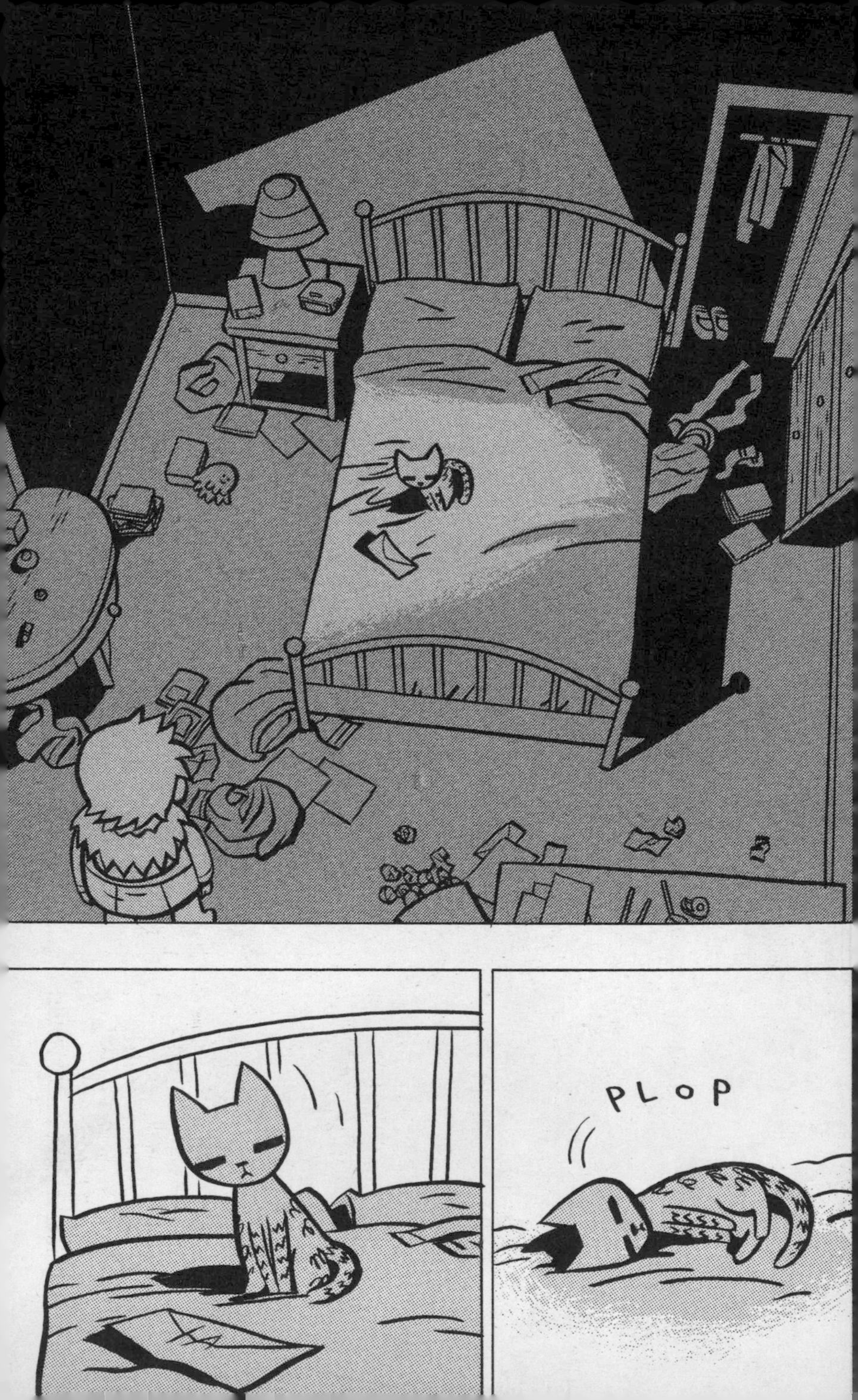
PLOP

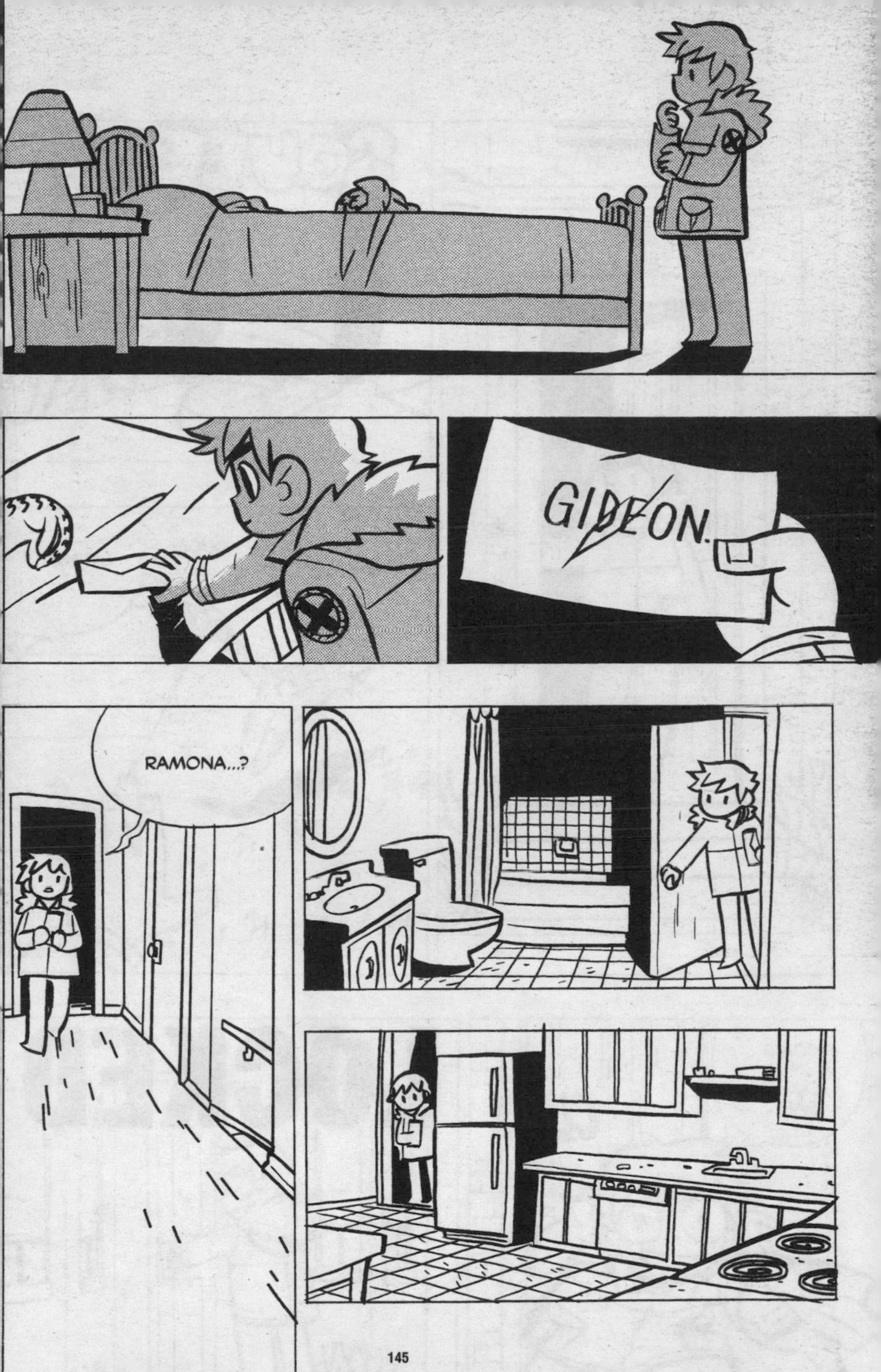
GIDEON.
RAMONA...?

31
WORLD of RUIN

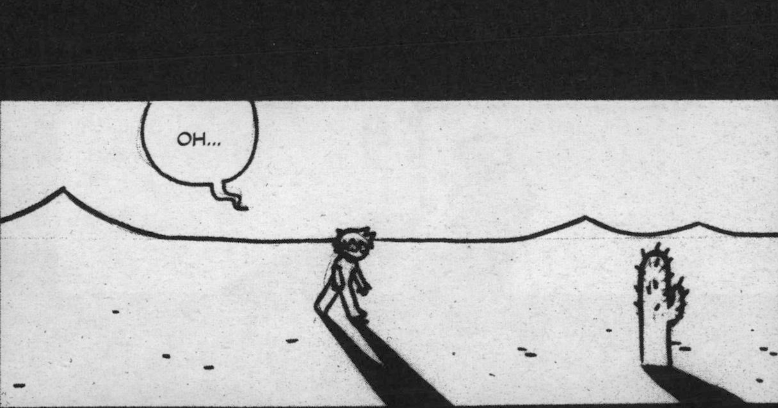

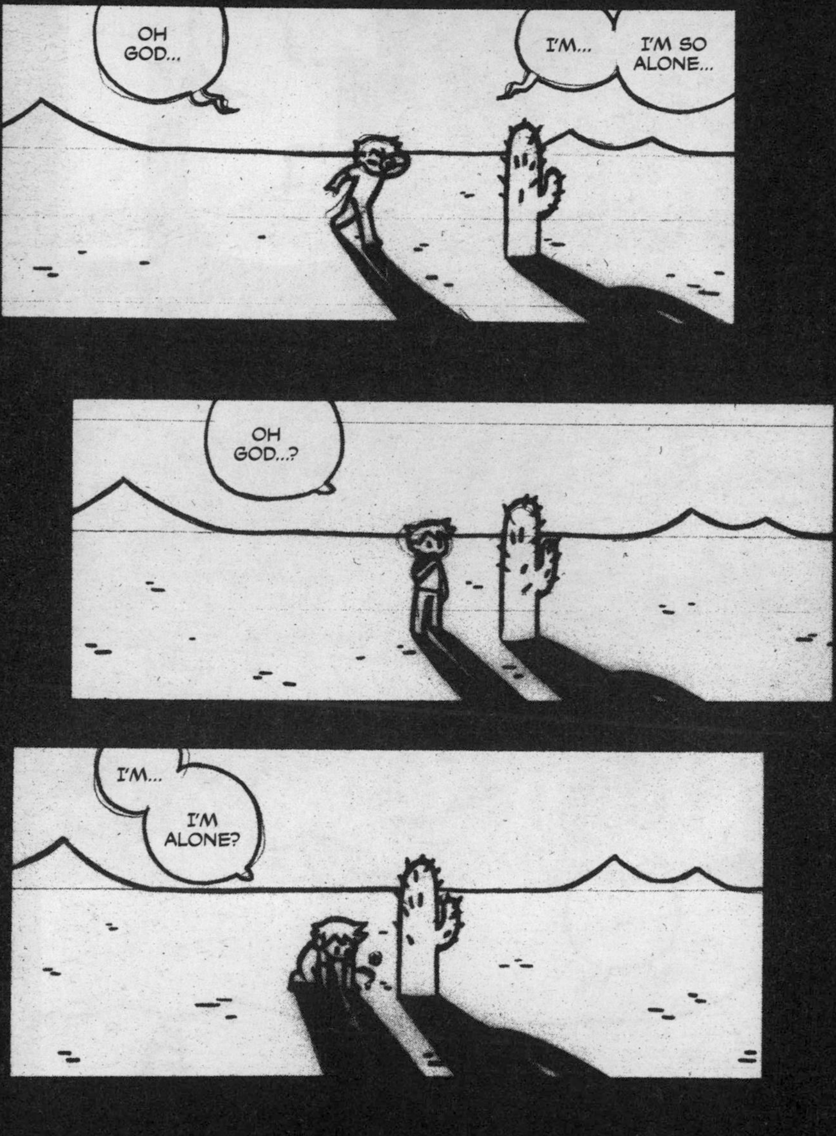
OH GOD...
I'M...
I'M SO ALONE...
OH GOD...?
I'M...
I'M ALONE?

GAME OVER

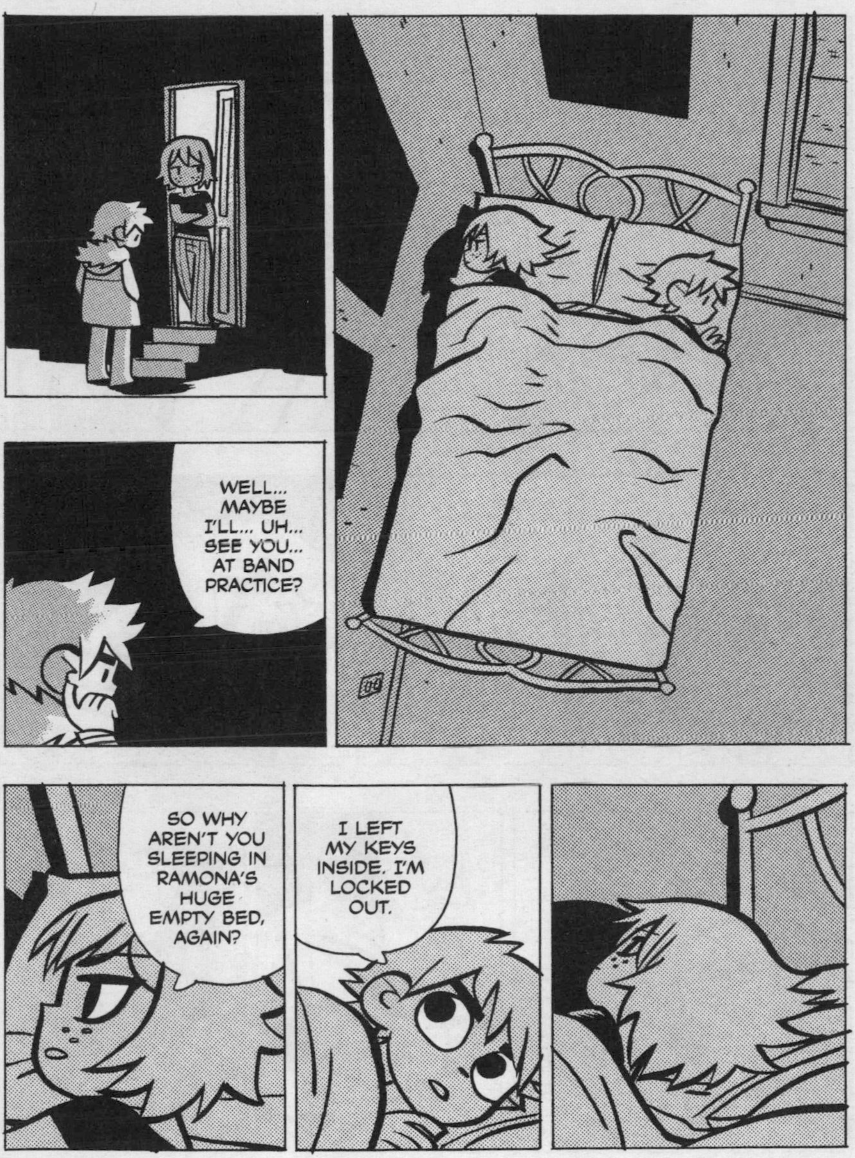
WELL... MAYBE I'LL... UH... SEE YOU... AT BAND PRACTICE?
SO WHY AREN'T YOU SLEEPING IN RAMONA'S HUGE EMPTY BED, AGAIN?
I LEFT MY KEYS INSIDE. I'M LOCKED OUT.

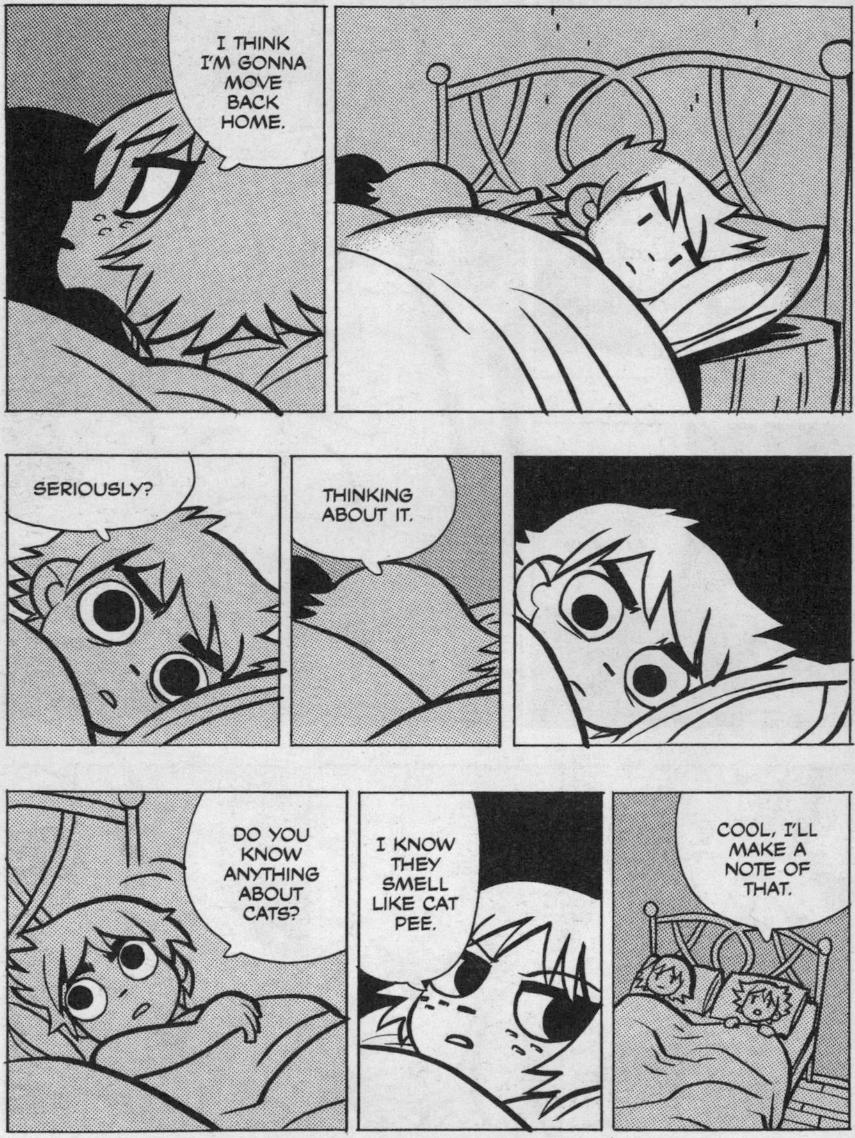
I THINK I'M GONNA MOVE BACK HOME.
SERIOUSLY?
THINKING ABOUT IT.
DO YOU KNOW ANYTHING ABOUT CATS?
I KNOW THEY SMELL LIKE CAT PEE.
COOL, I'LL MAKE A NOTE OF THAT.

THEY'RE DIRTY AND THEY LEAVE HAIR EVERYWHERE.

AND THE WAY THEY MOVE...

IT'S UNNATURAL.

SO YOU DON'T KNOW ANYTHING ABOUT CATS.

WHY ARE YOU EVEN ASKING ME?

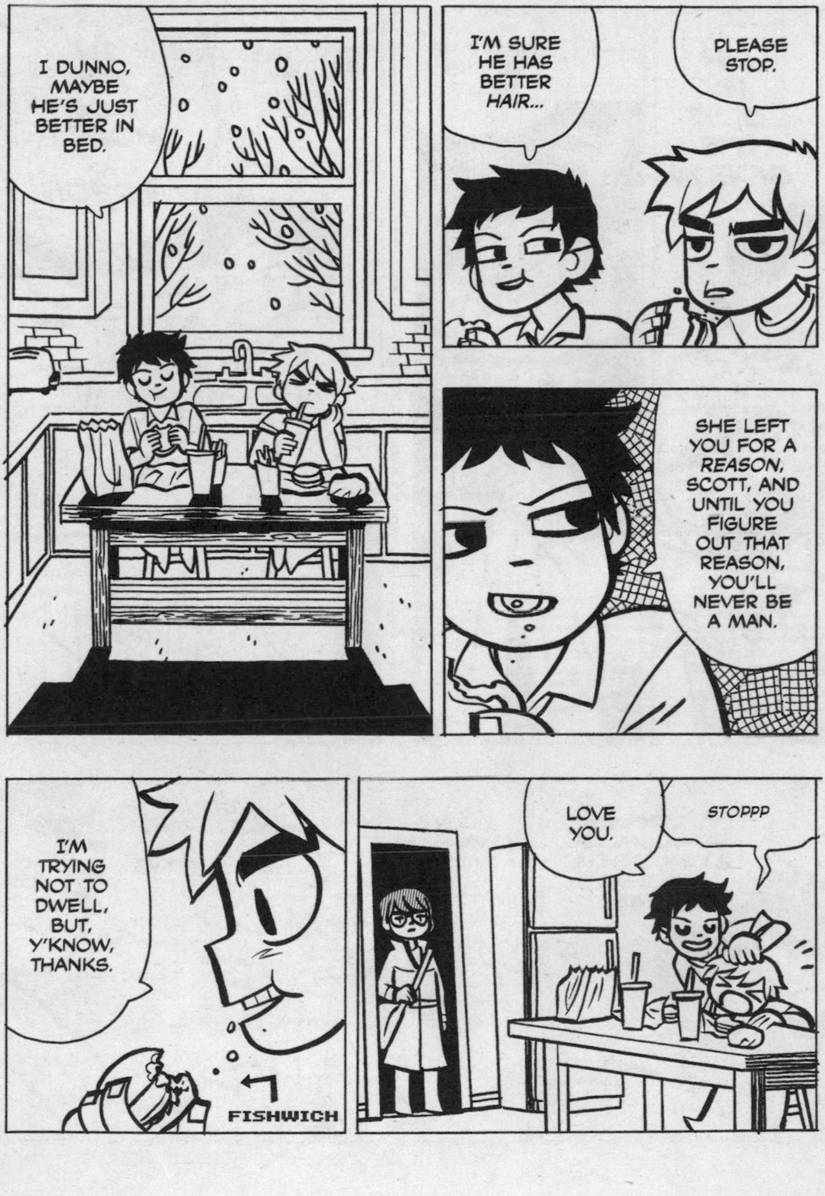
I DUNNO, MAYBE HE'S JUST BETTER IN BED.
I'M SURE HE HAS BETTER *HAIR*...
PLEASE STOP.
SHE LEFT YOU FOR A *REASON*, SCOTT, AND UNTIL YOU FIGURE OUT THAT REASON, YOU'LL NEVER BE A MAN.
I'M TRYING NOT TO DWELL, BUT, Y'KNOW, THANKS.
FISHWICH
LOVE YOU.
STOPPP

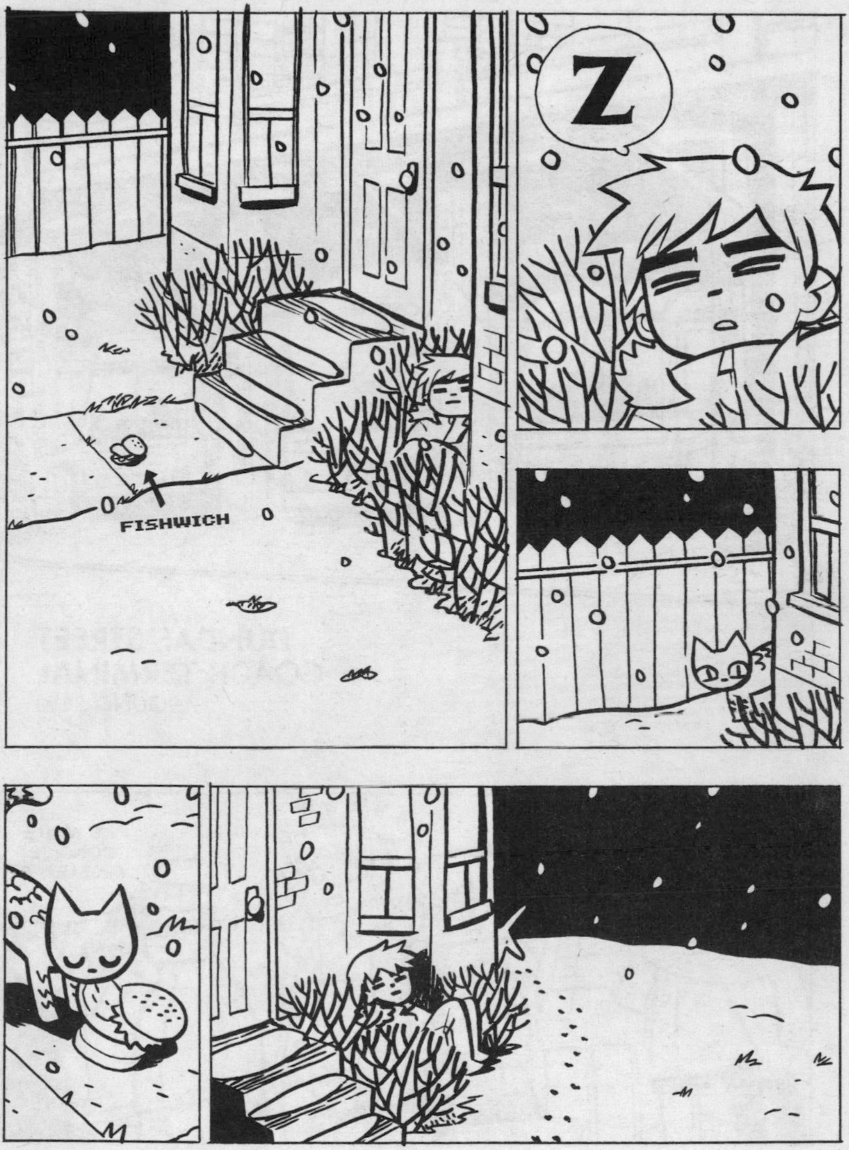
FISHWICH
Z

DUNDAS STREET
COACH TERMINAL
AROUND 5 PM

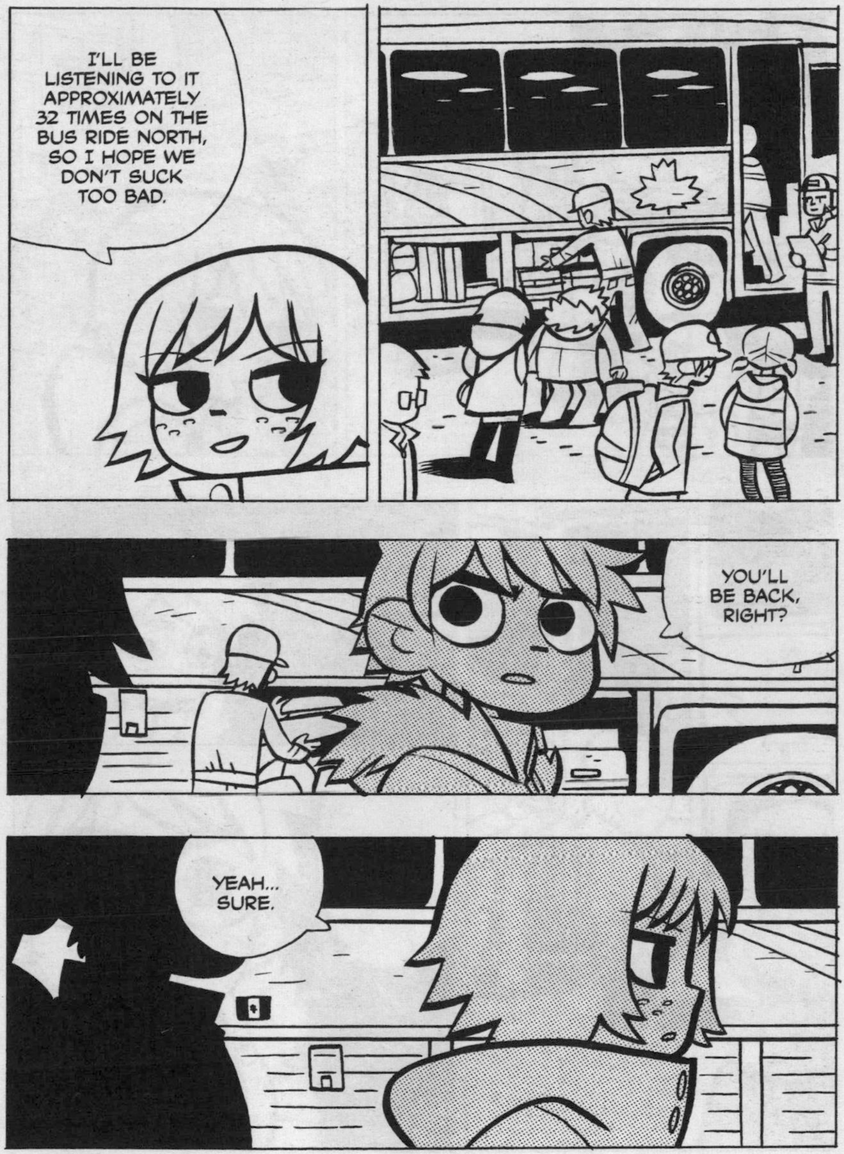
I'LL BE LISTENING TO IT APPROXIMATELY 32 TIMES ON THE BUS RIDE NORTH, SO I HOPE WE DON'T SUCK TOO BAD.
YOU'LL BE BACK, RIGHT?
YEAH... SURE.

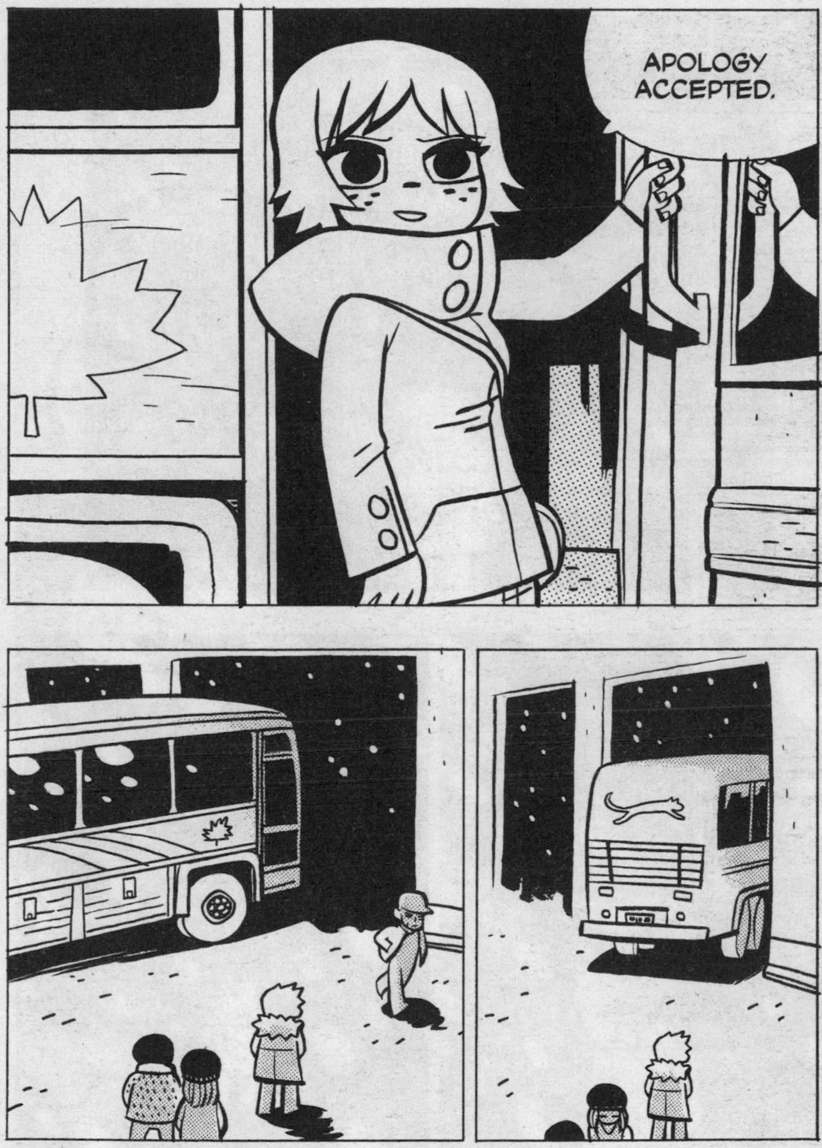
APOLOGY ACCEPTED.

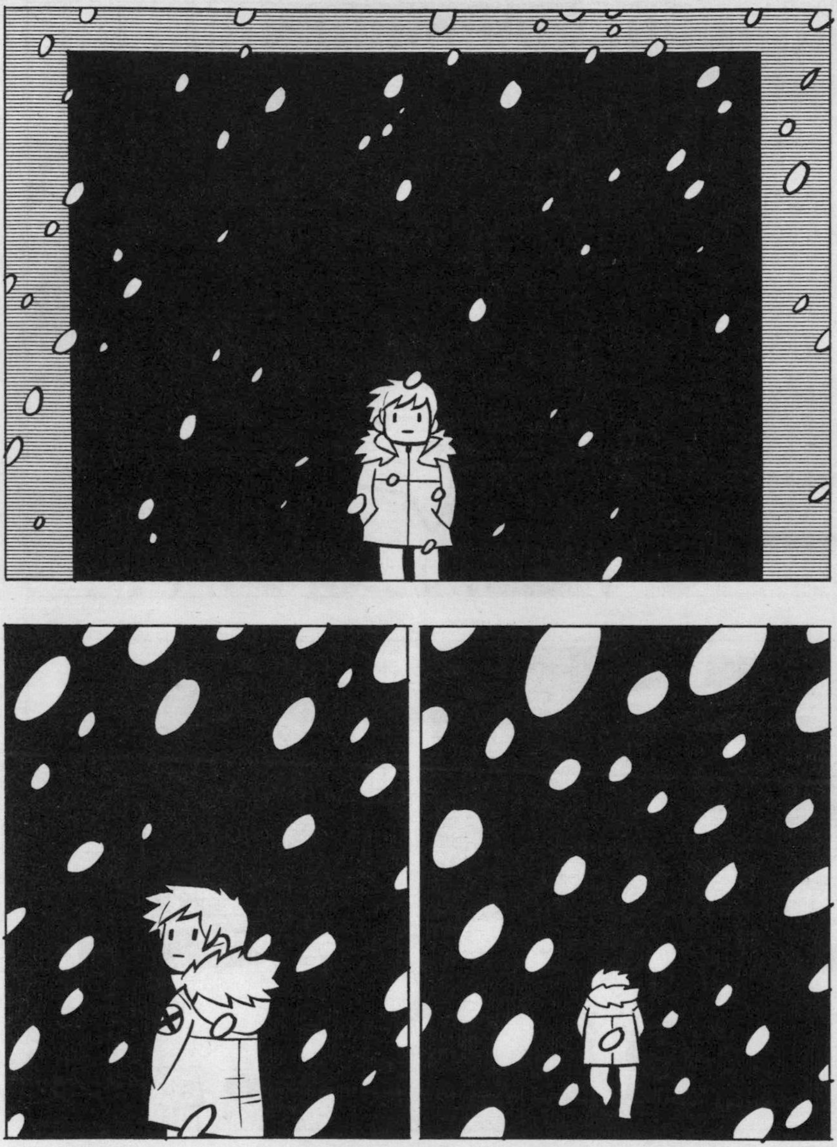

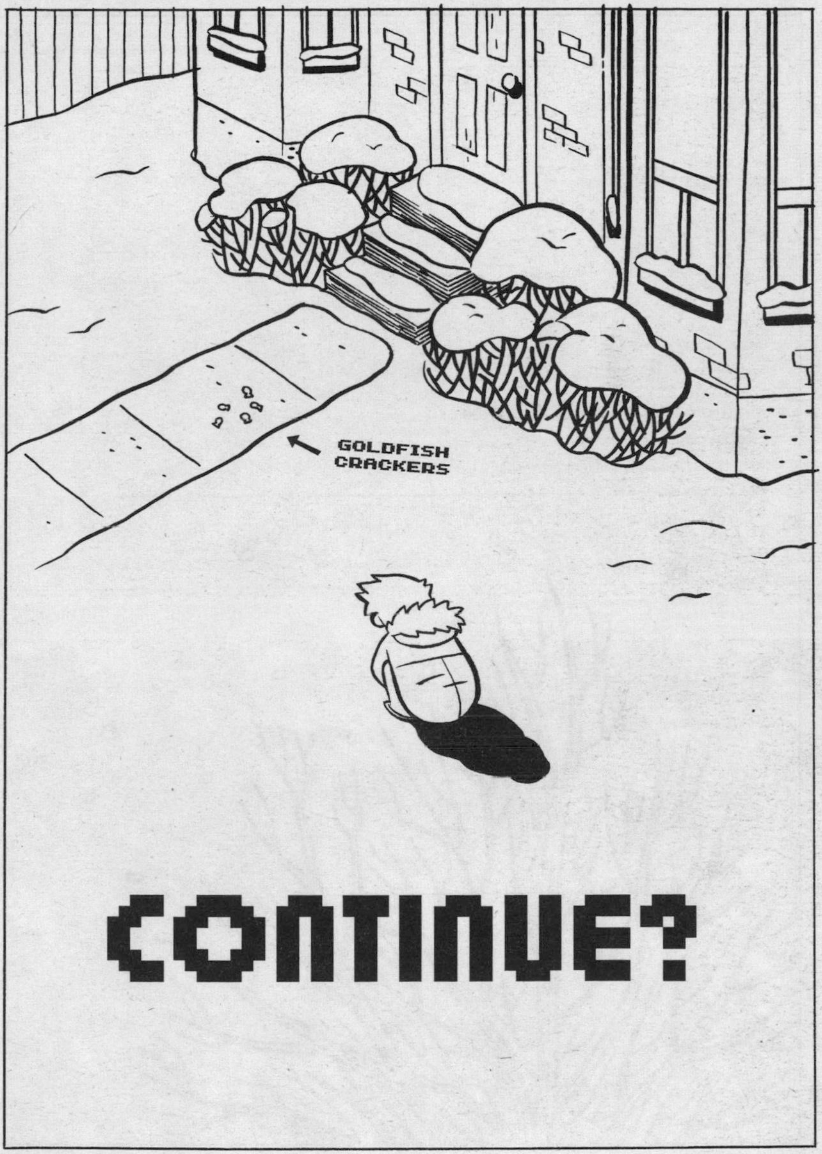
GOLDFISH
CRACKERS
CONTINUE?

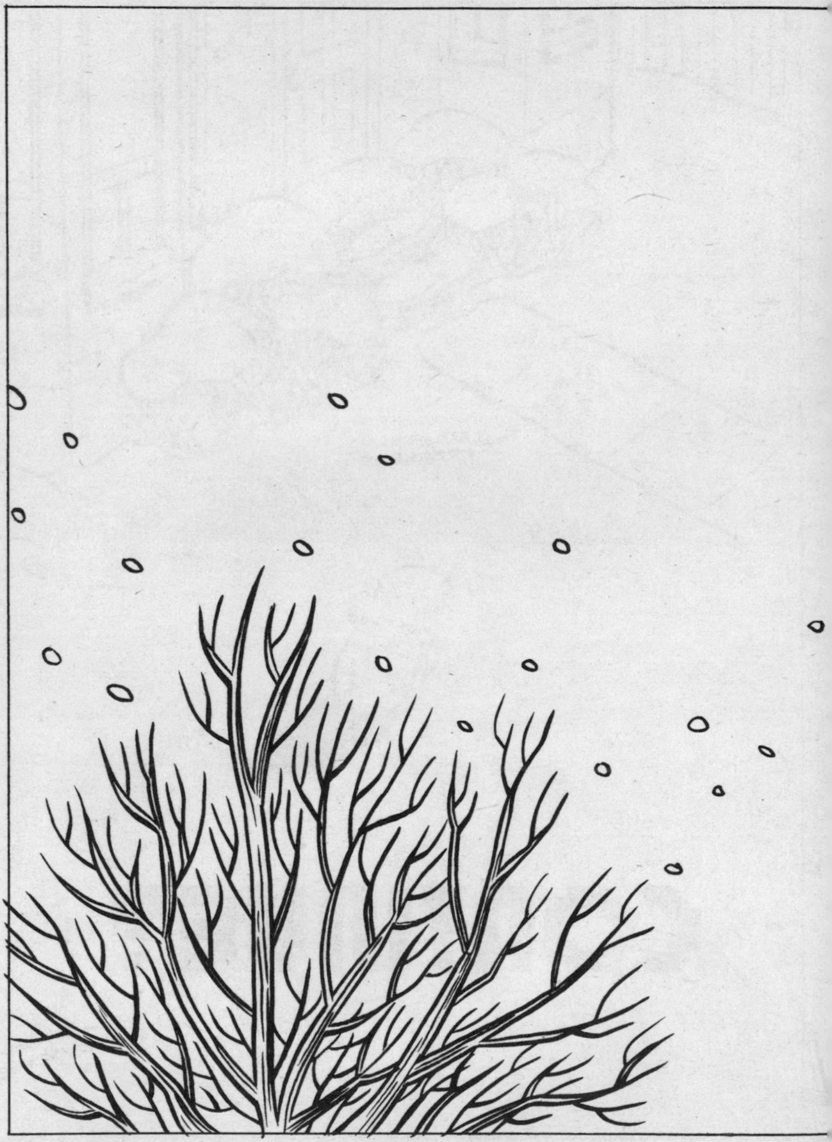

171

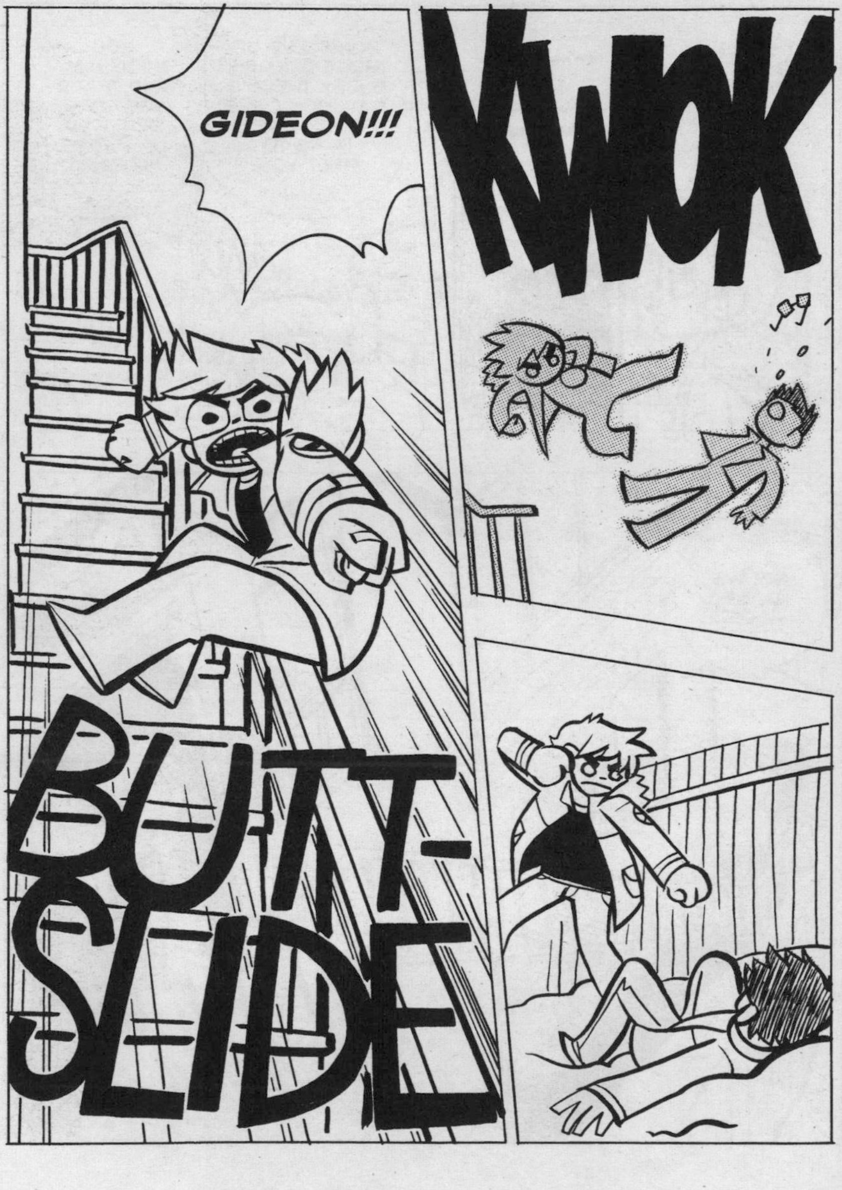
GIDEON!!!
BUTT-SLIDE
KWOK

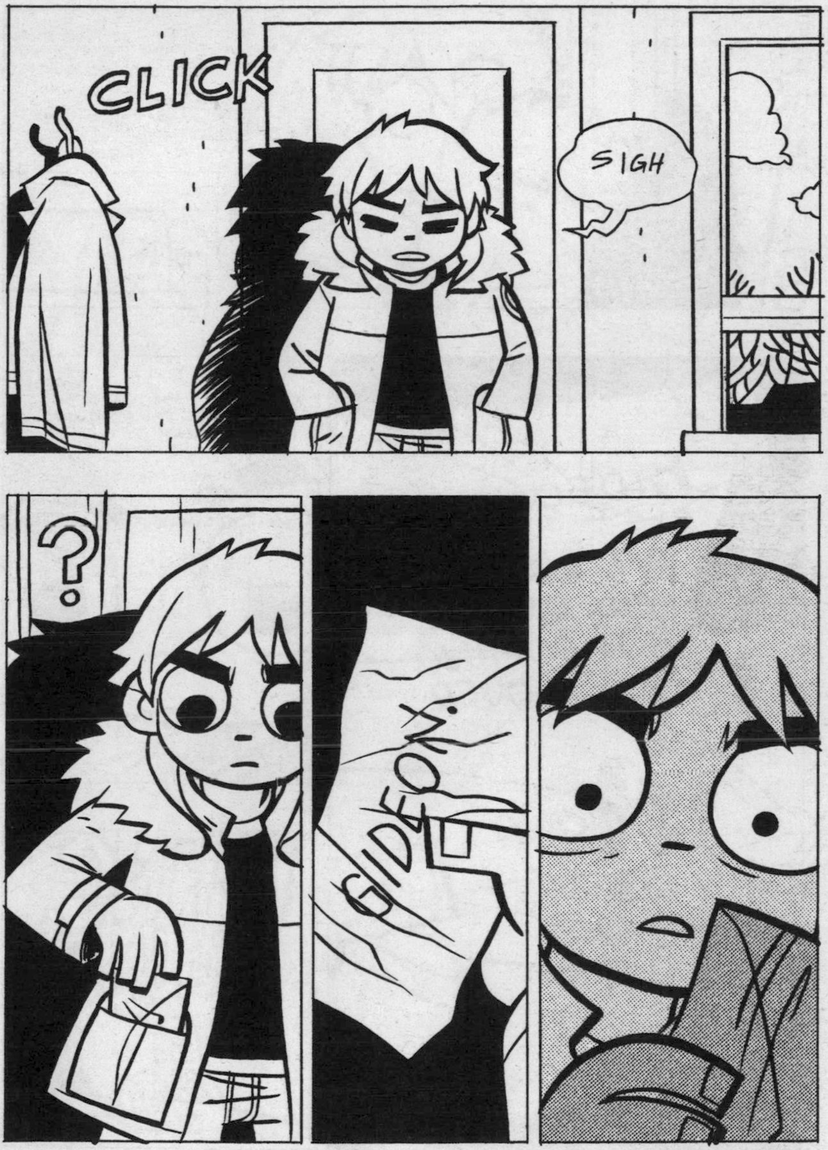
CLICK
SIGH
?
GIDEON

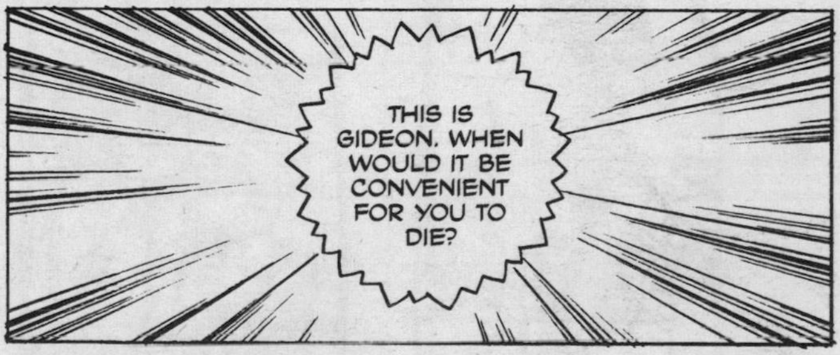
THIS IS GIDEON. WHEN WOULD IT BE CONVENIENT FOR YOU TO DIE?

NEXT:
ONE MORE TIME!

CREATING
SCOTT PILGRIM
FOR FUN AND PROFIT

By Bryan Lee O'Malley

SCRIPT

I like to write a full script for my books before I ever start drawing them. It looks kind of like the screenplay for a movie. A lot of cartoonists don't script this way, but I feel that I'm, ironically, not very visual-minded. I like words.

THUMBNAIL

After the script is totally finished (which in this case took a shockingly long time), it's time to break things down into comics. First I roughly determine how much content is going to fit on a page, and then I decide how the information will be laid out on the page. I like to draw these thumbnail sketches at a ridiculously small size, maybe an inch and a half high, otherwise I fear I'll spend too much time rendering them. The simpler they are, the better.

LAYOUT

I transfer the layout to a full-size page. I'm working at 9.5" x 14", which involves ruling and cutting a strip from an 11" x 14" sheet. I use Strathmore bristol and lately I like the vellum finish. I generally ink all of the panel borders before any actual drawing.

PENCILS

I work pretty roughly, with a light blue Col-Erase pencil. I like to place my word balloons as soon as possible - I already know where they'll be, from the thumbnail sketch, and often I can just put a balloon in the corner before I even begin to draw the figures.

The final lettering in the book is done with a computer font, and I space out the word balloons with a combination of letters, scribbles and straight lines. It's not the most scientific method, but I'm used to it by now.

When the pencils are done and I'm satisfied, I immediatoly ink in the word balloon outlines, using a cheap Pilot pen. I like those pens because they have a sharp point with great flexibility. They don't last very long, though.

Sometimes I will end up re-penciling a whole panel after having inked in the balloon outlines, trying to keep the figures in roughly the same location. Sometimes I have to paste in a new panel, when things get really bad.

INKS

Mostly done with a brush and ink (Rosemary & Co, #3 Kolinsky Sable, with Kohl-Noor drawing ink). Small details are drawn with the cheap Pilot pens again — things like wood grain, branches and leaves, floor tiles, etc.

I add or change certain things without re-penciling at all, like the angles of facial features, decorations and textures that I left blank, and shadows on the furniture and floors.

POST-PRODUCTION

Scanning, lettering, and screentones. Like everything else, these processes have been cobbled together from years of experience, tips and tricks learned from all over the place, and so they're difficult to explain. I use a variety of screentone effects, most of which I created myself in Photoshop, and which I've struggled to master the use of over the years. I'm definitely still struggling, and it'd be great if I had about twice as much time to really do a good job on toning.

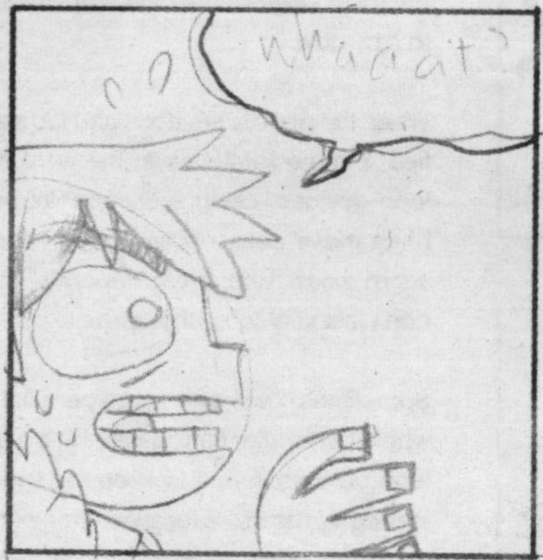

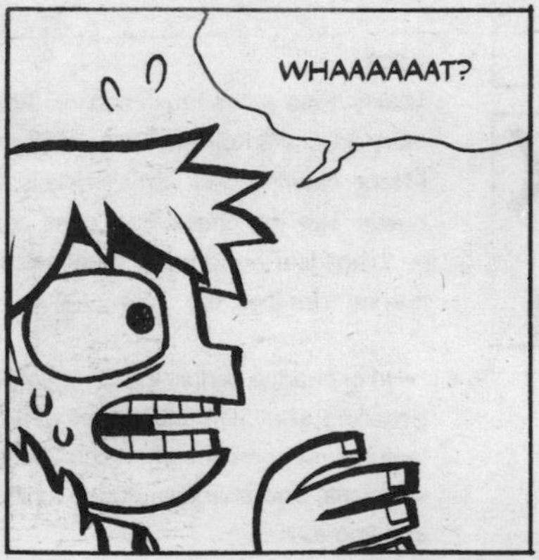
WHAAAAAAT?

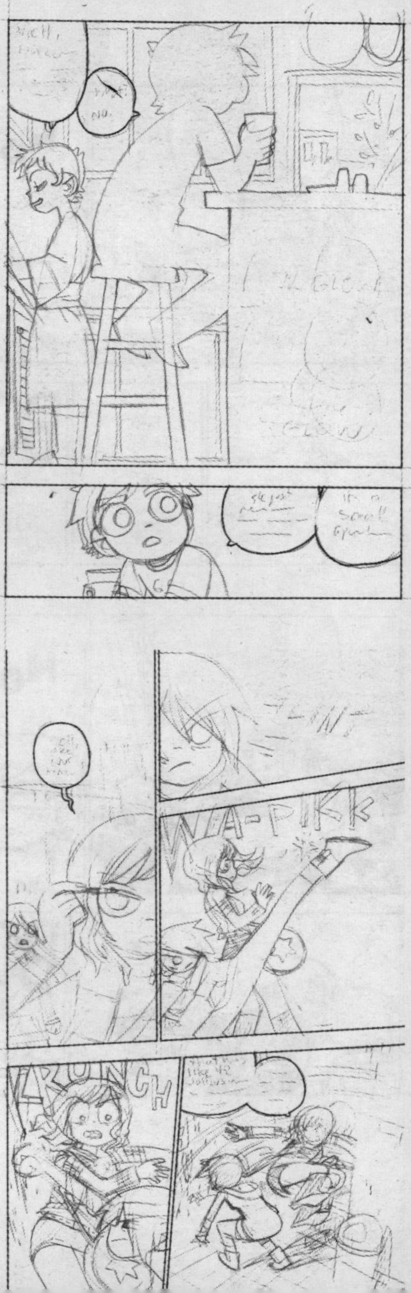

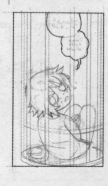

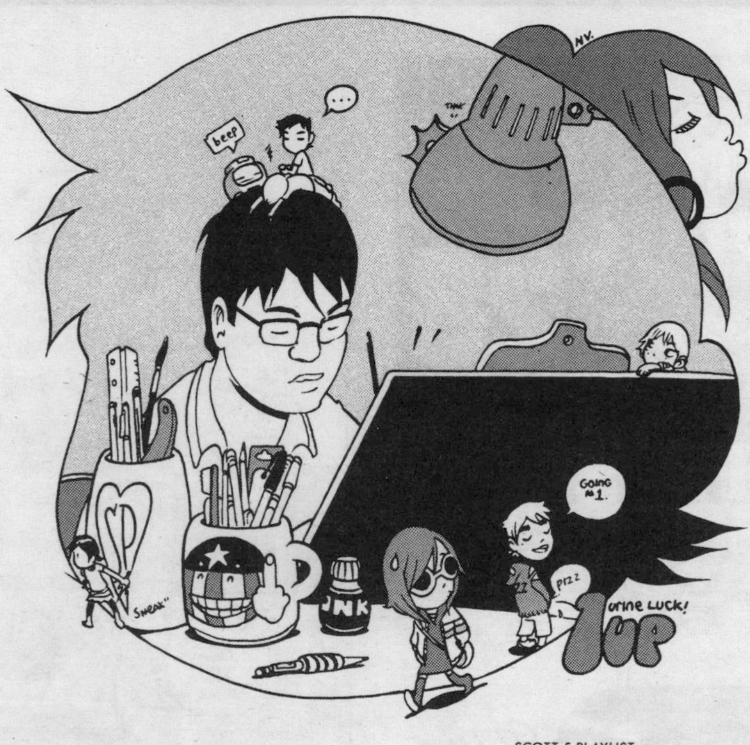
beep
NV.
GOING #1.
PIZZ
urine LUCK!
1UP

ABOUT THE AUTHOR

Bryan Lee O'Malley was made in Canada. This is the first book he has ever completed on schedule. He was 29. It was awesome.

SCOTT 5 PLAYLIST

Beulah - If We Can Land A Man On The Moon, Surely I Can Win Your Heart
Black Lips - Off The Block
Be Your Own Pet - October, First Account
Blondie - Heart Of Glass
The Rolling Stones - Under My Thumb
Neko Case - Lion's Jaws
Lou Reed - Perfect Day (Acoustic Demo)
Art Brut - Fight
Badfinger - Without You
Spoon - I Summon You
Sloan - I'm Not Through With You Yet
Fleetwood Mac - Don't Stop

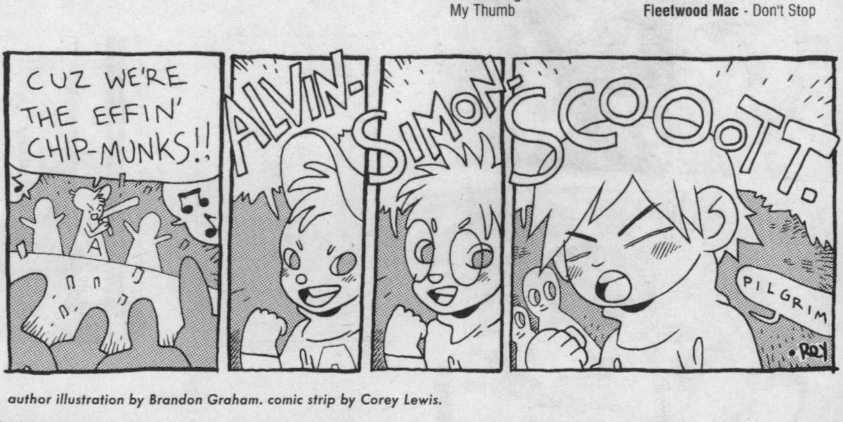
CUZ WE'RE THE EFFIN' CHIP-MUNKS!!
ALVIN-
SIMON-
SCOOOTT.
PILGRIM

author illustration by Brandon Graham. comic strip by Corey Lewis.